# Doing Research in Business and Management

## Pearson

At Pearson, we have a simple mission: to help people make more of their lives through learning.

We combine innovative learning technology with trusted content and educational expertise to provide engaging and effective learning experiences that serve people wherever and whenever they are learning.

From classroom to boardroom, our curriculum materials, digital learning tools and testing programmes help to educate millions of people worldwide – more than any other private enterprise.

Every day our work helps learning flourish, and wherever learning flourishes, so do people.

To learn more, please visit us at **www.pearson.com/uk**

# Doing Research in Business and Management

## An essential guide to planning your project

Mark Saunders and Philip Lewis

Second Edition

 Pearson

Harlow, England • London • New York • Boston • San Francisco • Toronto • Sydney
Dubai • Singapore • Hong Kong • Tokyo • Seoul • Taipei • New Delhi
Cape Town • São Paulo • Mexico City • Madrid • Amsterdam • Munich • Paris • Milan

**Pearson Education Limited**
KAO Two
KAO Park
Harlow CM17 9NA
United Kingdom
Tel: +44 (0)1279 623623
Web: www.pearson.com/uk

First published 2012 (print and electronic)
**Second edition published 2018** (print and electronic)

ISBN: 978-1-292-13352-2 (print)
        978-1-292-13353-9 (PDF)
        978-1-292-22231-8 (ePub)

**British Library Cataloguing-in-Publication Data**
A catalogue record for the print edition is available from the British Library

**Library of Congress Cataloging-in-Publication Data**
Names: Saunders, M. N. K., author. | Lewis, Philip, 1945– author.
Title: Doing research in business and management / Mark Saunders and Philip
    Lewis.
Description: 2nd edition. | Harlow, England : Pearson, 2018. | Includes
    bibliographical references and index.
Identifiers: LCCN 2017023723 | ISBN 9781292133522 (print) | ISBN 9781292133539
    (pdf) | ISBN 9781292222318 (epub)
Subjects: LCSH: Business—Research.
Classification: LCC HD30.4 .S277 2018 | DDC 650.072—dc23
LC record available at https://lccn.loc.gov/2017023723

10 9 8 7 6 5 4 3
22 21 20 19 18

Print edition typeset in 9/13pt Stone Serif ITC Pro by iEnergizer Aptara®, Ltd.
Printed and bound in Malaysia (CTP-PJB)

NOTE THAT ANY PAGE CROSS REFERENCES REFER TO THE PRINT EDITION

# Brief contents

# Contents

## Supporting resources

Visit **www.pearsoned.co.uk/saunders** to find valuable online resources:

**Companion Website for students**
- Multiple-choice questions to test your learning
- True or false questions to test your understanding
- Additional case studies
- Guides to SPSS and Qualitrics

**For instructors**
- Complete, downloadable Instructor's Manual
- PowerPoint slides that can be downloaded and used for presentations

Also: The regularly maintained Companion Website provides the following features:

- Search tool to help locate specific items of content
- Email results and profile tools to send results of quizzes to instructors
- Online help and support to assist with website usage and troubleshooting

For more information please contact your local Pearson Education sales representative or visit **www.pearsoned.co.uk/saunders**

# About this text

It is now 20 years since we collaborated in the writing of our first research methods book and six years since we wrote the first edition of *Doing Research in Business and Management*. The success of both books suggests that research methods is a popular subject with business and management students. This may be so. But we think that it has more to do with the fact that research methods is a complex area – one where it is easy to do things, but much less easy to do things right.

In writing the second edition of *Doing Research in Business and Management*, we have responded to the many comments we have received regarding the previous edition as well as recent developments in research methods and methodology. In particular this has led us to revise Chapter 4 to take account fully of the numerous sources of secondary data available online; Chapter 5 to incorporate fully revised sections on philosophical underpinnings of management research including a discussion of postmodernism, and on different approaches to theory development including a discussion of abduction; Chapter 6 to incorporate a new section on observation; and an appendix on how to reference. Alongside this we have taken the opportunity to also update examples and references as well as revise tables and figures. Inevitably, the body of knowledge of research methods has developed further since 2012, and we have revised all chapters accordingly. Our experiences of teaching and supervising students and working through the methods with them have suggested alternative ways to explain concepts, and we have incorporated these where appropriate. However, the basic structure remains the same as the first edition.

When we wrote the first edition of *Doing Research in Business and Management*, we had one overall mission in mind. That was to write a text that was clear and straightforward and explained things in a way that lost none of the complexity, or academic rigour, of the subject. In writing the second edition this mission has not altered. We still feel just as passionate about clear communication.

In fully revising *Doing Research in Business and Management*, we have taken into account that although some degree programmes require students to complete an assessed research project, they may be told that, rather than collect their own data, they should use only data that have already been collected for some other purpose (secondary data) or, alternatively, write an extended review of the literature. For a second category of students on undergraduate programmes, the extent of their research work is a research methods module which is assessed by a research proposal. There is a third category, those business and management students who opt not to do a research project at all. For those undertaking research to be assessed by a written project report, we aim to help in all aspects of the research process: from thinking of a topic through to writing the final submission. We therefore include material, in Chapter 3, on managing the research process, as well as chapters on using secondary data (Chapter 4) and reviewing the literature critically (Chapter 2). There are also two chapters (6 and 7) on collecting and analysing data, as an understanding of these is important for all types of research projects as well as preparing a research proposal. If you're taking a research methods module which is assessed by a research proposal, you will find that there is considerable emphasis on the preparation of a research proposal. Indeed, Chapter 8 deals specifically with writing the research proposal.

It may sound strange, but we think that business and management students in the third category, those who opt not to do a research project at all, can gain just as much from this book as those in the other two categories. As a student, you will spend much of your time studying material which is the result of careful research that has been scrutinised by the research community prior to publication. This scrutiny is a guarantee of good quality: that you should put your faith in what you have read. However, some of what you read may not have been through quite such a rigorous process. Knowing something about the research process enables you to ask the right questions of the material you are studying. It gives you the sense of healthy scepticism that is the hallmark of a university education.

## How you might use this text

We don't anticipate that you will read this text progressively from Chapter 1 through to Chapter 8. In fact, you may not read all the chapters, although we certainly hope that you will! The reason, we suspect, is that you will choose those chapters that meet your own needs. This may be because you are in one of the categories we mentioned earlier, have specific questions about the research process you need to answer, or it may be that your research methods lecturers specify certain chapters. We've written the chapters in such a way that they can be read on their own without recourse to the other chapters. To some extent, they draw inevitably on material from other chapters directly. Where this is so, we have cross-referenced to the relevant chapter. But the point remains that you can pick up any chapter in isolation and make sense of it.

This book is not a self-study text in the truest sense; there are no questions with model answers! However, we have included points in each chapter which facilitate an element of independent learning. Each chapter begins with a summary of content which we call 'Why read this chapter?' This gives you some idea of the chapter content and the approach we have taken on the topic being discussed. Each chapter contains a small number of examples of research called 'Research in practice'. These serve to illustrate in a practical manner some of the points being made in the chapter, in much the same way as a lecturer would give practical examples in a research methods lecture. Every chapter ends with a summary of the main points in the chapter and a section called 'Thinking about . . .' Here we make suggestions as to how you may test and reinforce the learning you have achieved during the reading of the chapter. Throughout the book, key research terms we use are isolated and placed in 'Definition' boxes to make it easy for you to refresh your understanding of these terms as you read through each chapter.

## What's in the text?

Chapter 1 deals with the first issue you will encounter in the research process: choosing the right research topic. We suggest some novel ways in which you may decide upon your topic, offer guidance in deciding what constitutes an effective research topic and consider some topics which may be problematic. In the latter part of the chapter, we deal with the issue of defining suitable research questions and objectives. The chapter ends with a discussion on what is meant by the all-important term 'theory'.

In Chapter 2, we approach the subject of the critical literature review. We offer some practical suggestions on the way you may go about approaching your literature review and actually conducting it, using full-text databases of academic articles. The chapter also explains what constitutes an effective critical literature review and offers guidance in how it may be structured.

Chapter 3 is concerned with practical issues regarding gaining access to organisations from which you may collect your own research data. In this chapter, we also consider the issues of self-management you may face in conducting your research, particularly the effective use of resources such as time. The management of other aspects of the research process is also discussed, such as your supervisor, university and those from whom you collect your data. We also help you to think about the ways in which you adhere to the code of research ethics that you will be required to observe.

In Chapter 4 we consider the use of secondary data. We discuss the valuable role which secondary data may play in your research and the reasons you may use secondary data. The ready availability of a wealth of secondary data online is considered. We also warn you about some of the pitfalls inherent in the use of secondary data and how to assess its value to your own research project.

The subject of Chapter 5 is research strategy. This involves a consideration of the main philosophies you may adopt and the ways in which they affect choice of strategy. We discuss the different types of research strategy, with an emphasis on the possibility of mixing strategies in one research project. We end the chapter with a discussion of the importance of validity and reliability: ensuring that your research results and conclusions are believable.

Chapter 6 gets to the core of the research process: the collection of data. We first explain how to choose a sample. We then consider three frequently used methods of collecting primary data in more detail. In this we look at how to design and distribute effective questionnaires, including the use of Internet questionnaires; conduct face-to-face, telephone and Internet-mediated interviews; and undertake structured and unstructured observations.

In Chapter 7 we deal with the process of data analysis. We discuss the two types of data – quantitative and qualitative – and the ways in which these data may be prepared for analysis and actually analysed. The use of statistics in both the presentation and analysis of data is explained with particular emphasis on the use of different software packages. We also discuss ways in which qualitative data may be prepared for analysis and analysed. As with the analysis of quantitative data, we emphasise the way in which you may develop theory from the analysed data.

Chapter 8 is devoted to the writing of your research proposal. We explain how the process of writing clarifies your ideas, and we emphasise the importance of treating the research proposal as an item of 'work in progress' by constantly revising it. The chapter also includes a discussion on what content the proposal should contain, how it may be structured and the appropriate writing style to be adopted. Finally, we suggest some of the criteria against which the quality of your research proposal may be assessed.

We hope you will learn a lot from this book: that's why it exists! But we also hope that you will enjoy reading it. Doing your research project should be fun!

*Mark and Phil*
*July 2017*

# About the authors

**Mark N.K. Saunders** BA, MSc, PGCE, PhD, Chartered FCIPD is Professor of Business Research Methods at Birmingham Business School and Director of Postgraduate Research Methods Training for the College of Social Sciences at the University of Birmingham. He is a Fellow of the British Academy of Management and member of the Fellows' College. Mark currently holds visiting professorships at the Universities of Surrey and of Worcester. He teaches research methods to master's and doctoral students as well as supervising master's dissertations and research degrees. Mark has published articles on research methods, and human resource aspects of the management of change including trust and organisational learning, in a range of journals including *British Journal of Management, Human Relations, Journal of Small Business Management, Management Learning, R and D Management* and *Social Science and Medicine.* He is co-author with Phil Lewis and Adrian Thornhill of *Research Methods for Business Students,* currently in its seventh edition and, with Bill Lee, co-author of *Doing Case Study Research for Business and Management Students.* He is also co-editor with Bill Lee and Vadake Narayanan of the *Mastering Business Research Methods* book series and editor of the *Handbooks of Research Methods in Management* book series. Mark undertakes research and consultancy in public, private and not-for-profit sectors. Prior to becoming an academic, he had a variety of research jobs in local government.

**Philip J. Lewis** BA, PhD, MSc, MCIPD, PGDipM, Cert Ed began his career in HR as a training adviser with the Distributive Industry Training Board. He then taught HRM and research methods in three UK universities. He studied part-time for degrees with the Open University and the University of Bath, from which he gained an MSc in Industrial Relations and a PhD for his research on performance pay in retail financial services. He is co-author with Mark Saunders and Adrian Thornhill of *Research Methods for Business Students,* currently in its seventh edition, and of *Employee Relations: Understanding the Employment Relationship;* and with Adrian Thornhill, Mike Millmore and Mark Saunders of *Managing Change: A Human Resource Strategy Approach;* and with Mark Saunders, Adrian Thornhill, Mike Millmore and Trevor Morrow of *Strategic Human Resource Management.* He has undertaken consultancy in both the public and private sectors.

# Acknowledgements

We are grateful to the following for permission to reproduce copyright material:

**Figures**
Figure 1.1 from *Competitive Advantage Maps*, Working Paper, Centre for Strategy & Performance, Institute for Manufacturing (Platts, K., and Khater, M., 2006), Reproduced with permission by Dr M. Khater from the Institute for Manufacturing; Figure on page 95 from Eurostat (2016) Copyright European Communities, 2016, Source: Eurostat, http://epp.eurostat.ec.europa.eu, © European Union, 1995–2017; Figure 7.3 from Organic farming. Organic crop area on the rise in the EU. Two million hectares more since 2010, *Eurostat News Release*, Source: Eurostat, http://epp.eurostat.ec.europa.eu, © European Union, 1995–2017.

**Screenshots**
Screenshot 2.2 from www.emeraldinsight.com, www.emeraldinsight.com; Screenshot 2.3 from https://www.ebsco.com, reproduced with permission of EBSCO Information Services; Screenshots on page 197, 7.7 from IBM SPSS Statistics Viewer, screenshots reprinted courtesy of International Business Machines Corporation, © International Business Machines Corporation. SPSS was acquired by IBM in October, 2009. IBM, the IBM logo, ibm.com, and SPSS are trademarks of International Business Machines Corp., registered in many jurisdictions worldwide. Other product and service names might be trademarks of IBM or other companies. A current list of IBM trademarks is available on the Web at "IBM Copyright and trademark information" at www.ibm.com/legal/copytrade.shtml.

**Tables**
Table 2.6 adapted from *Critical Reading and Writing for Postgraduates*, 3rd ed., Sage Publications Ltd (Wallace, M., and Wray, A., 2016)

**Text**
Extract 1.1 adapted from Rural broadband and digital-only services, Seventh Report of Session 2014–15, *House of Commons Environment, Food and Rural Affairs*, p. 3, Contains Parliamentary information licensed under the Open Parliament Licence v3.0; Extract 2.2 from SME innovation and learning: the role of networks and crisis events, *European Journal of Training and Development*, Vol. 38, Issue 1/2, pp. 136–49 (Saunders, M. N. K., Gray, D. E., and Goregaokar, H., 2014), doi: 10.1108/EJTD-07-2013-0073; Article 3.1 from Sweden leads the race to become cashless society, *www.theguardian.com*, 04/06/2016 (Henley, J.), Copyright Guardian News & Media Ltd. 2017; Extract on page 76 from *Research Ethics for Research involving Human Participants: Code of Practice* (2016),

https://www.brookes.ac.uk/Documents/Research/Policies-and-codes-of-practice/ethics_codeofpractice/, Oxford Brookes University Research Ethics Committee; Extract on page 94 from Eurostat (2016) Copyright European Communities, 2016, Source: Eurostat, http://epp.eurostat.ec.europa.eu, © European Union, 1995–2017; Extract on page 95 from *Methodological Manual for Tourism Statistics*, Version 3.1, p. 59 (2014), Source: Eurostat, http://epp.eurostat.ec.europa.eu, © European Union, 1995–2017; Extract 4.1 from http://www.edelman.com/insights/intellectual-property/2016-edelman-trust-barometer/global-results/, Daniel J. Edelman, Inc. and/or its subsidiaries and affiliates are the owners of the TRUSTBAROMETER trademark and copyright in the TRUSTBAROMETER surveys worldwide, which are used under license. These materials are not sponsored or endorsed by Daniel J. Edelman, Inc.; Article 5.1 from Emergence of 'serial returners' – online shoppers who habitually over order and take advantage of free returns – hinders growth of UK businesses, *Barclaycard*, Barclaycard 2017; Extract 7.6 from The influence of culture on trust judgments in customer relationship development by ethnic minority small businesses, *Journal of Small Business Management*, Vol. 52, Issue 1, pp. 67–8 (Altinay, L., Saunders, M. N. K., Wang, C. L.), Copyright © 2013, John Wiley and Sons; Extract on page 288 from *The Sociological Imagination*, OXFORD UNIVERSITY PRESS, INCORPORATED (MILLS, C. WRIGHT 1959) pp. 218–19, Reproduced with permission of OXFORD UNIVERSITY PRESS, INCORPORATED in the format Book via Copyright Clearance Center Inc.

**Picture Credits**
The publisher would like to thank the following for their kind permission to reproduce their photographs:

**Mark N. K. Saunders:** 205
Cover image: *Front:* **Mark N. K. Saunders**
All other images © Pearson Education

In some instances we have been unable to trace the owners of copyright material, and we would appreciate any information that would enable us to do so.

# Chapter 1

# Choosing your research topic

## 1.1     Why you should read this chapter

This is a big moment in your life. You are about to embark on a voyage of discovery. You will discover a lot about the research process, the topic you are going to research and, we hope, a lot about yourself too. For many of you, the research project is the one part of your course where you have an opportunity to choose what you are going to study and the way in which you study it. We hope that you see this as an exciting opportunity because we believe strongly that's what it is. It's your chance to express your individuality, your ingenuity and imagination, your resourcefulness and, above all, your personal organisational skills. These attributes have always been important. But in the twenty-first century, they are more important than ever. Why do we say this? It's because we think that all the social, economic and technological changes of the last few years have empowered us all to take charge of our own lives to a greater extent than ever before. So take charge of your research topic now!

The overall purpose of this chapter is to enable you to get your research project off to a good start by choosing a topic to research that will give you the best chance of succeeding and passing this important component of your course. It's worth bearing in mind that however good you may be at all the relevant skills that go into producing a good research project, you will give yourself a better chance of succeeding if you have chosen your topic wisely.

In this chapter, we talk about why choosing the right research topic is so important. We then explain why, for many of us, the choice of topic is so difficult. The choice is made easier if this decision-making process is tackled in a systematic way. In the chapter, we outline some of the procedures for adopting a systematic approach. Then, having got to the stage where you have chosen a topic, we examine ways in which the topic you have chosen can be refined in such a way that it is acceptable to your assessors and will provide you with the maximum amount of satisfaction.

We end the chapter with a consideration of what makes a good research topic, and some help on writing research questions and objectives.

## 1.2    Why choosing the right research topic is so important

It is possible, of course, that you may be constrained in your choice of research topic. Your university may define strict limits outside which you may not stray. Alternatively, it is possible that an employer has asked you to undertake a piece of research. In either case, some of the points in the next two sections on choosing the right research topic and generating research ideas may not apply to you directly. However, we encourage you not to ignore the points made. It may be that although you may not have a free choice of the general topic, the way in which you approach it may be entirely your decision.

Now let's look at some of the reasons why choosing the right research topic is so important.

### ● You have to live with it

The decision about which research topic to choose is something you will have to live with, maybe for as long as a year or more. We mean this in two senses. First, it is a topic you will become intimately familiar with, so it makes sense to choose something that you will enjoy. Ask yourself: what am I really interested in? OK, so it may be that football is your passion. Well, football nowadays is big business, particularly in the major leagues in Europe such as the English Premier League. So if your passion has a business dimension, then maybe there is a research topic to be pursued. One of our student's undergraduate projects explored the reasons why attendances at matches were generally lower when the match was screened live on television. This led into interesting areas such as the affiliation aspect of motivation theory, where some people, for example a football team's fans, have a need to be affiliated with like-minded people and are motivated towards interaction with these people, leading them to attend matches. This posed a question about the extent to which a comfortable armchair and the economic benefits of not attending the match in person overrode the need for affiliation!

The second sense in which we mean that the decision about your choice of research topic is something you will have to live with is that when you have chosen it, normally there is no going back. You will make life much more difficult for yourself if you find out after one half of the time period allotted to your research that you have chosen the wrong topic. It may be possible to change even at that stage, but you spend the rest of the allotted time playing catch-up. We talk later in this chapter about problems in choosing a research topic, and the consequences of making the wrong choice. So it is better to spend the time at the outset making sure it's right for you. It is a time-consuming process. Many students have remarked to us in the past that they thought that choosing their topic would be easy. It may be easy to choose one that interests you, but turning it into a viable proposition for your course may take much longer than you thought.

### ● It will be better choosing a topic that will both exploit and develop your knowledge and skills

As well as choosing a topic that you will enjoy, it obviously makes sense to choose a topic that you are capable of doing well. Making a list of your skills and knowledge seems a good starting point. Here are a few questions you can ask yourself to help you prepare the list.

### What are your personal strengths and weaknesses?

We are all better at some things than others. You may have discovered strengths on your course that you may want to exploit. These may relate to your background experience or particular skills that you can practise in the data collection and analysis stages of the research. The knowledge gained in previous or current work experience is a good knowledge source for many students. You are more likely to know your way around some of the areas that need specialist knowledge. In addition, this specialist knowledge will lead more easily to an informed research question that needs answering. Alternatively, you may be keen to learn about an industry that's new to you. For example, you may be fascinated by software design and want to learn more about that industry with a view to possible employment. In this case, you will need to ask yourself whether locating a research project in that industry will give you an equal chance of success compared to an industry with which you may be familiar. It's also a good idea to think about the modules you have studied and those in which you have had success. This will give you a confident start.

The data collection and analysis methods you adopt offer slightly different options. Here, you may be experienced at interviewing but less so at designing questionnaires. Do you exploit your expertise or decide to learn the skill of questionnaire design? Of course, you can include an element of both. The choices you make may be based on practical as well as personal development considerations. It's not much good having learned a lot but not passed the module!

### What knowledge and skills do you think you will need in the future?

This may be quite a difficult question to answer for many of us. Few of us could have predicted 25 years ago the extent to which we all now need information technology skills in both our work and home lives. Yet it may be possible for you to predict some of the generic skills you will need for effective personal performance. Some of these, such as influencing others and conducting meetings, you may have encountered during your course. The opportunity may present itself in your research to practise some of these skills, particularly in the data collection stage. In the same way, your choice of topic could help develop your specialist knowledge of an aspect of your chosen area of employment.

### What resources can you draw upon to help?

Perhaps the value of this question is most evident when it reveals the absence of resources. Most of you will have access to key people such as lecturers, managers and colleagues. The extent to which these can be of assistance will, of course, vary. It will be very valuable to be able to consult an 'expert' in the subject area you are studying for your research but, if you have chosen a fairly specialist field, the absence of such assistance may be a considerable block to your progress. You will, of course, have access to information technology, but such issues as the processing of questionnaire answers and the analysis of questionnaire data is a complex and demanding affair if you have no experience in this. Don't be afraid to ask for help!

### ◼ Will your choice of topic help you pass the whole course?

Although we have put the emphasis here upon self-development, the point remains that you must choose a topic that will allow you to meet the assessment requirements and will give you the best possible chance of ultimate success. If there is one fundamental lesson that we have learned as a result of supervising many research projects over the years, it is this: the earlier you start deciding upon your topic, the more likely you will be to choose the right one and ensure final success!

## 1.3    Why choosing a research topic is difficult

There is no question that for many of us, choosing the right topic is one of the most difficult aspects of the whole research process. At this stage, you are on your own! It has to come from you; and making decisions, which have important consequences, is often difficult for most of us. So, what are some of the reasons why this one may be particularly difficult? Let's have a look at some of them.

### ◼ There is simply too much choice

It's wonderful living in an age when so much information is available at the end of our fingertips. But this can lead us to think that there is no question that has not been asked and no problem which has not been solved. Whatever it is we are interested in, there appears to be a vast amount of information available, much of which there is never enough time to read. This results in the inevitable feeling that whatever it is you have in mind will have been done before. Well, it probably has, but maybe not in the way you intend to do it. But that doesn't mean that you can't tackle it. One of the most popular undergraduate research topics is worker motivation. 'What is that workers value most about their working lives?' is a frequently asked question. The textbooks are full of generic answers to this question, and your university library will be full of project reports which have asked the same question. Yet there are lots of managers in organisations who need to know the answer in respect of their own employees. In other words, even the most familiar topic can be applied to many different, specific situations.

### ◼ The fear it will be too difficult

The research process is challenging enough without making it more difficult by choosing a topic that stretches you too far. How will you know if that is the case? Have a look at the literature on a topic that interests you as a possible choice. Maybe the way in which the topic is covered has an overly theoretical approach which makes it too difficult for you to 'think your way in'. The motivation of people to work has a distinctly practical feel. But researching the way in which the brain operates to direct our enthusiasm to one interest rather than another seems to emphasise the biological aspects rather than the business perspective, for which your course has prepared you.

### ⬤ The fear that it will be insufficiently theoretical

It's quite understandable that you should feel a mild sense of panic when you go to your supervisor to explain with great enthusiasm your choice of research topic only to be greeted by 'yes, very interesting, but what role will theory play?'. This is where it starts to get tricky. But don't despair, because theory has a role to play in all project reports. It's just a question of how and where you use it. Later in this chapter we explore the role of theory in writing research questions and objectives. And in Chapter 5 we explain that theory can be used as a 'way in' to your research by setting up theoretical propositions which can be tested. It can also be used as a lens through which you can study your data, or a structure against which you can perform your data analysis.

In case you are unconvinced, just consider this statement: 'students read research methods textbooks in the hope that they perform more effectively in their research module'. That's a theory, and what you are doing right now is evidence that it is accurate!

### ⬤ The temptation to re-use work you have already done

It is tempting to take the easy way out and use an assignment which you have written for a previous purpose and just enlarge it to make it into a research project. There is a similar temptation for part-time students who perhaps have produced a research report at work. The trouble is that it never quite 'fits'. It's a bit like fitting a wheel to a bike that's not quite the right size. It may be OK, but it's never more than that. You are likely to spend more time getting it to fit than you would spend on thinking through a purpose-made topic.

## 1.4 Ten ways to generate ideas for a research topic

Now that we have given you some general guidelines on choosing a suitable research topic, let's look at some techniques for deciding on the topic itself. We have listed our favourite 10 of these in Table 1.1. They are in no particular order.

Table 1.1 Ten techniques for generating research ideas

| | |
|---|---|
| 1 | Thinking |
| 2 | Looking at past project titles |
| 3 | Using past projects from the university library |
| 4 | Using past course assignments |
| 5 | Using relevant literature |
| 6 | Following the news media |
| 7 | Brainstorming |
| 8 | Concept mapping |
| 9 | Making a note of ideas |
| 10 | Discussion with helpers |

## Thinking

We are bound to start with this one, because there is no escaping it! By thinking, we mean really thinking. Keep the need to select a topic in your mind all the time – when you watch TV, read a newspaper, browse relevant web pages, talk to colleagues, talk and listen in seminars, discuss issues with your lecturers. Probably, like us, prompted by your study of business and management, questions often go through your mind when you are in stores, airports and buses – questions such as 'How are the work rotas for these people organised?'; 'How can the cost of delivering this service be reduced while maintaining quality of service?' This is what you may call 'background thinking'. Now let's look at a series of more specific techniques for generating ideas.

## Looking at past project titles

You are not the first person to have trodden the path, so it's a good idea to look at what those before you have attempted. You may find a list of past research project titles for your course in your university library; alternatively, your course leader may have one. This will give you an idea of the sort of topic that may be suitable. It will also fire your imagination and help you to start thinking about how that title may relate to something that you have thought about. Don't worry about what you think may not be a particularly well-written title. And do bear in mind that in some universities, all past projects are placed in the library whether they are bare passes or distinctions. So the fact that a project is in your library does not necessarily mean that it's a good piece of work. The point is to generate ideas for your project, not work out what makes a good project.

## Using past projects

Having delved into the university library to look for past project titles, why not spend some more time checking the projects which have caught your attention? Raimond (1993) suggests a useful method for generating research topic ideas this way (see Table 1.2).

Table 1.2 Four steps for generating research topic ideas using past projects from the university library

| |
|---|
| **1**   Select six projects that you like. |
| **2**   For each of these six projects, note down your first thoughts to answer these three questions (if responses for different projects are the same, this does not matter): <br> (a)  What appeals to you about the project? <br> (b)  What is good about the project? <br> (c)  Why is the project good? |
| **3**   Select three projects that you do not like. |
| **4**   For each of these three projects, note down your first thoughts to answer these three questions (if responses for different projects are the same, or cannot be clearly expressed, this does not matter; note them down anyway): <br> (a)  What do you dislike about the project? <br> (b)  What is bad about the project? <br> (c)  Why is the project bad? |

Having completed these four steps, you will have a note of the things that you like and dislike about projects and, of equal importance, what you consider makes good and poor projects. What's more, that list will be personal to you. It's your opinion, and that is what you can use to guide your choice for your own research topic.

## Using past course assignments

Many students find that past course assignments serve as a good starting point for research topic ideas. It seems logical to develop the work of an assignment in which you have had some choice of topic, particularly when you have enjoyed it and received a good grade. However, do bear in mind the maxim that 'all research ends with ideas for more research'. Look hard at what you have done and ask yourself: 'Are there questions posed by my work which I have not yet answered?'

Beware of developing the assignment because you got a good grade! There must be scope for development, and it must meet the assessment criteria. For example, many universities have self-plagiarism rules to prevent students from re-using work that they have already submitted as an assignment.

## Using relevant literature

Since what you are going to tackle should use the literature relevant to your topic, it seems sensible to start examining that literature. Let's assume that you have decided to look at a possible research topic that is a development of a module you have enjoyed. Go back to your lecture notes and course textbooks on that topic and make a note of the names of relevant authors. This will give you a basis on which to undertake a preliminary search. This should help you to produce a list of articles, books, reports and other items.

A particularly valuable literature source of research topic ideas is academic review articles. They are valuable because they contain both a thorough review of the state of knowledge in that topic area and pointers towards areas where further research needs to be undertaken. Browsing recent journals in your field is also a good source of possible research ideas. For many subject areas, your project supervisor will be able to suggest possible recent review articles, or articles that contain recommendations for further work.

Books, by contrast, are often less up to date than journal articles. But they do often contain a good overview of research that has been undertaken, which may suggest ideas to you. Reports may also be of use. The most recently published are usually up to date and, again, often contain recommendations that may form the basis of your research idea. An example of such a report is shown as Research in practice 1.1.

### Research in practice 1.1

#### Using reports to generate research topic ideas

Access to broadband in the UK is inconsistent, the impact being particularly in rural areas where speeds are unacceptably slow. Written evidence to the House of Commons Environment, Food and Rural Affairs Committee explains how poor broadband can lead

→

to a range of problems: from reduced access to online learning resources for students, families being unable to use everyday online services and the effectiveness of rural businesses being severely affected. Slow broadband can produce a feeling of a two-tier society, with rural communities suffering markedly due to infrastructure problems which make them harder to reach.

The committee expressed concern that BT, the infrastructure developer, told it that the 2015 target of 95% of premises receiving superfast broadband by 2017 may slip. The committee recommended that the government unit overseeing broadband development should insist upon the 2017 target being met. Moreover, a target date for when the last 5% of premises will obtain access to superfast broadband coverage must be published.

The importance of good broadband for all is highlighted by the government's policy of providing its services 'digital-by-default'. This policy has clear ramifications when broadband access is limited or non-existent.

The report emphasised that it is vital that the last premises in the UK to have access to basic and superfast broadband are treated just as well as the first premises and are not left behind or forgotten.

*Source:* House of Commons Environment, Food and Rural Affairs (2015) *Rural broadband and digital-only services, Seventh Report of Session 2014–15.* London: The Stationery Office Limited.

Table 1.3 lists some useful questions to ask when searching articles and reports for possible research topic ideas. The answers to these can help progress your choice of topic.

**Table 1.3** Useful questions to ask when searching articles and reports for possible research topic ideas

- What did the authors conclude?
- What alternative conceptual models, explanations or hypotheses did the authors consider?
- What methods did the authors use to approach the problem?
- Do you accept the authors' conclusions? If not, are there other methods that could allow you to test their conclusion?
- Does the authors' research suggest new ways to interpret a different problem?
- Are there other problems that could be studied using the same methods?

## Following the news media

We would always encourage you to go to the academic literature as your first port of call, but don't ignore the value of keeping up to date with items in the news. News media can be a very rich source of ideas. The stories which occur every day in the 'quality' newspapers (e.g. *The Times, The Financial Times, The Guardian, The Independent* and *The Daily Telegraph*) in both print and online versions may provide ideas which relate directly to a possible research topic. Don't forget, there may be other ideas which flow from the main story. On the morning of writing this section in 2016, it was announced that the film *Batman v Superman: Dawn of Justice* had taken $424m (£300m) at the box office worldwide in its first five days, a record for a March debut and the sixth-highest US opening weekend. This suggests a research topic exploring the enormous amount of marketing spin-off opportunities presented by such a high-profile brand.

## Brainstorming

**Brainstorming** can be a useful and fun way of generating research topic ideas. It is particularly valuable when you brainstorm with a group of people, ideally those who really understand why you are doing this. You can brainstorm on your own – but it's much less fun!

To brainstorm, you start off by defining the general field you are interested in. Try to make this as precise as possible. In the early stages of formulating a topic, you may have to be pretty imprecise, such as 'I am interested the effects of the weather on food retailing, but I am not sure how I can turn this into a research topic'.

The next stage is to ask the other members of the group for suggestions, relating to the imprecise topic you have suggested. It's a good idea to arm yourself with a pen and a large sheet of paper and note down all the suggestions you receive. The following five rules are very important:

1 Do record as many suggestions as possible.

2 Do record all suggestions, however 'wacky' or 'off the wall' they may appear at first sight.

3 Don't criticise or evaluate any ideas until they have been considered.

4 Do consider all the suggestions and explore the precise meaning of each of them.

5 Do analyse the list of suggestions and decide which appeal to you most as research ideas and why.

> **Definition**
>
> **brainstorming:** a technique that can be used to generate and refine research ideas. It is best undertaken with a group of people.

## Concept mapping

Having completed your brainstorming, you may move on to use another technique which we find very useful in many contexts – **concept mapping**. This is a process which moves from a general idea that may have been the outcome of a brainstorm, or other idea-generating technique, to the creation of a map which represents visually the organisation of your thinking. Concept maps may be elaborate or simple; indeed, they

> **Definition**
>
> **concept map:** a diagram which represents visually the way we organize our thoughts about a set of related ideas.

may start out very simple and end up quite detailed. The purpose is to help you organize your thinking about a topic and get them into a coherent state. Concept maps are very useful in helping you recognise where you have gaps in your knowledge. This can help with planning further searches in the literature. They are also a good base from which you can move on to develop research questions and objectives. An example of a concept map is shown in Figure 1.1.

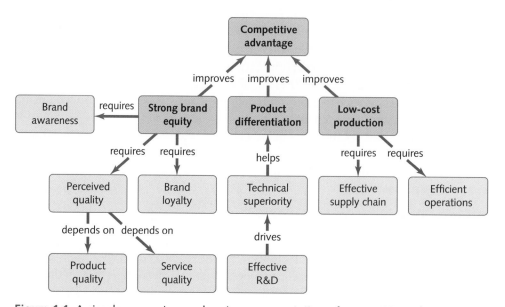

**Figure 1.1** A simple concept map showing representation of competitive advantage

*Source:* Competitive Advantage Maps, Platts, K. & Khater, M., Working Paper, Centre for Strategy & Performance, Institute for Manufacturing, 2006. Reproduced with permission from the Institute for Manufacturing.

## ● Making a note of ideas

Many of you will look at this title heading and say 'that's all very well for them but I never get any ideas!' You do; all of us do. Think positively and forget any notions that ideas are reserved just for the creative few rather than for the rest of us. It's perfectly normal to go through several days without having any ideas at all. Then, perhaps when you are thinking of something else entirely, an idea will come to you followed by more ideas. Sometimes, the ideas will come pretty quickly, so you will have to make sure you capture them before they are forgotten. When you start getting ideas, you will learn not to worry about the times when the ideas are not coming. It's just important to take full advantage of those idea flows when they happen.

So what about capturing those precious ideas when they come? It's important to voice-record or note ideas on your mobile phone or keep a notebook for this purpose. All you need to do is to note any interesting research ideas as you think of them and, of equal importance, what started you thinking of the idea. You don't have to go as far as Mark, who takes his notebook on holiday with him so he can jot down any flashes of inspiration that occur to him while sitting in a cafe!

## ● Discussion with colleagues, friends and lecturers

Don't forget the more usual sources of ideas and advice: your colleagues, friends and university lecturers. Project supervisors will often have ideas for possible student projects which they will be pleased to discuss with you. These may be based upon work done by other students which may be developed, or taken in a different direction. One of our students conducted an analysis of a food manufacturer's advertising strategy for launching a new brand with a view to discovering the optimum advertising expenditure level. We suggested a similar project using an insurance company. Each of the two students tackled the project in a different way. Both delivered very successful pieces of work.

You can also pick up useful ideas from talking to practitioners and professional groups. Find out if your local professional association has a students' evening. Here you can meet local managers who will be more than willing to discuss ideas with you. Most professional groups are pleased to welcome students to meetings where often interesting presentations are given which may spark off your ideas. Once again, do bear in mind the value of discussing possible ideas and make a note of them.

## 1.5    How to refine research topic ideas

## ● Refining topics given by your employing organisation

The choosing of a research topic may be less problematic than we have suggested above. At least, on the face of it, this may be so. We say this because you may be given a topic. This may apply particularly to you if you are a part-time student and your manager has given you a topic to research. The problem here is that it is not 'your' topic, and you may not be wildly enthusiastic about it. If you find yourself in this situation, you will have to weigh the advantage of doing something useful to the organisation against the disadvantage of a potential lack of personal motivation. Aim for a balance.

One of the problems in this situation is that the research project your manager wishes you to undertake is larger than that which is suitable for your course. This may not be an insurmountable problem. Within the larger project there may well be a smaller element which you can concentrate upon for your university research project.

In such cases, it may be possible to complete both by isolating an element of the larger organisational project that you find interesting and treating this as the project for your course.

### Research in practice 1.2

#### Refining a topic given by an organisation

Peng, a student of Phil's, worked for a large manufacturing organisation which felt it had a problem with communicating with its employees. She was asked by the HR manager to carry out an employee survey to establish what employees felt about the way in

→

which managers communicated with their staff, and the way the company in general delivered important news to employees. One of the motives behind this managerial initiative was the feeling of the HR director that the company should have a regular newsletter. (Not the least reason for this motive was the thought that this would promote the profile of the HR function!) This project was not one which Peng would have chosen. However, she was interested in the theoretical proposition that employees would feel more committed to the company if they felt trouble was being taken to communicate effectively with them. Peng talked this over with Phil and, with the approval of the HR manager, included some questions designed specifically to test this theoretical proposition.

Peng decided to treat the company research as one major piece of work with a separate element which was 'hers' for her university research project. This involved writing a large report for her employer and a smaller report for her university work.

Peng was very aware of the political dimension to her work. She knew that the HR director had a vested interest in the outcomes of her work. Phil advised her to keep this in mind but not let it compromise the element of the work she was doing for her university course. Peng and Phil agreed that it was important to have a clear stance with regard to her personal objectives, and to stick to them.

One final point about the potentially tricky job of 'serving two masters': the biggest potential problem may be one of your own making: to promise to deliver research outcomes to your employer and not do so. After all, don't forget that in this situation, as an employee, you get paid for what your employer asks of you.

## The preliminary study

Even if you have been given a research idea, it is still necessary to refine it in order to turn it into a research project. This is often called a **preliminary study**.

For some research ideas, this study need only be an initial review of some of the literature. This is similar to 'using relevant literature' and 'following the news media' in the 'ten techniques for generating research ideas' section (Table 1.1). You may think of this as the first attempt at drafting your critical review of the literature, a topic we deal with in detail in Chapter 2. Other research ideas may benefit from revisiting the techniques discussed earlier in this section, in particular looking at past project titles, using past course assignments and using past projects from the university library. Discussions with lecturers and managers may also be very valuable.

> **Definition**
>
> **preliminary study:** the process by which a research idea is refined in order to turn it into a research project.

Your university may require you to complete a research project which restricts you to collecting secondary data, data that already exists and was originally collected for some other purpose (see Chapter 4). If so, it is important that you establish that the data you require are available.

If your research is going to be conducted in an organisation, it is essential to gain a good understanding of that organisation. One good way of doing this is to shadow employees who are likely to be important in your research. They will usually provide useful insights into the way the organisation works as well as specific guidance for your research. Whatever way you choose to familiarise yourself with the organisation, don't forget that the underlying purpose is to gain a greater understanding so that your research question can be refined.

At this early stage you will be testing your research ideas. However, it may be that after a preliminary study, or after discussing your ideas with colleagues, you decide that the research idea is no longer viable. Don't despair too much if this is the case. It is much better to revise your research ideas at this stage than to have to do it later, when you have undertaken far more work.

## The Delphi technique

Another approach you may use for refining your research ideas is the **Delphi technique**. This technique involves using a group of people who are either involved or interested in the research idea to generate and choose a more specific research idea. To use this technique, you need to:

1 explain your research idea to the members of the group (they can make notes if they wish);
2 encourage group members at the end of your explanation to seek clarification and more information as appropriate;
3 ask each member of the group, including the originator of the research idea, to generate independently up to three specific research ideas based on the idea that has been described (they can also be asked to provide a justification for their specific ideas);
4 collect the research ideas in an unedited and non-attributable form and to distribute them to all members of the group;
5 conduct a second cycle of the process (steps 2 to 4) in which individuals comment on the research ideas and revise their own contributions in the light of what others have said;
6 undertake subsequent cycles of the process until a consensus is reached. These either follow a similar pattern (steps 2 to 4) or use discussion, voting or some other method.

| Definition |
| --- |
| **Delphi technique:** a technique which can be used with a group of people who are either involved or interested in the research topic to generate and select a more specific research idea. |

People generally enjoy trying to help one another, so this technique can be very effective. It is also very good for forging team spirit among groups of people. An example of the developing of a research question is shown in Research in practice 1.3.

### Research in practice 1.3

#### Using a Delphi Group

Kumar worked part time at The Sizzling Wok, a restaurant specialising in Asian fusion cooking. The owner of the restaurant, Virat, explained to him that while business in general was good, it was important that the restaurant generated more turnover in the traditionally slacker periods, i.e. during the day and on evenings in the early part of the week.

Kumar thought that a research project involving some consumer research and business costings would be useful for Virat and provide a project for his university course which would involve marketing, accounting and business planning.

Kumar was part of a small group of course colleagues which met frequently to discuss ideas and help each other with the more challenging parts of the study programme. He explained his research idea to the group members. As a result the group generated a series of research ideas for Kumar to explore. These were:

- Having 'special offers or special menus' at 'quiet' times, meaning that customers could eat more cheaply at these times.

- A loyalty scheme with points awarded to customers leading to free meals and extra points awarded at 'quiet' times.

- Promotions including features such as 'show cooking', where the chefs prepared special dishes responding to customers' wishes in the restaurant itself, thus generating interest and a sense of 'bonding' with the customer.

- Restricting the opening times of the restaurant to avoid opening for business at 'quiet' times.

- Examining the costs of opening at 'quiet' times (e.g. staffing costs) with a view to making these times more profitable.

Following on from the list of general ideas, the group then developed some more specific research ideas, among which were the following:

- how the restaurant may generate more business during the 'quiet' times of the week, and

- examination of the profitability of operating during the 'quiet' times of the week.

At the end of this process, Kumar was able to refine his thinking and decide upon a research idea with which Virat was pleased and his research supervisor was impressed. It was: 'How can The Sizzling Wok operate during the less busy times of the week in order to meet the demand of maintaining a consistent level of profitability at all trading times?'

Kumar was delighted with the outcome of the meetings and resolved to help his colleagues with the same level of commitment with which they had helped him.

## Narrowing down

The Delphi technique illustrates what is perhaps the most difficult aspect of refining your research ideas: the move from the general to the specific. Many of us start out with some idea of what we want to do for our research but find it tricky to narrow down.

One useful way of moving from the general to the specific is to think of research ideas as developing through a process which goes through three stages of idea classification. These are:

1 The general area.

2 The more specific field.

3 The precise focus of the research.

One of our students recently was following the marketing route through his degree. He was also very interested in environmental issues. These can be termed his general area of interest. More specifically, he was also very enthusiastic about exploring the different ways in which marketeers can learn about 'greener' ways of conducting marketing for their organisations. After much thinking and discussion, he developed the research questions: 'What methods do marketeers use to learn about "greener" ways of conducting marketing for their organisations?' and 'Why do they decide upon the methods chosen?'

## 1.6    What makes a good research topic?

The next section draws together some of the thoughts in the section 'Why choosing the right research topic is so important' as well as introducing ideas about what goes into making a good research topic choice. Some of the most significant of these ideas are listed below.

## It is a topic about which you are enthusiastic and which matches your career goals

Let's start with by repeating two of the points we made earlier. A good research topic is one in which you have a genuine interest because, as we said earlier, you have to live with it for possibly a few months or longer and you want to give yourself the best chance of success. A well-chosen topic is also one that matches your career goals.

## There are resources available, particularly data and time

We also referred to the question of resources, in particular those of your skills and knowledge and individuals, such as lecturers, who may be able to help you. But there are two other key resources to think about. The first of these is data. It is all very well thinking up and precisely defining an intriguing research idea, but it's of little use if you cannot get access to the data to explore it. You may, for example, be very interested in the effect on patients of specific management initiatives in the UK National Health Service. However, getting primary data from patients may be far from easy for all but researchers appointed by the Service. Secondary data may be available, but will it answer precisely the research question you have set?

The second question to ask yourself is: 'Is the research topic achievable within the available time?' This may be quite a difficult question to answer at the beginning of your research project because you cannot anticipate the potential delays. If you are dependent on data from other people such as managers, customers or colleagues, it is reasonable to say that this will not be as high a priority for them as it is for you. It is always a good idea to be realistic (or even pessimistic!) in your assessment of the time-scale necessary to gather data. Even the collection of secondary data may be less straightforward than you envisage, particularly that from non-official sources. The more realistic you are in setting your timescales at the beginning, the less stressful you will find the latter stages of the research process.

## ◼ The subject is topical

In the winter of 2015–16, Apple was locked in a bitter dispute with the FBI over the latter's desire to compel Apple to access the information on the iPhone of a mass killer. Apple obviously expressed the deep concern felt by most people about the reasons for the FBI request but refused, arguing that if the US government could make it easier to unlock an iPhone, it would have the power to reach into anyone's device to capture their data. The government could then extend this breach of privacy and demand that Apple build surveillance software to intercept an individual's messages, health records or financial data, location, or even access the phone's microphone or camera without the user's knowledge.

At the time of writing this dispute remained unresolved. But it is likely to be repeated in other cases, particularly as other technology organisations such as Amazon and Google came out in support of Apple.

This raises an interesting question about the ownership of digital data and the extent to which the privacy, which is at the heart of our relationship with many of the digital companies with which we deal, may be compromised in particular circumstances. This may be the basis of a marketing investigation about the degree to which technology companies can stress data privacy as part of their market appeal.

The Apple–FBI case may have been the catalyst for this project and serve as a useful example from which another research project may be developed.

## ◼ Whatever the outcome, you still have a worthwhile project

Let's say that you develop a research question such as 'How do severe winter weather conditions affect retail food supermarket trading patterns?' On the face of it, this sounds a reasonable question. It could be expected that there would be an effect, not only on the volume of trade but on the type of food purchased. However, it is possible that the answer may be 'there is no effect'. The consequence of the 'no effect' result for you is not only that it is rather dispiriting, but you don't have an interesting story to tell in your project report.

The trick is to define a research question that gives you results of similar value whatever you find out. In the example here, 'To what extent does the weather affect retail food supermarket trading patterns and why?' is a much wider question that will guarantee that you have the scope to write an interesting project report, whatever the outcome.

## The topic fits the specifications and will meet the assessment criteria set by the university

Your lecturers are likely to issue a set of guidelines to help you with completion of your research project. This will give you general ideas of what constitutes a successful project. A good place to start in your study of this is the assessment criteria. It's a good idea to check through these criteria to make sure that your choice of research topic will enable you to meet those criteria. So, for example, if there is a criterion that your research must aim to solve an organisational problem, it's of little use pursuing a study that analyses consumer expenditure data over a given time period. Similarly, if the assessment criteria state that you should only use secondary data, you should not design a questionnaire or interview people.

It is taken for granted that the chosen research topic should match the content of the course being undertaken. Yet we have seen a number of cases where this is questionable. An interest in the under-representation of women in management, for example, could easily develop into a study of the role of women in society in general, rather than in organisations specifically. This is an easy trap to fall into. One of the problems with a study chosen by you, and pursued by you, is that you become so close to it that you lose sight of the fact that you are wandering away from the initial brief. That is why talking to people is such an important part of the process.

As with all concerns you may have about the progress of your research, talk to your lecturer if you are not sure about the appropriateness of your topic choice.

## There is a clear link to the relevant literature

It is almost certain that your assessment criteria will specify the need to link your work to the relevant academic literature. It is essential here to ask yourself: 'Why am I doing this?' Too often the literature chapter in project reports we read is of the 'he said this, she said that and they said the other' variety (section 2.2). You should not use the literature in this way. Rather, an alternative way of thinking about the review of the literature is to call it a 'review of previous research on my topic'. From this you can extend this work. This can be done, for example, by setting your study in the context of the literature reviewed. A student of Mark's, for example, reviewed studies of workers who have some autonomy over the way in which their work is organised and applied this to her project on the work organisation of courier drivers. As well as locating your study in a different work context to that which has been covered in your literature review, you can set it in a different time context or national culture. Many of the classic management theories are several decades old. You may well ask the question: 'Does this still apply in the twenty-first-century post-industrial age?'

### ⬤ Fresh insights into the topic are provided

We hope it will have occurred to you that the previous points about the extension of your literature search will guarantee that your research will be able to provide fresh insights into your chosen topic. A fresh context leads to fresh insights. What is less easy to guarantee is the degree to which your project report's discussion conclusions are insightful.

### ⬤ Research question(s) and objectives are capable of being stated clearly

Perhaps the best test of the clarity of your research question(s) and objectives is the extent to which those who know nothing about your topic can understand what it is you plan to do. If you pass this test, and the others listed in Table 1.4, you are well on your way to developing a successful research topic. We say more about writing clear research questions and objectives in the next section.

**Table 1.4** Summary: what makes a good research topic?

- It is a topic about which you are enthusiastic and it matches the career goals.
- There are resources available, particularly data and time.
- The subject is topical.
- Whatever the outcome, you still have a worthwhile project.
- The topic fits the specifications and meets the standards set by the examining institution.
- There is a clear link to the relevant literature.
- Fresh insights into the topic are provided.
- The research question(s) and objectives are capable of being stated clearly.

## 1.7  How to turn a research idea into a research project

Settling on a suitable research idea is a great step forward in the research process. It is challenging and time consuming. But the early stages are not complete yet. The task of turning your big idea into precise and meaningful research question(s) and objectives is vital if you are to end up with reliable and valid data from which you can draw valid conclusions.

Do you need research questions and objectives? Well, we think that you do. We see them as a progression: from research questions, you then move on to define objectives. Perhaps this is clearer if we define what we mean by these two key terms. Research questions are those questions that the research process will address. They are often the forerunner of research objectives. On the other hand, research objectives are clear, precise statements that identify what you wish to accomplish as a result of doing the research. And research objectives are vital. Why? You've guessed it – because if you don't know where you're going, you're likely to end up somewhere else!

## Developing research questions

Rather like generating research ideas, defining **research questions** is not a simple, straight-forward matter. Here again, we come up against what is a suitable research question. For the answer to this, we go back to the last section, 'What makes a good research topic?' A suitable research question is one that reflects the the fact you have thought about what fits the specifications and meets the standards set by the examining institution, provides a clear link to the relevant literature and promises fresh insights into the topic you have chosen. Let us concentrate on that word 'insights'. Here we raise the point about two types of questions – those questions that are too easy and those that are likely to provide insights. An example will illustrate the difference. Let us say that your research idea involves examining the impact that Internet banking has had upon local bank branch closure. Asking the question 'How many local bank branch closures have there been in the period since Internet banking became widespread in my country?' would be too simple. It would merely describe a situation and not provide insights into the link between the growth of Internet banking and local branch closures. Questions that would promise more insights would be 'What effect has the growth of Internet banking had upon the uses customers make of branch facilities?' and 'Why do customers prefer to bank online in preference to visiting their local branch?' The answers to these questions may give some clue as to the eventual effect on branch closures of Internet banking. If, for example, you found that the overwhelming response to the question 'Do you still value your local branch?' put to Internet banking users was negative, then the obvious conclusion would be that the future for local bank branches is bleak.

Avoiding the asking of questions that promote descriptive answers, because they are too easy, is one way of ensuring that you do not ask unsuitable research questions. Another is asking questions that are too difficult. Earlier in this chapter, we cited the example of a research interest that many researchers have had in recent years in the under-representation of women in management. There are several ways you may be able to gain insights into the research question 'Why are women under-represented in senior management positions?' but it is a difficult question to answer definitively. In this case, as with most research questions, there is a simple response to the question of how to find out the answer: ask those who select the appointees to senior management positions. But the reality here is that it would probably be very difficult, if not impossible, to gain access to those key decision makers in large organisations. Without such access it would not be possible to get a good understanding of the subtle 'unofficial' processes that go on at staff selection which may favour one type of candidate over another. Overreaching yourself in the definition of research questions is just as big a danger as asking simple, descriptive questions.

To end up with a research question that is suitable, try subjecting it to the 'Goldilocks test'. This is what Clough and Nutbrown (2012) use to decide if research questions are either 'too big', 'too small', 'too hot' or 'just right'. By 'too big' they meant those that

| Definition |
| --- |

**research question:** the one overall question or a number of key questions that the research process will address. These are often the precursor of research objectives.

probably need significant research funding because they need too many resources. Questions that are too small are like those that we mentioned earlier – the ones that just promote descriptive answers. The 'too hot' questions are so called because they stray into sensitive areas, rather like our example of asking senior managers why they tend not to recruit women to senior management positions. There are other reasons why the context may be too sensitive. Many of these are likely to involve issues of status and power among subjects whom you wish to play a part in your research. Alternatively, the timing of the research may be inappropriate. One of our students was conducting research on redundancy. His requests to organisations were often met with refusals because the organisations that refused to participate were going through difficult times. Outside people talking about redundancies would have sparked off suspicion among employees that these organisations were planning redundancies. On the other hand, research questions that are 'just right' (Clough and Nutbrown, 2012: 43) are those that are 'just right for investigation at this time, by this researcher in this setting'.

## Research in practice 1.4

### Defining the research question

Rebecca was studying for a BSc in Management Studies and taking her placement year in Forsure, a multinational insurance company. The company's overall mission was: 'to help our customers live their lives with more peace of mind by protecting them, their relatives and their property against risks and by managing their savings and assets'. One of the company's strategic objectives was:

> To become the preferred company for all our stakeholders by strengthening our focus on the customer and fostering employee involvement through building a culture of trust and achievement.

During her degree Rebecca had become particularly interested in corporate strategy. She was particularly interested in the way in which the often rather ambitious mission statements were put into practice by organisations.

Rebecca was rather concerned that the strategic objective of her placement company quoted above contained two areas of her course-customer focussing and employee involvement- neither of which she had studied in depth on her course.

She confessed her concern to her research supervisor, Dr Hunt, who suggested that it might be useful for her to concentrate upon the process of delivering the strategic objective rather than the objective itself. This would lend the project an element of generalisability which would not be the case were it to focus on either customer focussing and employee involvement.

Together with Dr Hunt, Rebecca developed the following research question:

> How do the procedures and processes the senior management of Forsure use to cascade downwards support their strategic objective of becoming the preferred company for all their stakeholders by strengthening the focus on the customer and fostering employee involvement through building a culture of trust and achievement?

Another useful metaphor to help you think about clarifying your research question is Clough and Nutbrown's (2012) Russian doll principle. Here your research can be broken down from the original statement to something which strips away all the complicated layers and obscurities until the heart of the question can be expressed, in the same way as the Russian doll is taken apart to reveal a tiny doll at the centre. Table 1.5 has some examples of research ideas and the general focus research questions they suggest.

Table 1.5 Examples of research ideas and the focus research questions they suggest

| Research idea | General focus research questions |
| --- | --- |
| 1  The marketing of security in credit cards | To what extent does a credit card company market the measures it takes to ensure consumer security in order to gain competitive advantage? |
| 2  Organisations' employee newsletters | How effective are organisations' newsletters at gaining employee identification with the organisation in geographically diverse organisation structures, and why? |
| 3  The use of shelf display point-of-sale material in retail supermarkets | How does the use of shelf display point-of-sale material in retail supermarkets affect buyer behaviour? |
| 4  Sustainable accountancy | To what extent are organisations ensuring that environmental and social performance is better connected with strategy and financial performance, and why? |

In the examples in Research in practice 1.4 and Table 1.5, there is one general focus research question generated from the central research idea. Of course, this may lead to several more detailed questions or the definition of research objectives. In the next section, we deal with the development of research objectives.

## Developing research objectives

Having written your research questions, you may be asking yourself why it's necessary to develop **research objectives**. The answer is that it may not be. Your research project assessment brief may state that it's acceptable to write research questions or research objectives. In our view, it's better to do both. Why? Because we think that research objectives add an element of precision to research questions. In Table 1.6 we illustrate

---

**Definition**

**research objectives:** clear, specific statements that identify what the research process seeks to achieve as a result of doing the research.

**Table 1.6** Phrasing research questions as research objectives

| Research question | Research objective |
|---|---|
| 1  Why have organisations introduced employee communication schemes? | 1  To identify organisations' objectives for employee communication schemes. |
| 2  How can the effectiveness of employee communication schemes be measured? | 2  To establish suitable effectiveness criteria for employee communication schemes. |
| 3  Has employee communication been effective? | 3  To assess the extent to which the effectiveness criteria for employee communication have been met in published studies. |
| 4  How can the effectiveness of employee communication be explained? | 4a  To determine the factors associated with the effectiveness criteria for employee communication schemes being met. |
|  | 4b  To estimate whether some of those factors are more influential than other factors. |
| 5  Can the explanation be generalised? | 5  To develop an explanatory theory that associates certain factors with the effectiveness of employee communication schemes. |

this point by showing research objectives alongside the research questions from which they have been developed. In general, research objectives tend to be more acceptable to the research community. Research in practice 1.5 is an example of how an official research report prepared by the UK government expresses an overall research aim and then expands this into specific objectives.

## Research in practice 1.5

### Developing research objectives from an overall research aim

The UK Department for Work and Pensions (DWP) commissioned a leading public affairs research agency to explore how employers approach the recruitment and hiring process for unskilled and semi-skilled workers. This included the factors that influence recruitment decisions and how hiring decisions are made in practice. The purpose of the research was to support Jobcentre Plus* customers seeking work and further inform the Department's employer engagement practices.

A qualitative research study was carried out between May and July 2013 based on focus groups with small employers reflecting a range of industry sectors, and a small number of employer case studies which provided the opportunity to observe any differences in how employers describe their recruitment process and what they do in practice.

#### Research aim

The DWP wished to explore how employers approach the recruitment and hiring process, what influences recruitment decisions, and to understand how hiring decisions are made in practice.

With this key aim, research was designed to consider how DWP might firstly, support its customers who are seeking work and secondly, further inform the Department's employer engagement practices.

Within this overarching aim, there were four key objectives:

- to explore how employers approach the recruitment process, including:
  - the sources they draw on to identify potential candidates;
  - the recruitment processes and practices they use;
  - the candidate features that influence an employer's decision about whether to employ; and
  - the rationality of the recruitment process and the circumstances in which employers change their practices, either explicitly or implicitly;
- the effect of labour market and sector requirements on the recruitment process;
- experiences and views about Jobcentre Plus and third party agencies as recruitment organisations; and
- the impact of government initiatives on recruitment decision-making.

\* Job Centre Plus is a DWP agency providing services to those attempting to find employment.

*Source:* Department for Work and Pensions (2014) *Small Employer Recruitment Practices: Qualitative Research into How Small and Medium-Sized Enterprises Select Candidates for Employment.* Report No 855, July 2014.

Table 1.6 comes from research we did on an organisation's employee communication scheme. This was the forerunner of research on the scheme of a particular organisation who wanted to establish if their scheme was 'working'. This prompted us to explore a highly debatable question to which the literature offered no satisfactory answers.

Writing research question 1 as an objective prompted a consideration of the objectives of the organisations. This was useful because it led to the finding that there often were no clear objectives. This in itself was an interesting theoretical discovery. (How often management initiatives are introduced with no clear objectives in mind!)

Objectives 2 and 3 operationalise the matching research questions by introducing the notion of explicit effectiveness criteria. This is particularly important if measurement of success is to be attempted. Similarly, objectives 4a, 4b and 5 introduce an element of precision about factors that lead to effectiveness in question 4. The most significant difference between these questions and objectives is illustrated by the way in which question 5 becomes objective 5. Although similar, they differ in the way that the objective makes clear that a theory will be developed that will make a causal link between two sets of variables: effectiveness factors and employee communication scheme success.

You may find it easier to write specific research questions than objectives. But, as Table 1.6 demonstrates, research objectives add a further level of precision. Our view is that research objectives require more rigorous thinking, which derives from the use of more formal language.

We make one final point on the development of your research objectives. Think about adding personal objectives to those specific research objectives. These may be concerned with your specific learning objectives from your research or more general personal objectives such as enhancing your career prospects. You will be familiar with the SMART test, listed in Table 1.7. Try this when you have thought about your personal research objectives.

Table 1.7 The SMART test

| Check that the objectives are: | |
| --- | --- |
| **Specific** | What precisely do you hope to achieve from undertaking the research? |
| **Measurable** | What measures will you use to determine whether you have achieved your objectives? |
| **Achievable** | Are the targets you have set for yourself achievable given all the possible constraints? |
| **Realistic** | Given all the other demands upon your time, will you have the time and energy to complete the research on time? |
| **Timely** | Will you have time to accomplish all your objectives in the time frame you have set? |

## The part that theory plays in developing research questions and objectives

There is no more misunderstood word in the research vocabulary than 'theory'. In this section, we clarify what **theory** is by explaining what it is not. It's important that you get this clear. In Chapter 5, we explain the importance of theory in research design. We emphasise that the role of theory will play a key part in your study, as all projects will need to link to theory in some way. The most likely link will be to an existing theory explained in the literature relevant to your research topic.

Theory may be broadly defined as an explanation of the relationship between two or more concepts or variables. So, for example, the fact that you are reading this text is based (we hope!) on the theory that the outcome will be that you are better equipped to pursue your study.

We said we would clarify what theory is by explaining what it is not. Sutton and Staw (1995) help here and, although their article was written in the last century, it is still really helpful! In their view, theory is not:

- lots of data;
- lists of variables;

Definition

**theory:** an explanation of the relationship between two or more concepts or variables.

- numerous hypotheses;
- pages of references;
- frequent use of diagrams.

### Theory is not lots of data

We warned earlier in this chapter about developing research questions that are too easy. They often allow only for description of phenomena. Such questions lead to project reports which are full of **data** and little else. Data only describe what you have found out and, possibly, report on the patterns observed: theory explains the relationships between these patterns. As Sutton and Staw (1995: 372) say, 'data do not generate theory – only researchers do that'.

### Theory is not lists of variables

You may be tempted to list a series of **variables** in an attempt to explain the determinants of a given process or outcome. But simply listing variables which may predict an outcome is insufficient. For example, in a study of effective management decision-making, merely listing those factors which seem to be associated with effectiveness is insufficient. What is required for theory development is an explanation of why the factors associated with effectiveness are likely to be strong predictors of effectiveness.

### Theory is not numerous hypotheses

In section 5.5 we explain the role of hypotheses in a research design, and in section 7.3 we talk about **hypothesis** testing. Testing possible relationships between variables certainly has a part to play in setting up research projects. But they do not clarify why phenomena have happened and therefore do not constitute theory.

---

**Definitions**

**data:** facts, opinions and statistics that have been collected together and recorded for reference or for analysis.

**variable:** individual element or attribute upon which data have been collected.

**hypothesis:** tentative (usually testable) statement about the 'relationship' between two or more variables.

---

### Theory is not pages of references

'How many references should I include?' is a question you have probably been asked by student colleagues; you may have asked it yourself. It's as if the more references you include, the more 'theoretical' your work will be. OK, so it may (only may) indicate that you have done lots of reading, but that isn't theory. Theory is present when you outline *why* the things you describe occur.

### Theory is not frequent use of diagrams

Diagrams, boxes and arrows may help in clarifying patterns and causal relationships between variables, but they don't usually explain why the relationships have occurred.

So, to sum up, the key word to stress in establishing the presence of theory in your project report is 'why'. Why do certain things happen when particular variables are present and others absent? Why does A happen and B does not? Why do people behave in this way rather than the opposite way?

We made the point earlier that the fact that you are reading this text is based on the theory that it better equips you to complete successfully your research study. In that case, every purposive decision we take is based on theory: that certain consequences will flow from the decision. So, if your decision to read this text is theory-based, then so is, for example, every manager's meeting that is devoted to making decisions. Yet managers are unlikely to realise this. They are equally unlikely to want to acknowledge this! After all, theory is something that belongs in the university; it is not something which is part of the 'real world'. Yet, as Kurt Lewin (1945: 129) said, 'there is nothing as practical as a good theory'.

So, if theory plays an important part in our everyday lives and is implicit in the decision-making processes which go on, it's not something that you should be too scared about. What is important is that the element of theory in your research is made explicit, not left implicit.

### How 'grand' does my theory need to be?

Still feeling a bit scared about the idea of theory development? Well, let's try to put your mind at rest by looking at a three-type categorisation of theory developed by Creswell (2008). Creswell talks of 'grand theories', 'middle-range theories' and 'substantive theories' (Figure 1.2).

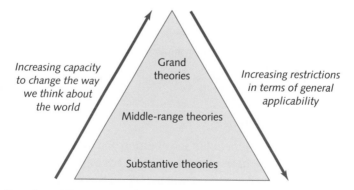

**Figure 1.2** Grand, middle-range and substantive theories
*Source:* Saunders et al., 2016; developed from Creswell, 2008.

**Grand theories** are those that are so significant that they make a major contribution to the way in which we understand the world around us. An example of one such grand theory is Darwin's theory of evolution. Don't worry; there is no need for you to think about following in Darwin's footsteps! Neither is there the need for you to be so ambitious as thinking of **middle-range theories**. These are not as world-changing in their scope as grand theories, yet they are clearly of great importance in their particular field of study. You will have studied many of these in your course. Examples are those concerned with motivation, leadership or creative thinking. Of course, you may apply one of these to your particular situation. But you wouldn't be expected to come up with an original theory of such significance, which could be generalised to many other contexts.

However, most of us are concerned with developing rather more modest theories – **substantive theories**. These are restricted to a specific context: a particular time, research setting, population or problem. So you may be concerned with a study of the reason why, for example, the introduction of a new computer system in a particular organisation proved to be a failure. The conclusion you draw would be prefaced by the word 'because' – a term which serves as a 'trigger word' for a theoretical statement (e.g. 'it failed because there was too little of A and not enough B and C'. Alternatively, 'it failed because management did not explain the reason for the introduction to staff concerned which led to staff discontent'. Either of these theoretical explanations may stand alone, or you may link them to well-established middle-range theories developed by other researchers.

Substantive theories may be more modest, but they may lead to 'middle-range theories'. And by developing substantive theories, we are doing our bit as researchers to develop our understanding of the world about us.

---

### Definitions

**grand theories:** theories that make a major contribution to the way in which we understand the world around us.

**middle-range theories:** theories which are not as world-changing in their scope as grand theories but are of great importance in their particular field of study.

**substantive theories:** theories which are restricted to a specific context: a particular time, research setting, population or problem

---

### Research in practice 1.6

## Writing a research question based on a middle-range theory

Aafreen was a part-time management student at her local university. Her full-time job was a practice manager at a large city health centre in which she was responsible for a team of over 30 administrative personnel whose main duties included reception work, patient record-keeping, financial control, stock control, prescription monitoring and general clerical duties.

→

In most respects, the local Health Service Trust and general practitioner doctors in the practice were happy with the operation of the practice, including the way it was administered by Aafreen and her team. However, a recent customer satisfaction survey concluded that the way in which the practice's performance was perceived by its clients was not as good as it could have been.

In management meetings this survey conclusion was discussed at some length, and a number of suggestions were made about how things could be improved. One central theme ran through those suggestions: that the practice needed to improve its rather dreary and pedestrian image. The management team, including, Aafreen, decided that the way in which all staff members, including the professional medical staff, presented themselves needed to improve.

Consequently, Aafreen was charged with the responsibility to implement a staff self-presentation programme with the intention that all staff should present an image consistent with a modern, professional health centre. She knew that this would have to be handled sensitively because a number of staff members, although excellent performers in their jobs, presented a somewhat dowdy image.

Aafreen had studied motivation theory in the early part of her course and guessed that the sure way for the initiative to fail was to impose it upon staff. She felt that the route to programme success was to use empowerment theory, giving the ownership of the programme to the staff members themselves, starting with a meeting where ideas could be invited.

Aafreen decided that she would implement her investigation and keep detailed notes of every aspect of it, and then write it up as her course project.

Aafreen felt that an initial research question would help her focus on both the practical project to be undertaken at the practice and her course project. After some thought, and trial and error, she wrote the following research question:

'How should a staff self-presentation programme be implemented effectively using the principles of empowerment theory?'

## Summary

- Choosing the right research topic is important because: you have to live with it for a considerable period of time; it should exploit and develop your knowledge and skills, and enable you to draw upon existing resources and help you to pass the course you are studying.

- Choosing an appropriate research topic is difficult because: there is too much choice; there are fears that it will be too difficult and insufficiently theoretical and there is a temptation to choose a topic that you have done before for another purpose resulting in repetition.

- Ten techniques for generating ideas for research topics are: thinking; looking at past project titles; using past course assignments; using past projects from the university library; using relevant literature; following the news media; brainstorming; concept mapping; making a note of ideas and discussion with helpers.

- Pursuing a research topic assigned to you by your employer poses its own problems. In such cases, you should aim for a balance between the competing demands of your employer and your university by, for example, isolating an element of the larger organisational project that you find interesting and treating this as the project for your course.
- Research topic ideas may be refined by the conduct of a preliminary study; application of the Delphi technique and a process of narrowing down.
- A good research topic is one: that you are enthusiastic about and it matches your career goals; for which resources are available; that is topical; that, whatever the outcome you still have a worthwhile project; where the topic fits the specifications and meets the standards set by the examining institution; that links to the relevant literature; that provides fresh insights into the topic and for which research question(s) and objectives are capable of being stated clearly.
- The next stage from choosing the research topic is the development of research questions and objectives. A suitable research question is one that reflects the that fact you have thought about what fits the specifications and meet the standards set by the examining institution; provides a clear link to the relevant literature and promises fresh insights into the topic you have chosen. Research objectives add an element of precision to research questions.
- All projects will need to link to theory in some way. The development of a 'grand theory' or 'middle-range' is unnecessary; 'substantive theory' development is sufficient.

## Thinking about your research topic

→ Look again at the 10 techniques available for generating research ideas (Table 1.1). Choose those that appeal to you most. Use these to try to generate a research idea or ideas. Once you have some research ideas, or if you have been unable to find an idea, talk to your project supervisor.

→ Evaluate your research ideas against the checklist 'what makes a good research topic?' (Table 1.4).

→ Choose a research report contained in an article in an academic journal relevant to your topic. Revisit the useful questions to ask when searching articles and reports for possible research topic ideas (Table 1.3) and apply these to the article.

→ Write a general focus research question related to your research topic. Try to ensure this is 'Why?' or 'How?' rather than a 'What?' question.

→ Use the general focus research question to write more detailed research questions and your research objectives.

→ Go back to the research report contained in an article in an academic journal relevant to your topic that you used with the questions in Table 1.3. Assuming that the research question and objectives are not made explicit, try to establish from the content of the article what the research question and objectives may have been.

## References

Creswell, J. (2008). *Qualitative, Quantitative, and Mixed Methods Approaches* (3rd ed.). Thousand Oaks, CA: Sage.

Clough, P. and Nutbrown, C. (2012). *A Student's Guide to Methodology* (3rd ed.). London: Sage.

Department for Work and Pensions. (2014). *Small Employer Recruitment Practices: Qualitative Research into How Small and Medium-Sized Enterprises Select Candidates for Employment.* Report No 855, July 2014.

House of Commons Environment, Food and Rural Affairs. (2015). *Rural Broadband and Digital-Only Services, Seventh Report of Session 2014–15.* London: The Stationery Office Limited.

Lewin, K. (1945). The Research Centre for Group Dynamics at Massachusetts Institute of Technology. *Sociometry*, 8(2), 126–36.

Raimond, P. (1993). *Management Projects.* London: Chapman & Hall.

Saunders, M., Lewis, P. and Thornhill, A. (2016). *Research Methods for Business Students* (7th ed.). Harlow: Pearson Education Ltd.

Sutton, R. and Staw, B. (1995). What theory is not. *Administrative Science Quarterly*, 40(3), 371–84.

# Chapter 2

# Reviewing the literature critically

## 2.1 Why you should read this chapter

Since you started your programme, your lecturers have expected you to read textbooks and academic journal articles as part of your studies. Sometimes your lecturers will have told you exactly which book chapters and articles they want you to read. At other times, such as when undertaking an assignment, you will have been expected to find at least some books and articles yourself, deciding whether or not they were relevant. This will have meant you searching in your university's library catalogue to see if there were any potentially useful books, as well as searching one or more of your university's online databases of academic journal articles. You will probably also have searched the Internet for relevant reports and articles using a general search engine such as Google or Bing. Having found some books and articles, you would then have read them quickly to work out whether or not they were relevant before reading them more carefully and using them in your assignment. Well done! You have already started to develop some of the skills you need to review the literature critically.

The overall purpose of this chapter is to help you further develop the skills and understanding you need to critically review the literature so that you can complete your research project. The skills you develop will also be helpful for your assignments. We explore the skills by looking at critically reviewing the literature as an iterative process consisting of four activities which you will need to go through a number of times to develop your literature review chapter (Figure 2.1).

However, before we do this, it is important that you understand what a critical literature review is, why you need to review the literature for your research project and are aware of the variety of literature available to you.

In this chapter, we therefore start by talking about what a critical literature review is and its purpose. We then go on to explain why it is important that you review the literature critically as part of your research project and describe the variety of literature available to you. Next, we consider the skills and understanding you will need to conduct a critical literature review. First, we look at how you will search for and obtain the literature using your

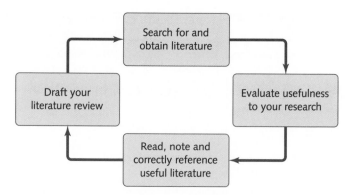

**Figure 2.1** The process of critically reviewing the literature

university's online databases of academic articles. As part of this we also consider briefly your use of the general search engine Google and the online encyclopaedia Wikipedia. Next, we talk about how you can evaluate the usefulness of the literature you have found for your own research project. We then explain how to read, note and correctly reference this useful literature, emphasising the importance of not passing off others' work as your own by mistake and so being accused of plagiarism. We end this chapter by talking about how you can structure and draft your literature review.

## 2.2    What a critical literature review is

You will find that, although there are numerous definitions of a critical **literature review**, these usually emphasise four aspects. In particular, it:

- offers an overview of significant literature available in your chosen topic;
- includes relevant items such as academic journal articles, books and other sources;
- provides a discussion and critical evaluation of these, the level of detail reflecting the significance of each item to your research questions;
- develops a clear argument to contextualise and justify your research.

This means your literature review is not like a book review, or series of book reviews, simply describing and summarising what each book or article is about. First, it includes only significant literature published on your research topic (Table 2.1. You will therefore have to decide what is significant to your research topic and why it is significant. This will involve you in assessing how relevant, if at all, each item you read is to your

> **Definition**
>
> **(critical) literature review:** a detailed overview of the significant literature available about your chosen topic, providing a discussion and critical evaluation, and using clear argument to contextualise and justify your research.

research and, on the basis of your assessment, deciding whether or not to include it. We talk about this more in section 2.6. For those items (mainly articles and books) you decide to include, you then need to ensure that your review is more than just a description of their contents. You will need to discuss those aspects of what has been said that are relevant to your research, and within your discussion you must be critical. We would be surprised if this was the first time you had heard the term 'critical'. It, or something similar such as the phrase 'critically evaluate', is often used in assignments and exam questions. However, it is worth pausing for a moment to explain what is meant by 'critical' in relation to your literature review. This word is crucial as it summarises what you must do when writing your literature review.

Within your literature review, being critical simply means you provide clearly justified, reasoned judgements about what you have read and are now writing about. To do this, you need to have a good knowledge of the literature on your topic that both supports and opposes your ideas, and show through your writing that you have this knowledge. This is often referred to as 'demonstrating familiarity with the topic' in assessment criteria and means that you also need to show you know whom the recognised experts in your topic area are. When you read and note the items that relate to your research topic, you will need to do so with some scepticism, questioning what you read. If you think an author's arguments, ideas or research findings are unclear, biased, poorly justified, inconsistent or need to be tested further, this may well mean that they are. However, it is not enough for you to just write that the author's arguments are unclear, biased, poorly justified, inconsistent or need to be tested further. In your critical literature review, you must also include clear reasons why you think this. By justifying the points you make, you are showing your critical judgement. Through this, you will also provide a reasonably detailed justified analysis of the key literature in your research topic area, including research that both supports and opposes your ideas.

**Table 2.1**  What a critical literature review is and is not

| A critical literature review . . . | A literature review that is not critical . . . |
| --- | --- |
| • identifies and includes the most relevant and significant research to your topic | • includes all research that may possibly be relevant to your topic |
| • discusses and evaluates this research | • just summarises and describes this research |
| • identifies the recognised experts (authors) | • fails to mention recognised experts (authors) |
| • contextualises and justifies your research questions | • fails to justify or mention your research questions |
| • highlights areas where new or further research is needed | • does not highlight where new or further research is needed |
| • considers and discusses research that supports and opposes your ideas | • only considers and discusses research that supports your ideas |
| • justifies points made logically with reference to published research and clear argument | • makes unjustified or poorly justified points |
| • distinguishes between fact and opinion | • mixes up fact and opinion |
| • includes recent relevant research | • misses out on recent relevant research |
| • references all items referred to fully | • fails to reference all or some items referred to |

## 2.3    Why it is important to review the literature critically

Now you know what a critical literature review is, it is important to understand why you need to undertake one and include it in your project report. While we have already provided you with some hints about the reasons for this in the previous section, we still believe it is worth talking about these and others in more detail.

### Provides the base on which you will build your research project

Reviewing the literature critically is one of the first things you need to do when you start your research as it will provide the base on which your research project is built. By reviewing the literature, you will be able to develop a good understanding of what research has already been undertaken on your topic area. This means that you will be clear about what is known about your topic, and also the context in which it is known, and will be able to write about this in your literature review chapter or chapters. Let's say your research topic is personalisation of marketing. As you review the literature, you will begin to find out not only how online marketers are using technology to provide potential customers with unique and customisable content, but also the reasons why organisations are personalising their marketing. You will also become aware of the countries and industry sectors in which this research was conducted – in other words, the context of the research. Eventually you will have sufficient knowledge from what you have read to discuss the broader context of your own research on personalisation of marketing. You will also be able to explain and justify your own research questions in relation to what is already known (and what is not known!) about viral marketing and in what contexts (section 1.6).

### Helps you decide on the topic you want to research for your project

You will have read about how reviewing the literature can help you decide on your research topic in section 1.4. In that section, you read about the importance of academic review articles in providing you with a thorough review of the state of knowledge in a topic area as well as with pointers towards areas where further research needs to be undertaken. You also read how browsing peer-reviewed journals could provide you with a good source of possible research ideas. You will find that such research ideas are often introduced under the heading 'Directions for future research' or with the phrase 'Further research is needed.' These articles are useful not only for the ideas, but also because they highlight areas where research is needed and give you a justification for undertaking your research to which you can refer. It is also likely that the theories these articles identify will be those you will explore further in your own research.

Although books may be less up to date than journals, they can also suggest research topics to you. In particular, edited books based on papers given at a conference or seminar often contain a final chapter that summarises the key findings from the earlier chapters and draws out key themes, including future directions for research (Research in practice 1.1).

In addition to reviewing academic journal articles and textbooks, you will also be reading trade and professional magazines. Reviewing this type of literature will provide you with an indication of whether your research topic is 'hot'. Returning to our example of personalisation of marketing, if this has been discussed in recent issues of marketing magazines such as *digital marketing magazine*, it is newsworthy and likely to be a 'hot' topic. This can be helpful, particularly if you are going to collect your own data. People are often keener to be involved in research they believe is topical and that will have immediate benefits for them or their organisation (section 3.2).

### Can give you insights into the secondary data that are likely to be available

It is likely that you will make at least some use of data that have been collected by others for some other purpose in your research project. Such secondary data are useful, not least because they give you access to far larger data sets than you could collect yourself and can also provide you with comparative and contextual data (section 4.3).

As you review the literature critically, you will become aware of the data that other researchers looking at your topic have used. In some articles and reports (and occasionally books) the data collected will be presented as tables. You can use these as secondary data for your own research, providing of course you reference the article, report or book as the source of the data! In other articles, reports and books the authors will explain how they have used data sets collected originally by someone else for some other purpose. Where these data sets are in the public domain, you will also be able to find, download and use them in your research, providing of course there is a full reference to the source of these data.

### Can give you insights into possible ways of collecting your own data

The literature you review will also give you ideas about how you might collect your own data. This is important because, if a method has been used before to collect similar data and worked well, it will hopefully work if you decide to use it. In particular, articles and book chapters that report research using data that the researcher has collected will nearly always describe how those data were collected in a section headed 'Method' or 'Methodology'. While you would hope that the description is in sufficient detail for you to be able to understand fully and repeat the same method, unfortunately this is not always true. However, even if the description is not particularly detailed, it can still provide you with an indication of how you might collect your own data. In addition, it is likely to include references to other items which you can read to find out more about the method used.

Let's say that you read an article on your research topic that has used a questionnaire to collect the data. This article provides both a detailed description of the method and, as an appendix, a blank copy of the questionnaire that the authors used to collect their data. This gives you a clear idea of the questions you need to ask if you decide to also use a questionnaire to collect your own data. If you think the questions are suitable for the people you are intending to collect your data from, you may decide to use the same questions. However, if you do this, you must give credit to the people who originally designed the questions and include the full reference to their article in your methods chapter. If you do not do this, you may be accused of plagiarism, as you are passing off the work of others as your own.

Alternatively, you may read an article in an academic journal that focuses on research methods, such as *Organizational Research Methods* or *Field Methods*, which explains the use of a particular technique for collecting data such as a form of interviewing or observation or a specific use of questionnaires. Such articles will provide you with helpful insights about how to conduct your own research and what to avoid. They are likely to contain more detail about particular techniques than we have been able to include in Chapter 6. Where you use the ideas from one of these articles for your own method, you should refer to that article in your methods chapter (Research in practice 2.1).

### ● Can give you insights into possible ways of analysing your own data

Academic journal articles can provide insights into how to analyse both data you collect yourself and secondary data. The techniques used to analyse data are usually named in the 'findings' or 'results' section. Where these are widely used techniques, in particular statistical tests, it is likely that, although the test is named, it will not be explained in any detail as it will have been assumed that the reader (you) will already be aware of and understand the technique. In addition, you will not see a reference to a journal article or a statistics textbook. This is not a problem as you will almost

---

### Research in practice 2.1

#### Insights into research methods from the literature

An article by Mark (Saunders, 2012) in *Field Methods* concludes by offering a series of recommendations about the use of web-based questionnaires for organisational research which may be helpful for your research. These include:

1  For research in organisations, the use of web-based questionnaires should be considered only where respondents are IT-literate and have ready access to the Internet at work.

2  Web-based questionnaires should be designed to allow the impact of people not responding to be assessed.

3  Caution should be exercised regarding the inclusion of questions on topics related to the use of the web or associated technologies.

4  Care should be taken when comparing responses to open (write in) questions from web-based questionnaires with those from questionnaires delivered using other methods, owing to the impact of the technology on response length.

certainly be able to find sufficient information about the test in your own statistics textbook or by using the Help feature of a statistics software programme such as IBM SPSS Statistics.

Where an academic journal article uses data analysis techniques that are not widely known, it is likely that the author or authors will have explained how to use the analysis technique. Hopefully, this will be in sufficient detail for you to be able to understand fully and use the same technique, although unfortunately this is not always true. However, even if the description is not particularly detailed, it can still provide you with an indication of how you might analyse your own data. In addition, it is likely to include references to other books and articles which you can read to find out more about the technique. Such articles are likely to contain far more detail than we have been able to include in Chapter 7, and where appropriate should be referred to in your method or findings chapter.

## 2.4     The types of literature available to you

The amount of literature available to you is expanding rapidly as more sources are made available online. In addition to the library catalogue, your university library's web pages will provide a comprehensive list of the other sources you can access and the types of literature they contain. Most of these other sources accessed are databases, so your library's web pages will usually include direct web links and details of any passwords needed.

We have listed the main types of literature you are likely to access through your library catalogue and databases for your critical literature review in Table 2.2, along with a brief description of their contents and an indication of their likely use for your review. Textbooks, such as those that have been recommended to you for your modules, will be very helpful as you start your literature review, providing an overview of your research topic and the recognised experts. However, academic journal articles which have been **peer-reviewed** (also referred to as 'refereed') will be the most useful to you in your literature review and will form the majority of items you use. These articles will have been read and evaluated by academic experts, called peer reviewers, to ensure they meet the quality criteria of the journal before they are published. Peer reviewers are usually anonymous and ensure quality by both detecting errors, which have to be corrected before the article is published, and providing a detailed assessment of the article. Where peer reviewers consider the quality is not sufficient or there are too many errors, the article will not be published.

> **Definition**
>
> **peer review:** the process of evaluating an article by experts to establish whether it meets quality criteria and is suitable for publication.

**Table 2.2** Main types of literature available to you

| Type | Contents | Use for your critical literature review |
|---|---|---|
| **Textbooks** | Written specifically for audiences such as students or professionals. Material usually presented in an ordered and relatively accessible form. Often draw on a wide range of sources including peer-reviewed academic journal articles. | Useful, particularly as an introductory source for an overview of your research topic and to find the recognised experts. |
| **Peer-reviewed (refereed) academic journal articles** | Provide detailed reports of research. Articles written by experts in the field and evaluated by other academics (peer reviewers) to assess quality and suitability. Pay rigorous attention to detail and verification of information. Usually contain an extensive list of references. Before publication, have usually been revised in response to comments. Not all academic journal articles are peer-reviewed (see below). | The most useful type for your literature review. |
| **Non-refereed academic journal articles** | Articles may provide detailed reports of research. Articles selected by an editor or editorial board with subject knowledge. | Relevance and usefulness varies considerably. Beware of possible bias. |
| **Professional and trade journal articles** | Articles written for members of professional or trade organisations, so related to their needs. Consist of a mix of news items and more detailed accounts of a practical nature. Articles rarely based on research, although some provide summaries of research. | Can provide useful insights into practice, although may be biased. Need to be used with considerable caution. |
| **Newspaper articles** | Articles written for members of public, most newspapers addressing a particular market segment. News presented is filtered dependent on events, priority being given to headline-grabbing stories that are likely to appeal to that newspaper's readers. | Good source of topical events and developments. May contain bias in reporting and coverage. |
| **Conference proceedings** | Selected papers presented at a conference, often published online, as a book or special edition of a journal. Usually peer-reviewed. | Sometimes difficult to find. Very useful if the theme of the conference matches your research. |
| **Reports** | Reports on specific topics written by academics and various organisations, including market research organisations and government departments. Often available online. Beware of possible bias. May not have gone through same review process as peer-reviewed academic journal articles, but those from established organisations often of high quality. | Often difficult to access or expensive to purchase. Can be a useful source of information when the topic matches your research. |

## 2.5   Searching for and obtaining literature

Although your skills in using general search engines such as Google and Bing are likely to be excellent, we have found that many of our students are unaware of at least some of the search features of full text databases of academic articles such as *Business Source Premier* and *Emerald Insight*. While you will have already used these or similar databases of academic journal articles for assignments, there are relatively simple things you can do to make your searches as fruitful as possible.

The process of searching for and obtaining the literature consists of five stages:

1  Decide on your topic.

2  Identify and note the search terms and phrases you will use.

3  Choose your online databases.

4  Undertake your search.

5  Download relevant publications.

We will now look at each stage in more detail.

### Decide on your topic

You have probably already got a reasonably clear idea of your research topic. However, if you haven't, don't worry. Just turn back to Chapter 1 and look at sections 1.4 and 1.5, which talk about generating ideas for your research topic and refining these ideas. This process of refining these ideas is important because, unless you have a reasonably clear and specific idea of the topic you wish to search for in the literature, most of the items you find are not going to be of use for your research project!

Let's say you've defined your research topic as 'financial management' and decide to search for items on this topic in one of the online databases to which your university subscribes. Because the topic of financial management is so broad, an initial search for 'financial management' will probably find more than 100,000 items – far too many for you to ever download, let alone read! However, if you define your topic as 'the impact of recession on financial management', you can be more precise in your choice of keywords with which to search the literature. By using keywords and phrases such as 'financial management' and 'recession' as search terms, you would be likely to find about 1,000 items, a slightly more manageable number for you to begin to look at. You might have been even more specific, defining your topic as 'the impact of recession on financial management budgeting'. Searching for this topic in the online database using keywords and phrases such as 'financial management', 'recession' and 'budget' as search terms would find fewer than 100 items. Not only is this a far more manageable number to look at, but it is also likely that a greater proportion will be directly relevant to your research topic.

### Identify and note the search terms and phrases you will use

Databases find relevant items by matching specific words and phrases with either the full text or part of the publication such as the abstract (summary) or title. You will have found when searching with Google or Bing that the more specific the word or phrase you type in, the more likely you are to find relevant web pages. You will have also found that if the word or phrase you type in is too specific, you don't find the web pages you need. The same principle applies to searching databases, including those of academic journal articles. You therefore need to think carefully about the **search terms** you will use while searching, and, as when searching using Google or Bing, you need to be prepared to try a variety of keywords and phrases.

> **Definition**
>
> **Search term:** a word or phrase that describes your research topic, question(s) or objectives and can be used either on its own or in combination with other phrases in databases.

Your ideas for possible search terms and phrases, such as 'financial management' and 'recession', are likely to be based upon what you already know about your research topic and any reading you have already done. In addition, you will probably find some of the techniques to generate research topics outlined in section 1.4 helpful. Techniques such as looking at past project titles, brainstorming, concept mapping and discussing your ideas can all help you clarify your thoughts and come up with possible search terms and phrases. You will also find that dictionaries and encyclopaedias (including Wikipedia) are often helpful for suggesting alternative words and phrases. We have listed six things to think about when identifying your search terms in Table 2.3. They are in no particular order.

Table 2.3  Six things to think about when identifying your search terms

| Using: | Example |
| --- | --- |
| Terms appearing regularly in literature you've read | Downsizing and Redundancy |
| Both broad and narrow terms | Services and Restaurant |
| Different words with the same meaning (synonyms) | Motorcycle and Motorbike |
| Alternative spellings of the same word | Organisation and Organization |
| Abbreviations and the full term | EU and European Union |
| Old and new place names where these have changed | Peking and Beijing |

## Choose your databases

Your choice of databases will, not surprisingly, be dictated primarily by those available through subscriptions paid by your university. We have listed those most frequently available in Table 2.4, along with a brief description of what they cover and therefore what you can search for using your search terms and phrases. Of these, the most widely used by business and management students such as you are Business Source Premier and Emerald Insight. We would recommend that you start your literature search using these. However, these databases do not have such a good coverage of older items, particularly those published over three to four decades ago. You will find the database JSTOR a useful source for journal articles, particularly when you need to obtain a copy of that seminal article recommended by your supervisor.

**Table 2.4** Frequently used online databases of academic articles in business and management

| Database | Description |
| --- | --- |
| **Business Source Premier** (sometimes called EBSCO) | Full text articles for over 2,900 English-language journals published worldwide. Covers all areas of business and management with access for some titles back to 1886. Embargo of up to a year for full text of articles from the most recent issues of some journals. Also includes Datamonitor company profiles for the world's 10,000 largest companies, Datamonitor industry profiles for various industries and Economist Intelligence Unit country reports. |
| **Emerald Insight** | Full text articles for over 160 English-language management journals and reviews from over 300 management journals. Covers all areas of business and management. |
| **JSTOR** | Full text articles for science, social science, arts and humanities journals. Coverage usually extends back to volume 1, issue 1 of journals and more of the current issues of journals are also becoming available. Often the best place to find 'old articles'. |
| **Blackwell Reference Online** | Blackwell Encyclopaedia of Management, Blackwell 'Handbooks' and 'Companions' in business and management. |
| **Wiley Online** | Includes over 1,100 full text journals covering the sciences, business, law, humanities, psychology and social sciences. |
| **Google Scholar** | Scholarly literature consisting of articles, theses, books, abstracts or court opinions from many disciplines and sources. Usually provides a web link, but access can depend on subscription. Literature ranked according to the full text of each document, where published, author(s), how often and how recently cited in other scholarly literature. |
| **Nexis** | Full text of articles in newspapers across the world and UK national and regional newspapers as well as company information and reports. |

You will notice that we have included Google Scholar in Table 2.4. This is because it has a number of useful features to support your search of the literature and is readily available. In particular, once you know the names of recognised experts researching your topic, you can find out who has referred to (cited) their work by simply searching for their names. Google Scholar will rank all the recognised experts' publications and, for each, list the full references of other documents that have cited (referenced) the publication. This means you can see which of your experts' publications have been cited most, and you can find these other documents that have cited these publications subsequently.

You will have also noticed that, in contrast, we have not included Wikipedia in our table. There is no doubt in our minds that Wikipedia is useful if you want to find out something quickly. However, the level of detail provided is unlikely to be sufficient for your research project. As you know, Wikipedia articles can be edited by anyone and are allowed to be imperfect. Despite Wikipedia's clear editing policy and their request that contributors ensure the information they add is verifiable, errors and misinformation can and do occur. While these errors are usually put right quickly, an article may be wrong at the time you read it. Finally, although Wikipedia expects articles to be phrased to reflect the present consensus on a subject, people with rival opinions do compete to change what is written, resulting in the information you find changing overnight. We therefore recommend that you do not use Wikipedia as a source for your critical literature review.

## Undertake your search

Now you have identified the search terms and phrases you are going to use and chosen your databases, all you need to do is click on the links on your university library's web page and you are ready to start searching.

Most databases allow you to undertake a variety of searches ranging from 'basic' or 'quick' to 'advanced' in their complexity. Basic searches, as their name suggests, are relatively simple, often limiting the number of search terms you can type in. More advanced searches, as we will see shortly, allow you to specify your search more precisely. In addition, many databases have a browse facility allowing you to look through electronic copies of journals by title or by subject.

The first thing you need to do for a basic search is to type in the search term. If you look at the basic search screen for the online database Emerald, you will see that you can type in one term or phrase as a search term (Figure 2.2, point 1) and have only one option, selecting the content you want to search, in this case 'articles and chapters' (Figure 2.2, point 2). When you click on 'Search', this will retrieve all relevant items in the database containing the search term, in this example 'articles and chapters' articles about 'service quality'. For this example, this is likely to be over 100,000, as the search term is very broad!

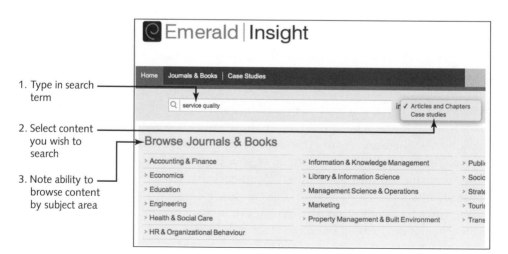

**Figure 2.2**  Quick search using Emerald Insight

*Source:* Emerald Insight, reproduced with permission.

For more advance searches, again the first thing you need to do is to type in your search terms (Figure 2.3, point 1) using Boolean operators to link two or more search terms (Figure 2.3, point 2). Boolean operators are the words you use to join together your keywords and phrases for your search. If you look at the advanced search screen for the online database Business Source Premier (Figure 2.3), you will see that the search terms 'supply chain' and 'power' are joined by the Boolean operator 'AND'. This means that when you undertake this search, you will retrieve only items that contain both these search terms. In other words, the word 'AND' is narrowing your search to retrieve items that contains both search terms. Other Boolean operators that you may find useful are 'OR' and 'NOT'. The word 'OR' broadens your search by retrieving items that, in this example, contain either the search term 'supply chain' or the search term 'power' or both search terms. The word 'NOT' narrows your search by excluding items. This means that if you searched for 'supply chain' NOT 'power', you would retrieve only items that included the search term 'supply chain' but that did not also include the term 'power'.

In many databases, you can amend your search by truncating your search terms or using wildcards. For most databases, the truncation character is *. If you truncate the

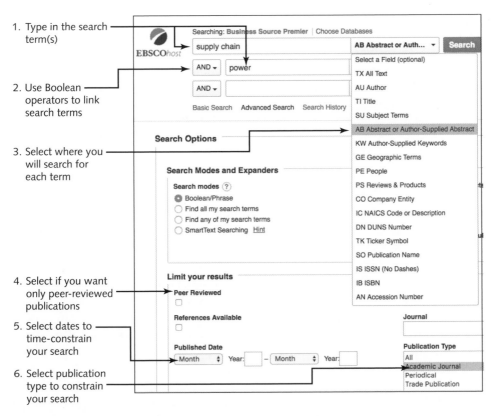

**Figure 2.3** Advanced search using Business Source Premier

*Source:* EBSCO Information Services, reproduced with permission.

keyword 'learning' to 'learn' by typing in the search term 'learn*', the database will retrieve all items that include the word 'learn', including 'learn', 'learning' and 'learner'. Wildcards are useful if you have to deal with spelling variations, particularly between US and UK English. The wild-card character differs between databases, but is often '?'. So, if you type in 'organi?ation' as a search term, you will retrieve items with both the US spelling organization and the UK spelling organisation.

You will find it is best to start most searches by looking for your search term or terms only in the abstract field (Figure 2.3, point 3). **Abstracts** are summaries of articles, books or reports that normally provide sufficient detail for you to decide whether or not they are likely to be useful for your research. By only searching for your search terms in the abstract, you will exclude literature that does not focus on your topic, even if your search terms appear elsewhere in the main text.

Most online databases, including Business Source Premier, allow you to check ✓ whether you want to retrieve all items or only those where the full text is available and you have access to it. Similarly, you can often check whether you want to retrieve all items, or only those that have been peer-reviewed (Figure 2.3, point 4). You can specify the dates for which you want to retrieve publications (Figure 2.3, point 5) and the type of publication (Figure 2.3, point 6). This can be useful if, say, you want to retrieve only items that have been published in the last five years in academic journals.

---

**Definition**

**abstract:** a summary of an article, book or report, providing an overview of what it contains and sufficient information for the original to be located.

---

## Download the relevant publications

Before you obtain a copy of a relevant publication, usually by downloading an article in an academic journal, it is worth making a quick assessment of its likely usefulness to your research project. You can usually do this by reading the abstract on the screen (Research in practice 2.2).

Obtaining articles is very easy if you have checked the box for only retrieving articles where full text is available. For most journal articles, you will only have to click on an icon to download an electronic 'PDF Full Text' copy which you can read using Adobe Reader (if you have not already downloaded this, you can do so for free). For articles where an electronic copy is not stored in the database, you will often be able to click on a different icon and download the 'Linked Full Text'. Again, you will usually be able to be read this using Adobe Reader. For those articles not available electronically, your library may well have a print copy. If not, you may be able to order it from another library as an inter-library loan. You will probably be charged for this service, so use it very sparingly.

## Research in practice 2.2

### Using an abstract to assess likely use of an article

Jaimie's research project was about entrepreneurial learning in small and medium-sized Enterprises (SMEs). In a search using the Emerald Insight database, she had found an article in the peer-reviewed academic journal *European Journal of Training and Development* by Saunders and colleagues (2014) that she thought would be useful. She decided to read the abstract online to check.

#### Abstract

**Purpose:** To contribute to the literature on innovation and entrepreneurial learning by exploring how SMEs learn and innovate, how they use of both formal and informal learning and in particular the role of networks and crisis events within their learning experience.

**Design/methodology/approach:** Mixed method study, comprising 13 focus groups, over 1000 questionnaire responses from SME mangers, 13 focus groups and 20 case studies derived from semi-structured interviews.

**Findings:** SMEs have a strong commitment to learning, and a shared vision. Much of this learning is informal through network events, mentoring or coaching. SMEs that are innovative are significantly more committed to learning than those which are less innovative, seeing employee learning as an investment. Innovative SMEs are more likely to have a shared vision, be open-minded and to learn from crises, being able to reflect on their experiences.

**Implications for research:** There is a need for further process driven qualitative research to understand the interrelationship between, particularly informal, learning, crisis events and SME innovation.

**Implications for practice:** SME owners need opportunities and time for reflection as a means of stimulating personal learning – particularly the opportunity to learn from crisis events. Access to mentors (often outside the business) can be important here, as are informal networks.

**Originality/value:** This is one of the first mixed method large scale studies to explore the relationship between SME innovation and learning, highlighting the importance of informal learning to innovation and the need for SME leaders to foster this learning as part of a shared organisational vision.

The abstract confirmed that the **Purpose** of the article was to explore how SMEs learn and innovate using both formal and informal networking. More detail was given in the **Findings** and **Research limitations/implications** sections of the abstract. The **Design/methodology/approach** indicated that the research had been undertaken in the United Kingdom using a questionnaire answered by over 1,000 SMEs' managers as well as 13 focus groups.

Based on this information, Jaimie decided that the article was likely to be useful to her research project, so she downloaded and saved the PDF file.

## 2.6    Evaluating the usefulness of literature to your research

You have already started evaluating the usefulness of the literature to your research through reading the abstract (Research in practice 2.2). Inevitably, the usefulness of any item will depend on your research question and your aim and objectives. This means that an article, which may be very useful for your friend's research project, could be of little or no use for your research project. As you review the literature, you will need to read as much of the literature that is closely related and of value to your research question as time permits. Let's say your topic is one where research has been ongoing for some years. If this is the case, you should find plenty of literature of value that relates directly to your research question. However, if your research question is about a new topic, you may find that not much of value that is closely related has been published. You will therefore have to review the literature more widely and set your own research in a broader context of what is already known.

Each time you evaluate the usefulness of publication for your research project, you are asking yourself questions about two interrelated aspects: its relevance and its value. At the same time, you are also probably asking yourself 'Have I read enough articles yet?' Any item's relevance to your research project depends on the appropriateness of the research reported and the connections you can make with your own research project. A publication's value to you depends on the quality of the research that is reported. This includes things such as how well methods and theory have been used, as well as the quality of the argument. In contrast, the answer to the question 'Have I read enough articles yet?' is about you having read sufficient publications to allow you to position your research project in the wider context of what is already known, and to cite the main writers with confidence.

Our students have found the questions in Table 2.5 helpful when they have been evaluating the relevance of a publication to their research, and we hope that you will also find them helpful for your own research.

Table 2.5 Questions to help evaluate the relevance and value of literature

| Question | Comment |
|---|---|
| **Relevance** | |
| 1  Is the item recent? | Although more recently published items are often more relevant, do not discount items just because they are old! |
| 2  Is the topic of the research similar to your own? | If it is, you may be able to compare and contrast your findings. |
| 3  Is the context of the research similar to your own? | Beware: do not discount items just because the context is different; you can often still get useful insights. |
| 4  Is this item cited (referenced) in other items that you have also found useful? | If it is often referred to in other items, it is probably important. |

**Table 2.5** Continued

| Question | Comment |
|---|---|
| 5  Is the author cited (referenced) in other items you have found useful? | If yes, then the author is probably a recognised expert. |
| 6  Does the author contradict or support the arguments you will make? | In either case, it is likely to be useful! |
| **Value** | |
| 7  Does the author use emotional words, illogical argument or seem to only choose examples that support the points being made? | If the author does, the item is probably biased and needs to be used with caution. If you do use it, you should comment on the possible bias and give reasons why you think this is so. |
| 8  Does the author describe theory clearly and in sufficient detail? | Even if there are gaps in the description of theory, the item may be useful for the references to the original theory. |
| 9  Is the method used described clearly and in sufficient detail? | Even if there are gaps in the method, the item may still be of use. If you do use it, you may need to comment on those aspects of the method that are less clear. |
| 10  Does the author highlight gaps in current research or offer suggestions for future research? | If the gaps or suggestions relate to your research topic, they could provide a useful justification for what you are doing. |
| 11  Is there an extensive list of references at the end? | A long list of references will often include relevant publications that you have not yet discovered – a great help. |
| **Sufficiency** | |
| 12  Do you recognise the author and her/his ideas from other things you have read? | If you do, you are getting closer to having read sufficient publications. |
| 13  Have you read the publications by those considered to be key researchers in the field? | If you have, you are getting closer to having read sufficient publications. |
| 14  Can you write about the topic and associated research with confidence? | Confidence normally only comes if you know the topic well. |

*Source:* Developed from Saunders et al. (2016).

## 2.7  Reading, noting and correctly referencing useful literature

### Reading and noting

You may be one of those people who, as they read an article or book, only uses a highlighter pen to mark those pieces they think are useful. If you are, beware! Just highlighting sentences and paragraphs that are likely to be useful will not help you concentrate nearly as well as making notes in the margin or on a separate piece of paper. Your notes can remind you why you thought the passage in the article was important, how an idea fits with your own research topic or even why you disagree with what you have just read. Making notes will help keep your mind focused on what you are reading and to remember what you have read.

Harvard College Library (2011) suggests that as you read, your note taking should focus on:

1  summarising;

2  comparing and contrasting.

When you write a summary of what you have just read in your own words, you probably find the process quite difficult. This is not surprising, as by summarising in your own words, you have to understand fully what you have read. In contrast, copying sentences just shows that you can copy. Copying sentences can also be a problem if you later forget they were copied and include them in your project report as your own words. Most **plagiarism** detection software will highlight your copied sentences as actual direct quotes and suggest their original source. If you have not put the copied sentences in quotation marks and also stated their source as a reference, you will, quite rightly, be accused of plagiarism. You can minimise this problem by making notes in your own words that summarise what you have read and always acknowledging the source of the ideas. If you decide you must copy a sentence exactly, enclose it in quotation marks and note the full reference and page number next to it.

As you make your notes, ask yourself how the item you are reading compares or contrasts with other articles and books you have read and your own thoughts upon reading it. Within this you need to think carefully about the clarity of the arguments and whether they are justified by the evidence presented. Let's say you have already read Hofstede et al.'s (2010) book *Culture and Organizations* about national cultures. The article you are now reading by McSweeny (2002) is very critical of Hofstede's research and in particular the assumptions on which he bases much of the research in this book. You are not sure who to believe, but you no longer feel so positive about Hofstede's theories! You therefore emphasise in your notes that McSweeny believes Hofstede's arguments are flawed, the reasons why and that you don't feel so positive towards Hofstede's theories about national cultures. You also find your notes on Hofstede's book and add a brief comment, 'See McSweeny (2002) for critique', to help ensure you do not forget to include this information in your literature review.

Five questions that can help you to read critically and make useful notes are listed in Table 2.6, along with a brief comment on each.

> **Definition**
>
> **plagiarism:** presenting the work and ideas of other people as it were your own, without acknowledging and referencing the original source.

Table 2.6  Five questions to help critical reading and noting

| Question | Comment |
| --- | --- |
| 1  Why am I reading this? | This question will help you focus on the reason or reasons you are reading the item, rather than be side-tracked by the author's agenda. |
| 2  What is the author (or what are the authors) trying to do in writing this? | Your answer to this question will help you to decide how useful the material that you are reading may be for your research project. |
| 3  What is the author (or what are the authors) saying that is relevant to my research topic? | Your answer to this question will give you the focus of your summarising notes. |
| 4  To what extent am I convinced by what is being said and why? | Your answer to this question will help you make notes that compare and contrast what you are reading with the other items you have already read. |
| 5  What use can I make of what I have read in my research project? | This question forces you to think about how you will write about what you have read in your literature review. |

*Source:* Developed from Wallace and Wray (2016).

## Referencing

As you write your project report, you will need to record the sources of all the information, research findings, theories and other ideas to which you refer in your writing. This process is known as referencing and allows you to acknowledge and give credit to the work of others, also helping ensure you are not accused of plagiarism. It allows you and anyone else who reads your project report to find the original source of this work. You reference work by identifying the source of the ideas briefly in your main text and then provide full details as a **list of references** or **bibliography** at the end of your project report. As a general rule, it is better to avoid quoting directly. However, if you do use a quotation, you must enclose this in quotation marks and state the number of the page from which it was copied. So, if you were quoting directly from a book Mark and Phil wrote with their colleague Adrian Thornhill, you would write:

"For some project reports you will be required to include a bibliography. Convention dictates that this should include all the relevant items you have consulted for your project, including those not referred to directly in the text. For others you will be asked to include only a list of references for those items referred to directly in the text." (Saunders et al., 2016: 107)

### Definitions

**(list of) references:** list of those items you have consulted, used and referred to directly in the text. Your university will specify the precise style.

**bibliography:** list of all relevant items you have consulted and used, including those you do not refer to directly in the text. Usually in alphabetical order. Your university will specify the precise style.

You would then provide the full reference at the end of your project report. We have provided a guide in Appendix 1 to a version of each of the most commonly used styles of referencing in business schools: Harvard and the American Psychological Association (APA).

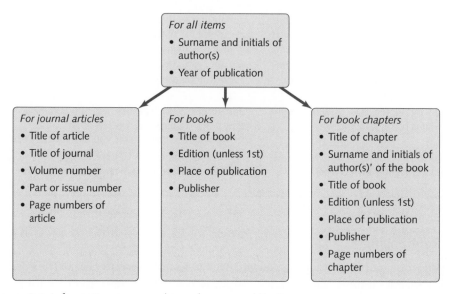

**Figure 2.4** Information you need to reference publications

However, rather than just using one of the two formats we suggest, please check to see if your own university or faculty has a preferred referencing style for recording articles, books and chapters in books as well as other items you have referred to in your literature review and elsewhere in your project report. If it does, it is essential that you obtain a copy of this and follow it exactly. Sloppy referencing suggests you do not care about your work and is likely to lose you marks. Whatever referencing style you use, the information you will need to record for the most common publications you reference is listed in Figure 2.4.

The most common referencing style in Business and Management is the author–date system. When using this system, you usually use the author's (or authors') surname(s) and the year of publication to identify documents in the main text as you refer to them. All these references are then recorded in full in one alphabetical list by author's surname at the end of your project report under the heading 'References' (Research in practice 2.3). Another referencing system you may come across in your reading is the footnotes system. Footnotes systems (such as Vancouver referencing), identify references in the main text with a number that is usually in superscript. All these references are recorded in full in the order to which they were first referred, usually in one sequential list at the end of your project report under the heading 'References'. This means that, if you use the footnotes system, your list is unlikely to be in alphabetical order (Research in practice 2.3).

## Research in practice 2.3

### Footnotes and author–date (Harvard) systems

Amina had used the footnotes system to reference the books and journal articles she referred to in the first draft of her literature review on strategic change. This is shown in the following two extracts from her literature review and list of references:

#### 2.3 Barriers to strategic change

. . . The cultural web[22] offers a way of auditing an organisation's culture and the barriers to change that culture can present. It has been argued that the web can be used to help build a vision for the new organisation, which managers can then compare with the web for their existing organisation.[23] Despite the numerous obstacles to strategic change, summarised by Franken and colleagues[24] as . . .

#### References

22. Johnson, G., Whittington, R., Scholes, K., Angwin, D. and Regnér, P. (2014) *Exploring Corporate Strategy* (10th ed.), Harlow: Pearson.
23. Balogun, J., Hope Hailey, V. and Gustafsson, S. (2016) *Exploring Strategic Change* (4th ed.), Harlow: Pearson.
24. Franken, A., Edwards, C. and Lambert, R. (2009) Executing strategic change, *California Management Review*, 51(3), pp. 49–73.

In his feedback her supervisor commented that, although she had used the footnotes system correctly, the University's assessment criteria asked for the Harvard author–date system. Amina checked the guidance notes on referencing provided by her university and amended her draft so that the references were in Harvard format. This is shown in the following two extracts:

#### 2.3 Barriers to strategic change

. . . The cultural web (Johnson et al., 2014) offers a way of auditing an organisation's culture and the barriers to change that culture can present. It has been argued that the web can be used to help build a vision for the new organisation, which managers can then compare with the web for their existing organisation (Balogun et al., 2016). Despite the numerous obstacles to strategic change, summarised by Franken et al. (2009) . . .

#### References

Balogun, J., Hope Hailey, V. and Gustafsson, S. (2016) *Exploring Strategic Change* (4th ed.), Harlow: Pearson.
Franken, A., Edwards, C. and Lambert, R. (2009) Executing strategic change, *California Management Review*, 51(3), pp. 49–73.
Johnson, G., Whittington, R., Scholes, K., Angwin, D. and Regnér, P. (2014) *Exploring Corporate Strategy* (10th ed.), Harlow: Pearson.

## 2.8    Drafting your critical literature review

### Deciding on the structure

Your critical literature review is likely to form either one chapter or a series of chapters in your project report. In being critical you will need to discuss different themes and compare and contrast what different authors say about them. Your own opinions will also need to be justified through your writing.

Many students' early drafts of their literature reviews are simply listings of everything they have read, in which each author's ideas are described one after another for those themes they have discussed (vertical arrows in Figure 2.5). If you do this, your literature review will be boring and uncritical. You, and your readers, will find it much more interesting if you take a thematic approach and write about one theme at a time. As you compare and, where necessary, contrast those authors who have said something about each theme, you will be writing critically (horizontal arrows in Figure 2.5).

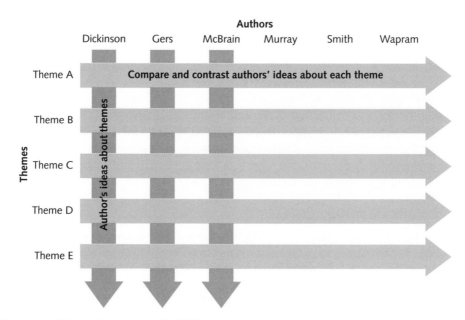

Figure 2.5 Structuring your critical literature review

In our book *Research Methods for Business Students* (2016), we suggest that you should think of your literature review as a thematic funnel. This means you should take the following steps:

1 Begin by providing a more general overview of your research topic before narrowing down to your research question or research aim and objectives.

2 Start by providing a brief overview of the key themes and ideas in the literature reviewed.

3  For each theme, summarise, compare and contrast the research of recognised experts.

4  Within each theme, highlight previous research you have found that is most relevant to your own research, including work that may not be by recognised experts.

5  Provide a detailed account of the findings of this previous research and show how they are related to the theme.

6  Use your review to highlight those aspects where your own research will provide fresh insights, linking these explicitly to your research questions or objectives.

7  Tell your reader that these aspects will be explored in subsequent sections of your project report.

8  Finish with a summary that links to your next chapter.

The key to you drafting an interesting and critical literature review is therefore to link the different ideas you find within each theme in the literature, and then link the themes to form a clear, well-justified argument. You need to ensure that this places your research in the context of what is already known and justifies why your research is worth doing.

## Getting on with writing

Although you will not be able to start writing until you have done some reading, it is important you begin to draft your literature review before you have completed reading all the literature. The process of drafting your literature review will help you get your ideas about your research clear in your own mind. As you read more, you can update and revise your draft as necessary.

You, like everyone we know, will find drafting your literature review difficult. As you write, you have to get your ideas clear in your own mind and put them into words such that anyone who reads them can understand. Phil refers to this writing process as the 'rewriting process', emphasising the need to improve early drafts of what you have written. Your literature review writing process will be no different, and you should expect to have to rewrite your critical review more than once. Indeed, what you write at the start of your literature review will almost certainly have to be updated and revised as you read more over the course of your research project.

We often compare a poor literature review to a shopping catalogue. This describes what your literature review should not be like. If you wrote your literature review as a shopping catalogue, you would:

- Include every item you have read.
- Group each of the items you have read in some way.
- Sort the items within each theme in some way, such as by date or author.
- Describe each item using a similar number of words.

Obviously, your literature review will be far more than just a shopping catalogue, as you need to be critical. Your writing, therefore, needs to show that you have:

- Reflected on the value of the findings of each item you have read.
- Reflected on the value of the ideas of each item you have read.
- Made reasoned judgements about the value of each item you have read.

- Included only those items that are relevant.
- Organised the ideas and findings into a coherent logical argument by theme.

Look at the project report extracts in Research in practice 2.4. You will notice that in the first extract, Ben simply lists the ideas from the literature one after the other like in a shopping catalogue. The order in which he has written about each of the items does not appear to be logical, the more general ideas of Rousseau et al. and of Schoorman et al. being described after his summary of more specific and focused arguments by Möllering. In addition, Ben has only listed the items and has not linked the authors' ideas together to form an argument. At the end of this extract, he quotes a Wikipedia definition rather than discussing the definitions used by academic researchers, something which is unlikely to please his supervisor.

## Research in practice 2.4

### Writing – a shopping catalogue or critical review?

Ben was feeling pleased. He had spent a great deal of time reading the literature and felt he had described clearly everything he had read. He emailed the first draft of his literature review to his project supervisor in advance of his supervision meeting. At the meeting his supervisor was obviously not impressed by Ben's writing. She commented that his draft was 'more like a shopping catalogue than a critical literature review' and needed to be 'completely rewritten'. Ben listened carefully to his supervisor's comments and went back to his room to redraft his work as a critical literature review.

This extract is taken from Ben's first draft:

> . . . Möllering (2001) argues that trust develops from favourable expectations based upon interpretations of the reality to which trust relates, enabled by a suspension of disbelief and a corresponding leap of faith. Rousseau et al. (1998) argue that the development of trust theory has, to date, been disparate, focusing on a range of levels of analysis from the interpersonal to the inter-organisational. Schoorman et al. (2007) recognise that there is a need for a context specific understanding of trust. Wikipedia (2017) states that trust is the willingness of one party to be vulnerable to the actions of another party, with the reasonable expectation that they will behave in a beneficial way . . .

This is the same passage after Ben had redrafted it as a critical review:

> . . . Development of trust theory has, to date, been more disparate, focusing on a range of levels of analysis from the interpersonal to the inter-organisational (e.g. Rousseau et al., 1998) and recognising the importance of context (Schoorman et al., 2007). Although this has resulted in a variety of definitions of trust, these exhibit a number of common elements, including notions of 'favourable expectations' and a 'willingness to become vulnerable'. Möllering (2001) has sought to use and develop these common elements in his research, arguing that trust develops from favourable expectations that are based upon interpretations of the reality to which the trust relates, enabled by a suspension of disbelief and a corresponding leap of faith. This suggests that . . .

Now re-read the second extract in Research in practice 2.4. You will notice that, unlike in the first extract, the order in which Ben writes about the ideas from the literature appears more logical, going from more general to more specific ideas. He starts with a general summary statement, referring to two sources as examples (Rousseau et al., 1998; Schoorman et al., 2007). In the next sentence, he provides a more detailed evaluation, highlighting similarities between authors. Ben uses the phrase 'although this has . . .' to link these two sentences. He then introduces Möllering's more specific and focused arguments, repeating the term 'common elements' from the previous sentence to help emphasise a clear link. This time Ben does not refer to Wikipedia. His final phrase 'This suggests that . . .' provides a link between his summary of Möllering's ideas and what he is going to write next.

Finally, a quick reminder. Don't forget to look at section 8.5, where we talk about the process of writing in much more detail.

## Summary

- Your critical literature review should offer an overview of significant literature available in your chosen topic, including relevant peer-reviewed academic journal articles, textbooks and other sources. It should provide a discussion and evaluation covering each of these, the level of detail reflecting the significance of each item. It should develop a clear argument to contextualise and justify your research.

- Critically reviewing the literature is important because it will provide the base on which your research project is built, helping you to decide on your precise topic and place it in the context of other research findings. It will also provide insights into secondary data that are likely to be available, as well as possible ways of collecting and analysing your own data.

- The amount of literature available to you is expanding rapidly. In addition to the library catalogue, your university library web pages will provide a comprehensive list of the other sources you can access as a student and the types of literature they contain. The most useful sources will be the databases of academic journal articles.

- Your literature review will consist predominantly of peer-reviewed academic journal articles, although you are likely to find textbooks helpful, particularly early on in your reviewing.

- The process of searching for and obtaining the literature consists of five stages: (1) decide on your literature search topic; (2) identify the search terms and phrases you will use; (3) choose your databases; (4) undertake your search and (5) download the relevant publications.

- The usefulness of any item will depend on your research question and your aim and objectives. When you review the literature critically, you will need to read as much of the literature that is closely related and of value to your research question as time permits.

- As you read, you should make notes in your own words of ideas that are useful to your research. Your notes should provide a summary of the item and remind you why you thought the particular idea was important, how an idea fits with your own research topic or even why you disagree with what you have just read. Making notes will help keep your mind focused on what you are reading and to remember what you have read.

- As you write your project report, you will need to record the sources of all the information, research findings, theories and other ideas to which you refer in your text. This process is known as referencing and allows you to acknowledge and give credit to the work of others, helping ensure you are not accused of plagiarism.

- The most common form of referencing in Business and Management is the author-date systems (e.g. Harvard, APA). Your university will probably have a preferred referencing style and, if it does, it is essential that you obtain a copy of this and follow it exactly.

- Think of your literature review as a thematic funnel in which you link the different ideas you find within each theme in the literature and then link these themes using a clear, well-justified argument.

## Thinking about your critical literature review

→ If you have not yet begun to think about critically reviewing the literature, start now.

→ Write your research question or aims and objectives on a piece of paper and refer to them frequently to keep focused. (If you are still unsure what to do for your research project, turn back to sections 1.4 and 1.5.)

→ Based on what you already know about your research topic, identify the terms and phrases you will use to search. Be prepared to use a variety of different terms and phrases.

→ Use the databases available through your university and your university library catalogue to search the literature for useful items. Although you will find textbooks listed in the library catalogue useful in the early stages of your review, you should focus mainly upon finding peer-reviewed academic journal articles, using databases of journal articles.

→ Obtain the articles and other items that seem likely to be useful and assess their relevance and value (usefulness) to your own research.

→ Use Google Scholar to find more recent items written by others that refer to those items you have already found that you feel are most useful to your own research.

→ Make your own notes about these useful items and include a summary in your own words. As you make notes, write about how the item compares with other items you have read.

→ Note the full reference of each item, using your university's preferred style of referencing.

→ Begin to draft your critical literature review, using a thematic structure and comparing and contrasting what each author has to say about a theme. Be mindful that you will have to redraft your review more than once.

## References

Harvard College Library (2011) *Interrogating Texts: 6 Reading Habits to Develop in Your First Year at Harvard*. Available at: http://bsc.harvard.edu/files/interrogating_texts_six_reading_habits_to_develop_in_your_first_year_at_harvard.pdf [Accessed 12 October 2016].

Hofstede, G., Hofstede, G.J. and Minkov, M. (2010) *Culture and Organizations: Software of the Mind* (3rd ed.). Columbus, OH: McGraw-Hill.

McSweeny, B. (2002) Hofstede's model of national cultural differences and their consequences: a triumph of faith – a failure of analysis. *Human Relations,* 55(1): 89–118.

Saunders, M.N.K. (2012) Web versus mail: the influence of survey distribution mode on employees' response. *Field Methods,* 24(1): 56–73.

Saunders, M. N. K., Gray, D. and Goregaokor, H. (2014) SME innovation and learning: the role of networks and crisis event. *European Journal of Training and Development,* 38(1/2): 136–49.

Saunders, M., Lewis, P. and Thornhill, A. (2016) *Research Methods for Business Students* (7th ed.). Harlow: Pearson.

# Chapter 3

# Managing the research process

## 3.1　Why you should read this chapter

In Chapter 1 we noted that doing a research project gave you the chance to develop a number of skills. Much of this chapter focuses in part upon the development of your personal organisational skills. Also in Chapter 1 we talked of the importance of managing your own learning through choosing a research topic that will develop your skills and knowledge as well as, possibly, your employment opportunities. We also noted the importance of choosing a topic that matched the resources available to you, in particular time and data. All of this suggests the importance of you taking control of the research process. It is a process which you should lead, not one where you allow yourself to be led. In fact, we would go as far as to say that self-organisation is a crucial factor in determining a successful outcome to your research project.

So what are these components of the research process that need to be managed by you? Well, assuming that you are doing primary research in a work organisation, the organisation itself in the form of its key personnel, or its customers, are obvious starting points. You will need to get access to the organisation in the first place. Then there are the people from whom you wish to get the data. Obviously, paying attention to these key resources is vital. Then there is the management of the components over which you have more control. First, we concentrate upon the key component of managing oneself, where attention needs to be paid to wider topics than just managing your time. Then there is the relationship you have with your supervisor. Managing this does not mean that you 'take charge' of your supervisor. It's more subtle than that. Many students (and lecturers, for that matter) talk of unsuccessful student/supervisor relationships. We help you to ensure that your situation is successful. We then cover the relationship you have with the university through, for example, the importance of paying attention to the standards that are demanded of you. We represent the management of the research process in Figure 3.1.

**Figure 3.1** Managing the research process

The final part of this chapter is about the ethics of doing research. This is a central consideration in the conduct of research. It's essential that you consider the ethical implications of your research in order to avoid falling foul of the expectations of your host organisation, respondents, university and project supervisor.

## 3.2 Getting access to your research organisation, respondents and participants

So your research questions and objectives mean that it's necessary to gain access to an external organisation, or a number of organisations, to do some research. Much of this section assumes that you will not be doing research using your employing or placement organisation as the main context, so it's one with which you are unfamiliar. (However, we deal with issues that arise from being the 'insider' later in the section.) It's possible, of course, that you have had some introduction to the organisation, from a friend or a previous connection. But even if that is so, there are still key issues that you need to consider. These issues are divided into two main parts in this section. First, we consider some of the main problems that you are likely to face when attempting to gain access to your chosen organisation. Second, armed with an awareness of some of these problems, we talk about how you may overcome them to achieve your goal of organisational access.

It would be good to think that the organisation in which you wish to do research will be keen to help you. You may be lucky; it may. But the reality is that most will not be keen. So what are some of the reasons for this possible lack of keenness to help?

### ⬤ What's in it for us?

The reaction of the manager who receives the request is likely to be, 'What's in it for the organisation?' Managers are busy people who are paid by the organisation to help achieve the organisation's goals, not your goals! This seems a most obvious point, but how often when we plan for a job interview, for example, do we concentrate upon what we want and what we can offer and not think about the needs of the employer?

## Oh no! Not another request!

Be aware of the fact that your request may be one of many. You will be aware that there has been huge growth in the number of degree students in recent years, including business and management students. This means that research access requests are much more commonplace, particularly in a large national organisation.

## Oh no! Not another student! Yet another demand on our time!

You must accept the fact that you may be a source of concern. This is probably the first time you have done something like this, so the manager has to balance the wish to help you (and many managers do genuinely want to help) and the risk that you may waste valuable organisational time.

The manager receiving your request is going to be mindful of the resources that will need to be devoted to you. That manager will need time to consider who may be responsible for dealing with your needs. In turn, the likelihood is that you will need to demand the time of other people, for example, more junior employees. This will impact upon the ability of people to do the jobs for which they are paid.

## Who is going to get hold of this information?

There is also likely to be a worry about what you going to do with the information you get from the organisation. We are not talking just about commercial secrecy here, but organisational politics. Many managers are very sensitive about who knows what in their own organisation, so they are going to be even more concerned about the public availability of that knowledge outside the organisation. This may not necessarily be particularly rational – the information may not on the face of it seem sensitive. But we are talking about human behaviour here, which isn't always as rational as we may think!

Clearly you will need to give assurances about treating such information that you collect with strict confidentiality, assuming that this is what is required. You may also need to promise that your participants or respondents will be anonymous so that their identity cannot be traced.

## Well maybe, but not right now . . .

Organisations will often cite reasons why they are not able to grant research access at the time when you approach them. Of course, there may be an element of putting you off here, in the hope that you will go somewhere else and leave them alone! But sometimes the reason may be perfectly valid. It may coincide with a particularly busy period, such as new product launch, or a sensitive time such as the announcement of a redundancy programme.

The discussion here refers to what may be called **physical access**, or the 'gatekeeper' level of organisational access. But you will usually need to get through the 'gate' to see

---

**Definition**

**physical access:** gaining access to an organisation to conduct research.

other people. Although 'gatekeeper' access is essential, it may also be necessary for you to gain acceptance and consent from those within the organisation order to gain **cognitive access** to the data that they are able to provide. These people may be other managers, or their employees whom you may need to see as individuals or in groups. So, let's face it, the problems you may face when dealing with the **gatekeeper** are equally relevant at other levels.

---

**Definitions**

**cognitive access:** gaining agreement from individuals to providing research data, such as by the answering of questions.

**gatekeeper:** the person, often in an organisation, who controls research access.

---

## 3.3 What about access to information?

So far we have dealt with the question of access to the organisation in order to get into a position where you can get the information you want. Now let's deal with access to that information itself. Here you need to be clear about precisely what data you wish to collect and the method or methods you intend to use to collect those data. This raises two key questions:

1 Have you thought through fully the extent of the access that you will require in order to be able to answer your research question(s) and meet your objectives?

2 Are you able to gain sufficient access to answer these research question(s) and meet your objectives?

Both these questions point to the need for thorough preparation on your part – which is a topic we will deal with in the next part of this chapter when we deal with strategies to gain access.

### Should organisational access be seen as a single event?

Your research question(s) and objectives may mean that you need to gain information from people at different levels of the organisation, and from different parts of the organisation, say different divisions or departments or geographical locations. Or it may be that you need to gather data in fragments, separated by time. All of this suggests that access is a continuing process and not just an initial or single event. So access negotiation becomes an even more important part of the management of the research process. Indeed, it may be continuous.

### Getting access to the organisation as an 'insider'

We mentioned at the start of this chapter that you may be an employee of the organisation in which you wish to do research, or you may be, or have recently been, a placement student in the organisation. This is great because people in the organisation will know you and, hopefully, have positive views about you. But you are still likely to face problems in getting the data you need. However, they may be rather different to those faced by the 'outsider'.

The likelihood is that, as the 'insider', you may still need to get formal approval to conduct the research. The larger or more geographically diverse the organisation, the more likely this is. All you may have is an introduction, so you may only be one step in front of the 'outsider'.

As the insider, you may come across the same issue of status. And it may not be just because you are seen as quite a junior member of the organisation (indeed, you may be quite senior). It will be an issue if, say, you belong to a part of the organisation which is seen to be more powerful than the one in which you wish to do the research. Feelings of suspicion may be even greater if you have been asked by your manager to take part in the research project. ('What are *they* up to now?') You may not feel much like a management pawn, but that's the way you could be seen.

There is another disadvantage as the 'insider' researcher. You may feel reluctant to ask very basic questions (e.g. 'What job does Mrs X actually do?' 'Who is our biggest client?') because you feel you should know the answer. As the outsider, you would not be expected to know the answers to these questions, so you can gather information that you really need to know to set your research information in context.

## 3.4  Six strategies for making sure that you get the organisational access you want

It sounds as if we are being totally negative in this chapter so far! Well, getting access to your research organisation certainly does pose challenges. But this chapter is all about managing the research process, so you need to manage the challenges.

You will have to plan your approach carefully. How do you do this? We explain in this section six strategies you can adopt to manage the process.

### Strategy 1: Try to use your existing contacts

It's undoubtedly easier to use any existing contacts you have to get access to an organisation to do your research. These contacts may come from friends, family, student colleagues, lecturer suggestions or contacts that you may make at meetings of the professional association related to your specialism. Having an introduction at least avoids that difficult stage where you approach the organisation as a complete unknown. Although using a contact who has mentioned you may not put the manager who receives your request under any obligation to give you the access, you are more likely to have the chance to make your request than in the case of asking when you do not know anyone.

We have mentioned the possibility of using your work placement organisation as your research organisation already in this chapter. If your placement has been a success, you will have made useful contacts that may be able to help you. Potentially, this is much better than using contacts given to you by someone else. You are known and trusted, and the organisation's managers will know that you are familiar with the context of the organisation's work. So your demand on resources may not be as great. It may be even better to build on the work you did on the placement by doing a research project that relates to this work. This may lead to the ideal situation, access to an organisation in which you are welcomed to conduct some research that is valued by the organisation!

You may also consider using the organisation with which you are familiar as a 'launch pad' for your research, facilitating access to another organisation from which you may gather your data. (Research in practice 3.1 is an example of this approach.)

---

### Research in practice 3.1

#### Negotiating organisational access in an organisation unknown to you

Nazaneen was a part-time business studies undergraduate who worked full-time in one of the major banks. She was very interested in the issue of cashless pay, both the technology that facilitated this development and the way in which it had the capacity to change consumer behaviour.

She had followed the media coverage of this topic for some time and was intrigued in the extent to which cashless pay had spread in Sweden where cash transactions made up barely 2% of the value of all payments made in 2015 – a figure some see dropping to 0.5% by 2020 (Henley, 2016). In Swedish shops, cash is now used for barely 20% of transactions, half the number five years ago, and way below the global average of 75%.

In the United Kingdom, a major milestone on the path to a cashless society was passed in 2015. This was the first year that consumers used cash for less than half of all payments, according to Payments UK, the organisation which represents the major banks, building societies and payment providers. As an example, the UK ready-to-eat food chain Pret a Manger reported that 65% of their customers use contactless payment cards and, increasingly, mobile 'phone systems' (e.g. Apple Pay) to make their purchases.

Nazaneen's reading of the relevant literature suggested to her that the main stumbling block to the widespread adoption of cashless pay in the United Kingdom was the reluctance to embrace its use by small retail businesses. So she concluded that the best way to understand their reluctance was to interview them. She was a bit wary of just going around to small shops on a 'cold call' basis and speaking to the owners, and she thought that something a bit more formal may be more appropriate.

Nazaneen talked over the matter of access with her research supervisor, who suggested that she contact the relevant trade organisation, which in this case is the National Federation of Self Employed & Small Businesses Limited. This she did by establishing the identity of the executive who seemed the most appropriate to her needs and then writing to that person with a full explanation of her project.

The letter which Nazaneen sent (she decided against using email – see strategy 4 in this section), which included a copy of her formal research proposal, impressed the executive concerned. It resulted in a helpful interview at the organisation's HQ. She was also given a list of small businesses to approach which would be able to provide more data to give a richer understanding of the nature of the perceived problems of the small retailer.

### Strategy 2: Put yourself in the shoes of the manager receiving your request

If the organisation is likely to be resistant to your approach, you have to think about why that organisation is likely to be resistant. Put yourself in the shoes of the manager receiving your request and think about how to overcome some of that resistance. Strategies 3–6 offer specific guidance on practical steps you take to overcome resistance. All these need you to think through how your request is likely to be seen by the manager receiving your request.

We noted above that the reaction of the manager who receives the request is likely to be 'What's in it for the organisation?' which seems a reasonable reaction. So it's important to think about any possible benefits to the organisation. And there may be some. Frequently, we have experienced participants who have confessed to us after an interview that they viewed the prospect of being interviewed as a bit of a chore. Yet we have been delighted to hear from them that they found the interview helpful. Rarely do they have the opportunity to talk through issues with an interested outsider. The more probing your questioning, based on thoughtful listening, the more value the participant is likely to get from listening to the responses.

Participants(s) may also appreciate a summary report of the interview, although it is not normally appropriate to send them a copy of your project report. The report is for a different purpose. An interview summary helps in three ways. First, it enables the participant to check the accuracy of your summary, second, it allows the addition of material which may have been overlooked during the interview and last, it shows that you have actually done something as an end product of the interview.

Let's go back to the worry the manager may have that you will take too much valuable organisational time. Your request for access is more likely to be accepted if the amount of time you ask for is kept to a minimum. And it's important to be realistic about the amount of time you ask for. Be honest. For example, falsely stating that each interview will last for only 30 minutes, and then deliberately exceeding this, may very likely upset the person you are interviewing and prevent your gaining further access.

### Strategy 3: Make sure you give yourself sufficient time to set up the arrangement

We hope that one of the messages that come across clearly in this book is that of giving yourself plenty of time to complete your research project. To summarise this message: start early!

Nowhere is this message more significant than the issue of allowing sufficient time to set up access to your research organisation. It can take weeks of delay between your original request and the final approval to go ahead (or, regrettably, the refusal). Even where the go-ahead is granted there will be further delay before you gain access to the people from whom you wish to get information.

Assuming that you are not using an existing contact (and even where you may be), you are unlikely to receive a direct reply to your first approach. There will be delay while you wait for this, and then for a response to your follow-up. This raises the question of the amount of time you should wait, and the 'tone' you adopt when sending your 'reminder'. You must ensure that you keep to the right side of the line between persistence and pestering. Whether you use email, telephone or letter (or a combination of the three) depends on the situation. We have found that a telephone approach with a written follow-up can be very effective.

The larger the organisation, the more time consuming the access negotiation process may be. Where you have no existing contact, it may be necessary to make several telephone calls simply to establish the best person to ensure that your request for access will be considered. If you use a contact given to you, you will still experience delay while your request is considered and an interview meeting arranged at a convenient time. This may take a number of weeks.

More time will be needed for access requests that are more complex. You may wish to get data in a variety of ways from across the organisation which, of course, has the potential for more delays. The official go-ahead from the organisational gatekeeper may mean that you are 'in', but you still have to gain cognitive access: the consent, support and trust of those participants you will depend upon for your research data.

One final note to emphasise is that the worst may happen and you receive a refusal. Not only is it essential to have a plan B (or even C and D!), but make sure the necessity to enact plan B does not seriously jeopardise your overall timescale. Following experimentation, psychologists recently have concluded that time passes quickest when we are busy. Many of our students have told us that this is not true: it passes like lightning during the time allocated to a research project!

## Strategy 4: Make your written request professional

Putting your request for research access into writing is highly advisable. Unless you read from script, it is unlikely that you could achieve the same level of precision in a spoken telephone request.

There are several reasons why it is advantageous to put your request in writing in a clearly written manner. Among these are:

1 It allows people to be aware precisely of what will be required from them. This is important because asking them for their help without being clear about your needs will probably lead them to be wary, since the amount of time you require from them may be more than they may reasonably expect to give.

2 It gives you the opportunity to set your request in context. You can explain the overall purpose of the research, the reason you are doing it, the university and department in which you are studying and the course you are completing.

3 It gives you the opportunity to enhance your credibility by presenting a professional image through a well-written and carefully considered request.

Your written request should outline briefly:

- the purpose of your research;
- how the person being contacted might be able to help;

- the demands being made of those taking part in the research;
- a guarantee of anonymity (where appropriate);
- what you will do with the information you get from each person involved, including any intention you may have of sharing the information during or after the data collection stage;
- your contact details so that the person can reply to you.

Should your written request be an email or a traditional letter? The advantages of an email are clear, but don't discount the value of a letter. The impact of the letter may be greater as it is more unusual these days; it is much less easy to delete or mislay; and it gives you greater opportunity to personalise and, therefore, impress. Whichever method you choose, it is essential that your communication achieves the highest standard of which you are capable. This warning is especially appropriate in the case of emails. We all know how easy it is for normal writing standards to drop when we send emails and how tempting it is to hit 'send' without double- and triple-checking in the same way that we may do with traditional written forms of communication. Don't be tempted. The person reading your email may (like us!) be a stickler for correct written English, and may reject your request on these grounds alone (see Research in practice 3.2).

### Research in practice 3.2

#### Writing your research request

Below is a copy of the letter Nazaneen sent to the National Federation of Self Employed & Small Businesses Limited regarding her planned research which we explained in Research in practice 3.1.

Dear Ms Armfield

Further to my telephone call to your assistant, Stephanie Dixon, last Friday April 11th, I would like to introduce myself and explain the reason for me contacting you.

My name is Nazaneen Ghorbani. I am a part-time business studies undergraduate at the University of ................... I also work full-time in one of the major banks. As part of my course I have to complete successfully a research project. I am very interested in the issue of cashless pay, both the technology that facilitates this development and the way in which it has the capacity to change consumer behaviour. This is the subject of my project.

In my review of the large amount of research material available on this topic it seems that the widespread adoption of cashless pay has particularly large important implications for smaller retailers. I would like to gain a closer understanding of the attitudes of small retailers to cashless pay by speaking to you and a number of your members. I hope you are able to help me in this regard.

The details of my research plan are in the attached document called 'Nazaneen Ghorbani Research Proposal'.

At the end of the document I suggest a set of topics/questions for the interviews I plan to conduct, which I hope will be valuable for you in thinking about this prior to my visit. I assure you that I will take no more than one hour of your time and that the information you give me will not be credited to you in any report that I subsequently write without your approval.

I very much hope that you are able to help. If so please email me at Nazaneen@isp.com or call me on 07123 456789. I will then contact Stephanie Dixon to fix an interview at a time and place suitable for you.

I hope we are able to meet in the not too distant future. Meanwhile, thank you for reading this letter.

Yours sincerely
Nazaneen Ghorbani

## Strategy 5: Work hard to ensure there are no concerns about the way in which you will use the information

You will have noticed that one thing that virtually all organisations have in common is that they like to present a positive front to the world! Even if the news is bad, they work hard to put a less negative aspect on that news than perhaps is justified. Why else would large organisations spend millions on public relations specialists? There is a message here for those of us who want to pursue organisational research. You are unlikely to gain research access if the subject of your research can be perceived as negative. So an inquiry into the reasons for an organisation's market failure in a particular product area is to be avoided. However, you may learn from the public relations experts and lend a positive emphasis to this by, for example, using the organisation of your choice as a context for an inquiry into the changing nature of the demand for a particular product area and what may be learned. Your choice of language in the written request will have to be very carefully considered to ensure that no hint of negativity is suggested.

A more predictable area of concern is that of anonymity. This relates to that information which is given to you and what you do with it once it is given. Some topics, some organisations and some people will be extremely sensitive about anonymity. While this occasionally may be hard to understand, the point remains that it is their information, and you must respect their wishes.

The introductory email or letter offers you the opportunity to give a guarantee of confidentiality in writing at the time of making the request for access. This is a good time to make the initial guarantee, as confidentiality may be uppermost in the minds of the managers who will consider your approach. But do think of this as only the initial guarantee. As you meet more people, you will need to repeat any assurances about confidentiality. This can be done, for example, with an assurance that any information given to you will not be attributed to any individual. It is essential that you honour this assurance, not only for your credibility, but for those researchers who may follow you.

It is quite common for the organisation to ask you to not place your written report in the university library, although you may not have identified the organisation or any individuals. You must check the course requirements here with your supervisor, but whatever the regulations, the confidentiality wishes of your research organisation come first.

## Strategy 6: Underline your credibility!

Perhaps this sixth strategy is a result of the efforts you have put in making your request as professional as possible. The more credible you seem, the more likely you are to receive a favourable response to your request for research access. But there is one point we haven't mentioned so far which we think will really underline your credibility: find out as much as possible about the organisation before requesting access. The more you know about the organisation's context, such as their products and services, markets, competitors, trading position, current challenges and development plans, the better. This will really impress the person you're approaching, particularly if that knowledge blends thoughtfully with the information you are seeking and your research question(s) and objectives.

## In the end, do what's possible

Like many research considerations, getting access to your research organisation is a balance between what is ideal and what is possible. OK, so you want to make sure that you get a representative sample, conduct your interviews in a uniform way and collect sufficient data to ensure the answers to your research question(s) and objectives are valid and reliable. But life isn't perfect. People will deny you access to information, limit your interview time, lose your questionnaire, go on holiday, and leave the organisation in the middle of your research. You are at the mercy of events. You can manage much of the process, but you can't control the uncontrollable!

**Table 3.1** Checklist of points to follow to increase your chances of getting access to your chosen research organisation

- Be clear about the overall purpose of your research project.
- Write your research question(s) and objectives.
- Use existing contacts where possible.
- Consider using your work placement organisation (if appropriate) as a setting for your research project.
- Approach relevant appropriate local and/or national employer, or employee, professional or trade bodies to see if they can suggest contacts.
- Make a direct approach to an organisation to identify the most appropriate manager.
- Think about the possible benefits for the organisation, should access be granted to you.
- Offer a report summarising your findings.
- Allow yourself plenty of time for the entire process.
- Allow sufficient time to contact intended participants and gain their consent, once access has been granted.
- If you make your initial request for access by telephone, follow this with an email or letter to confirm your request.

**Table 3.1** Continued

- Make sure the construction, tone, language, spelling, grammar and presentation of an introductory email or letter are all likely to persuade the person to help you.
- Consider how you will address concerns about the amount of organisational time you would take up.
- Ensure you have considered any sensitivities concerning your research topic.
- Assure participants or respondents you have recognised any needs for confidentiality and/or anonymity.
- Think about a range of contact methods for potential participants to use to reply.

## 3.5    Managing yourself

We now move on to consider the management of those components of the research process over which you have more control: managing yourself, your supervisor and your university.

### Managing your time

We have already mentioned in this chapter elements of time management, particularly those that refer to the process of gaining access to your research organisation. Here we consider time management more widely, both in terms of your research project schedule and the allocation of time to your research.

It is important that you complete a research project plan at the beginning of your research. Indeed, this may be a university requirement, as it helps your supervisor assess the viability of your research proposal. It's useful if you divide your research plan into stages. This will give you a clear idea as to what is possible in the given timescale. But don't forget that however well your time is organised, the whole process seems to take longer than you planned. An example of the sort of schedule you may develop is shown in Table 3.2.

**Table 3.2** Research project schedule

| Task | To be completed by |
| --- | --- |
| Generate list of research ideas | 10.10.2016 |
| Choose research topic | 1.11.2016 |
| Undertake preliminary literature review | 1.11.2016 |
| Define research questions and objectives and submit research proposal | 10.11.2016 |
| Main literature reading | 10.12.2016 |
| Literature review written | 31.12.2016 |
| Methods chosen and draft method chapter written | 10.01.2017 |
| Fieldwork commenced | 20.01.2017 |
| All data collected and fieldwork notes completed | 01.03.2017 |
| All data analysed ready for draft findings and conclusions chapters to be written | 20.03.2017 |
| Final draft submitted to supervisor | 15.04.2017 |
| Final submission | 30.05.2017 |

Even if the inevitable happens and you find that you have some slippage in your schedule, at least you know what you are slipping from! Not having a schedule is simply unthinkable.

Just as important as the project schedule is your personal timetable which shows the amount of time you are going to devote to your research. Here you will have to be realistic. You have other demands. Other modules require lecture preparation and assessment completion. But it is all too easy to fall into the trap of allocating time by 'what's the next most important deadline'. Of course, there is always another deadline looming, but the trouble for your research project is that the big deadline of final project submission is months away for most of the year and it's forever being left until later. It's best to schedule some time regularly, say each week, to do something towards your research. Do this at the start of the year and get into the habit of it. The beauty of personal timetables is that they become part of a 'self-contract'. If you meet your contractual obligation, you can feel pleased with yourself; if you don't meet it, make sure you feel suitably guilty! There is no substitute for getting into a routine. You will probably have heard this before when you started university, but it's the same for doing research, or for us in writing this text. Get into the habit of doing something towards your research right from the start on, for example, Monday afternoons in the library. It's always easy to find other things to do when the deadline is not pressing. Just try not to be like Oscar Wilde, who could resist everything except temptation!

One final point about time management. We have known students who have been perfectionists and 'just do enough to pass' types. Our advice is to be neither. The perfectionist runs into time management problems because of the need to polish everything until it dazzles. This is great if there's time: but there never is. 'Just doing enough', on the other hand, can often lead to not doing enough and the necessity to re-submit the report.

## ◉ Keeping up your motivation

You are likely to be doing your research project for an extended period, so expect your motivation to vary over that period. You may start and end on a high, but there will be times in between when you can't see your way forward. There are ways in which you can overcome this. Let's look at three of these.

First, set for yourself short-term goals. Sports coaches are renowned for using this technique to improve participant performance. You can distinguish between long-term goals, for example, breaking the world record or successfully completing your degree; intermediate goals, such as lowering the 100-metre sprint time by one second or getting all your fieldwork done on time, and short-term goals. Short-term goals may concentrate on each training session, or, in research project terms, the completion of a set of notes at the end of a two-hour session reading a particular article. Do remember that it's important that your short-term goals are SMART (specific, measurable, achievable, realistic and timely) (see Chapter 1, section 1.7).

Second, while we are on the subject of goals, think about setting some fresh learning goals. Learning how to conduct an interview effectively; use a new statistical analysis package or how to sift, label and categorise qualitative data in a systematic way will not only add to your repertoire of business skills but give you a sense of achievement.

Third, do keep focused. You can do this by keeping in touch with your supervisor and talking through your progress. This can be quite motivational, either because you are further on than you thought, or in giving you a refreshed sense of direction if you have lost your way. Another important way of keeping focus is to review regularly your research question(s) and objectives. It's so easy to wander away from the main point of your research into all sorts of interesting diversions. A regular review of progress against your research question(s) and objectives is a vital way to keep focused. OK, so this may involve some revision of your question(s) and objectives, but at least this will mean that you're on track.

### ⬤ Keep in touch with individuals who can help

We have already mentioned the need to keep in touch with your supervisor. Don't forget there are other people who can help. It is useful to talk to these people regularly. Among these are those student colleagues who helped you think about your research topic in the first place and family and friends. It may also be useful to talk to the specialist librarian in your research topic area. This expert may be able to point you in the direction of new resources and to suggest different perspectives on your research.

## 3.6   Managing your supervisor

When you look back on your time at university and remember your research project, it's certain you will remember your research supervisor. Usually, this is for the right reasons, because the relationship has been a fruitful one where both you and your supervisor have had your expectations met. But, of course, it can all go horribly wrong. Fortunately, this happens rarely. But it can happen, so in this section we look at the expectations that you should have of your supervisor, and those that your supervisor should have of you. Being aware of these, and acting accordingly, should mean that your eventual memories of your supervisor are as favourable as those that we hope our students have of us!

### ⬤ What should you expect of your supervisor?

Your supervisor is there to advise you at every stage of your research project, from formulation of the project through to completion of the final report. However, do remember that it is your research project, and your supervisor is not there to write it for you.

What expectations should you have of your supervisor? Here are some:

### *You receive assistance with the selection and planning of a suitable and manageable research topic*

You should not expect your supervisor to impose a topic upon you; it has to be your choice. But you should be prepared to have your ideas both praised and criticised. You want encouragement, but if your supervisor thinks an idea is a non-starter, you should be told this.

### Your supervisor is sufficiently familiar with the field of research to provide guidance

This can be quite a problematic area. With the increasing amount of students who require supervision comes the need of the university to resource this requirement. This sometimes means that there is not an ideal match between your research topic and your supervisor. However, do bear in mind that your supervisor will concentrate on the research process rather than simply on the topic. In our view, the more effective supervisors are those who are familiar with guiding their students on how to conduct the project rather than those who are subject-only specialists. However, talk to the supervisors who are specialists about your research plans. Getting them interested may mean that you end up with both a subject specialist and someone who can guide you successfully through the project.

### Your supervisor should be available for consultation and discussion about the progress of your research

How often you see your supervisor will depend upon several factors, not least of which will be the norm as it applies in your department. Usually, you will meet during the early stages of the project as things get going. As you become more confident, and you immerse yourself in reading or data collection, you would expect less frequent meetings. We usually find that our students value contact with their supervisor in the early and late stages of their project, when they are setting up and writing up. But do bear in mind that in most universities, the onus is upon you to initiate meetings, although your supervisor may contact you to arrange the first meeting. You should check with your supervisor what the procedure is here.

At the end of each meeting with your supervisor, it is good practice to arrange the time of the next meeting and to agree what you should have done by that meeting. You then have the basis of an agenda for the next meeting. There may also be a procedure where a record is kept of the content of the meeting.

### Your supervisor should respond to the work that you have completed

If you have sent your supervisor written work, as agreed between you, it is reasonable to expect that your supervisor will respond to this. You should expect to have helpful suggestions about how the work may be improved.

### Your supervisor should point you in the direction of facilities or research materials

Again, the onus is upon you to make arrangements to negotiate access to organisations, or libraries where you need secondary data. But it's reasonable to expect that your supervisor will have some ideas as the sort of data that may be of help to you and where this may be available. As you make progress in your research, you will probably find that you know more than your supervisor about your research topic. However, in the early stages you are hungry for ideas, and it's to be expected that your supervisor will provide some of these.

## What your supervisor should expect from you

*You should, in conjunction with your supervisor, develop a plan and timetable for completion of the stages of your research project, and meet all deadlines*

Meet all deadlines, you say! Well, yes. But for all sorts of reasons which we touched on earlier in this chapter, some delays may not be in your control. But your supervisor will expect you to pay attention to the set deadlines and make your best attempt to meet them. Treating deadlines in a trivial way is a sure path to a hurried and ineffective conclusion to the project. The more you have to rush at the end, the less value you can expect from your supervisor's comments at that vital late stage when you are drafting your report.

*You should meet with your supervisor when arranged and report fully and regularly on progress and results*

It would be good to say that it's rare for students to not turn up for an arranged meeting, or to show up having not done the work that was agreed at the last meeting. But, unfortunately, it's not that rare. You will want to get the best out of your supervisor, so make sure that you demonstrate that you are businesslike and do what you have agreed to do. That way, your supervisor will respond in a similar way and a fruitful relationship will develop.

*You should give due consideration to the advice and criticisms received from your supervisor*

It would be foolish to ignore criticism from your supervisor. But that's not the same as saying that you should follow slavishly every word. Indeed, when your confidence grows as your work progresses, you may choose to listen to criticism but decide, after careful thought, to stick to your guns. After all, it's your project and you will have to live or die by the final outcome. But bear in mind that your supervisor has probably seen many similar projects in the past and is likely to be one of the people assessing your project report, so do consider carefully any critical comments you receive.

*You should keep yourself up to date on the subject of your research topic*

The likelihood is that you will write your critical literature review early in your project's lifecycle. Try to avoid the temptation of then closing your mind to this aspect of your work. There may be important developments in your topic area during the course of your work, so don't miss out on these. Ignoring recent news in some highly topical subject areas, such as new technological developments, will damage the credibility of your work and threaten the success of your final submission.

*You should keep in touch with your supervisor and make yourself available for regular meetings at mutually convenient times*

Most lecturers will tell you that the students who keep in touch with their supervisor are the ones who usually complete the research project successfully, while those they rarely see are on course for failure! This may be because the more diligent students usually are successful. But we like to think that research supervisors can pass on a wealth of experience and know-how which you would be foolish to ignore.

## 3.7  Managing your university

At the beginning of your course, or research project, you should receive from your programme leader a guide which will specify such items as aims, objectives and learning outcomes of the research project. The guide should also list the relevant regulations for the completion of the project. These regulations will cover such topics as any requirements to attend seminars, meet specific deadlines, submit the written report in a specified style and, of course, the academic standards you should meet in order to be awarded a pass for your project. It is this last aspect of the university's requirements that we concentrate upon here.

The learning outcomes of any research project summarise much of what we cover in this book as they emphasise the process of doing research. Table 3.3 is a good example of a statement of such learning outcomes.

**Table 3.3** Example of a statement of learning outcomes for research project module

Upon completion of this module, students will be able to:

(a) show resourcefulness in the sourcing and selection of material;

(b) demonstrate the ability to exercise sound judgement in the selection of material;

(c) engage critically with the chosen material;

(d) organise complex information in such a way that data collected is integrated with pre-existing material;

(e) structure clearly and logically a substantial piece of work;

(f) produce a clearly defined and usable outcome within a specified timescale;

(g) demonstrate a level of expert knowledge in a particular subject or issue;

(h) manage their own efforts effectively.

At the end of the successful completion of the module, the student will have completed a submission in accordance with the course and thus fulfilled the aims outlined above.

You should also pay particular attention to the assessment criteria, which should be contained in your research project guide. Table 3.4 is a good example of clearly defined criteria which you can use as a checklist as you work through the research process and, in particular, write your final report.

The criteria specified in Table 3.4 should come as no surprise to you, as they may well be similar to criteria you have come across earlier in other modules. But do use

Table 3.4 Example of marking scheme guide for research project final report

| Criterion | Strong | Weak |
| --- | --- | --- |
| Definition of aims and objectives | Clear and informative definition of the aims and objectives of the research or study topic/problem to be investigated. | Absent or weak and cursory description of research topic/problem to be investigated. |
| Method and methodology | Correct selection of and justification for chosen method. Full understanding of values and limitations of method. Clear rationale and understanding of limitations. | No justification for selected method. Inadequate data collection. No evidence of understanding of method and limitations. |
| Understanding and coverage of the literature | Excellent understanding and insightful knowledge of the subject matter. Comprehensive expert account of topic. Fully referenced using Harvard referencing. | No understanding of the subject. Confused thinking and inadequate knowledge. Limited and inadequate referencing. |
| Critical analysis, examination and presentation of findings | High-level analysis using appropriate techniques. Thorough examination of results to present clear findings linked to evidence. | Weak and unacceptable analysis. No critical evaluation of results. Findings presented not linked to evidence. |
| Conclusions and/or recommendations | Logical and insightful conclusions based on findings presented. Recommendations for action based on conclusions and findings and relevant to the context of the study. | No attempt to present conclusions and/or recommendations. |
| Structure and presentation | Excellent layout. Conforms to all stated requirements. Clear, logical writing style with correct use of English. Clear presentation of all tables, figures, etc. | Unacceptable layout in terms of structure and logical argument. Key requirements ignored. Inappropriate use of English. Serious deficiencies in presentation. |

*Source:* Developed from the University of Plymouth (2016).

these for your research project. We even urge you to have a session with your supervisor as you approach the writing-up stage to discuss the precise meaning of these criteria in relation to your written project report.

## 3.8  The ethics of doing research

Your university will expect you to conduct your **research ethically** and has hopefully made you aware of the ethical responsibilities you have while conducting your research.

> **Definition**
>
> **research ethics:** the appropriateness of the researcher's behaviour in relation to the rights of those who become the subject of a research project, or who are affected by it.

Let's be clear about what we mean by ethics. Generally, ethics means 'standards of behaviour that guide the moral choices we make which govern our behaviour and our relationships with others'. Since virtually all research using primary data, that is data which we collect specifically for the purposes of our research, involves our relationships with others, this is clearly something we shouldn't ignore. Or can we? Well, even if you wanted to act in an amoral way towards your research participants, the rules of your university will stress the need for you to behave in an ethical way in the conduct of your research (see Table 3.5).

Table 3.5 Example of code of practice for ethical standards involving human participants

- No research should cause harm, and preferably it should benefit participants.
- Potential participants normally have the right to receive clearly communicated information from the researcher in advance.
- Participants should be free from coercion of any kind and should not be pressured to participate in a study.
- Participants in a research study have the right to give their informed consent before participating.
- Where third parties are affected by the research, informal consent should be obtained.
- The consent of vulnerable participants (e.g. children) or their representatives' assent should be actively sought by researchers.
- Honesty should be central to the relationship between researcher, participant and institutional representatives.
- Participants' confidentiality and anonymity should be maintained.
- The collection and storage of research data by researchers must comply with the Data Protection Act 1998.
- Researchers have a duty to disseminate their research findings to all appropriate parties.

*Source:* Oxford Brookes University (2016). Full version available at: www.brookes.ac.uk/Documents/Research/Policies-and-codes-of-practice/ethics_codeofpractice/

In this section, we explore some of the ethical issues you may encounter through the different stages of your research. Ethical considerations impact upon how you decide upon your research topic; design your research and gain organisational and individual respondent or participant access; collect your data; process, store and analyse your data and write up your research findings. At all these stages you will need to ensure that the way you design your research is both methodologically sound and morally defensible to all those who are involved.

Here we consider the ethical issues at three main stages of the research process: research design, data collection and reporting. Of course, these issues don't fit neatly into each of the main stages. Nonetheless, we cover some of the main ethical points which we then summarise at the end of the section in Table 3.6.

## What are the ethical questions you should consider at the research design stage?

### Getting participants' and respondents' informed consent

The main issue to consider at the design and access stage of your research involve the issue of respondent or participant consent. Look again at Table 3.5. Following the principles here means that your respondents and participants should understand what the research is about and what is expected of them, should be free from coercion of any kind and should not be pressured to participate in a study. Coercion is unlikely to be the issue when you are approaching a senior manager as an organisational gatekeeper, but it may be relevant when the senior manager arranges for you to interview participants more junior than that manager. You should be particularly sensitive to this situation. It is extremely unlikely that such people will refuse to cooperate, even if a feeling of being coerced by a senior manager exists. However, you will need full support from your participants rather than grudging acceptance. Full support is more likely if you give assurances of confidentiality before the interview in a bid to secure informal consent.

The ethical situation relating to data collected by questionnaire is rather more straightforward. The return of a completed questionnaire by a respondent is such that completion by itself implies consent. However, this is not the same as giving you consent to use the data collected in any way you think fit. You should bear in mind that when respondents agree to participate, this does not necessarily imply consent about the way in which the data provided are subsequently used. You should still tell them in the introduction to the questionnaire how you will use the data. Don't ignore another of the principles in Table 3.5: that honesty should be central to the relationship between you and your respondents. Consider the example of the phone caller who calls you at the most inconvenient time posing as a researcher but who, in reality, is a salesperson. This is infuriating, and quite the opposite of the standards you should be aiming at!

### Consent – not coercion!

Conducting research in your own employing organisation presents different concerns. You may be tempted to apply pressure to others (colleagues or subordinates) to cooperate. They may cooperate from a feeling of social obligation to you. But the same effort to obtain informal consent applies as discussed before. And like all respondents and participants, you should emphasise their right to withdraw from your study at any time.

If you are being asked by the organisation to conduct your research project, you have a right not to be forced to choose a research project in which you are uninterested. This prejudices a valuable learning opportunity for you. It also threatens one of the most important ethical obligations you have to all concerned – to produce research of the highest possible quality.

### Your ethical obligation to use the time you have been granted by the organisation is a way that is of benefit to the organisation

If you are using an organisation as your research context, you will have an ethical obligation to use the time you have been granted by the organisation in a way that is useful to the organisation. That is not to say that you will necessarily tell the managers what they want to hear. But even if your conclusions are unfavourable, then the organisation has a right to expect that you frame your conclusions in a positive and constructive way. At the same time, you have a right not to be coerced by the organisation's managers to misrepresent the data which you have uncovered so as to portray the organisation positively.

### Respondent and participant vulnerability

Clearly, some topics carry a greater risk of a breach of ethical standards than others. A brief look at Table 3.5 shows that the standard of seeking the consent of vulnerable participants or their representatives is one that is potentially sensitive. On the face of it, this may relate more closely to schoolchildren, medical patients or social services clients. Yet, vulnerability may apply to employees whose jobs are changing or being made redundant; or it may relate to sensitive areas such as poor employee performance. If your research topic has obviously sensitive implications, you will need to pay attention to the ethical dimension in your research proposal.

## What are the ethical questions you should consider at the data collection stage?

### The importance of confidentiality

Often confidentiality is an important condition that your research organisation makes when granting you research access. Organisational gatekeepers often insist that you do not disclose the organisation's identity in any way. We deal with how to cope with this in your report in the sub-section on 'confidentiality and anonymity at the reporting stage' later in this section.

It is often more important to guarantee confidentiality to individual respondents and respondents. This is particularly important in relation to names, addresses and personal data that may allow them to be identified. Not only is the issue of confidentiality important, but harm may be done to individuals by information that you have obtained being attributed to them. You may, for example, have gained the trust of a participant to the extent where you are told the individual's career plans, something that may be better kept from management. Again, as with the organisation, do make sure that your participants' identities are not revealed accidentally in anything you write. You can use the same 'participant A' method, or adopt a style such as 'one participant told me . . .' The key point here is not to break your promise of confidentiality.

It's not just in reporting your data that you may reveal the identity of your participants. This can happen in interviews. As you collect more data, you may develop themes which have emerged during the process. Developing these themes may mean that your participants can guess what previous participants have said from the questions you are asking. This can lead to participants indirectly identifying the person responsible for raising the earlier point that you now wish to discuss with them.

The confidentiality points mentioned earlier relate mainly to the collection and reporting of qualitative data. Such issues are equally important when it comes to the collection and reporting of quantitative data. Here your main concern is to report aggregated data, in order to establish the patterns that emerge. So making quantitative data anonymous is less problematic. However, you still need to take care. Presenting a table that reports agreement with the questionnaire statement 'This organisation is a great place to work' is not anonymous (and could cause problems) if it showed that the two senior managers in a named department both 'strongly disagreed'.

### Causing harm through the collection of primary data through interviewing

In addition to confidentiality, conducting interviews raises other ethical considerations. The potential to harm your respondents can arise in many ways. We deal with three here.

First, it is important to be sensitive to any reluctance that your participant may have to answer your questions. As your confidence in interviewing builds, it may be easy to start pressing participants for answers without realising that what they are experiencing may be quite stressful for them. It's important to make clear to participants that they have a right to refuse to answer any question, for any reason. It doesn't happen often, particularly when you have built rapport with the interviewee, but it can.

Second, do be careful that the questions you ask are not likely to be harmful to your participant. These may relate to personal circumstances or be of such a nature that they humiliate your interviewee. Such questions may be quite unintentional. They may not form part of your planned interview schedule. But it's easy for a follow-up question to come out in a way that had not planned.

Third, do be mindful of the circumstances of your participant. Simple things such as setting a time, location and interview duration that is convenient to your participant is important. If the interview participants are quite junior in the organisation, it's important that you stick to agreed arrangements as they are likely to have less time flexibility. Be on guard for signs of discomfort because, for example, you're running over the agreed time. Not only is this discourteous, but, once again, you may be causing stress and inconvenience to your participants.

### Causing harm through the collection of primary data by observation

Should you wish to collect some or all of your data by observation, you will face particular ethical problems. Let's say, for example, that you want to observe the behaviour of airline cabin crew members as they deal with customers, in order to establish the extent of the engagement that they demonstrate. Central to this is the choice you have over whether you should disclose your purpose to those crew members you intend to observe. Given everything that has been said so far in this section, this seems a clear-cut decision: you should disclose your research purpose.

However, you then face the problem of '**reactivity**' (or 'observer effect'), which is a particular problem with observation. This happens when those you are observing adapt their behaviour as a consequence of your observation. Obviously, this threatens the reliability and validity of your data. So you have a choice: you disclose your purpose and seek approval of the organisation and the crew members in the normal way, or you go ahead and do your observation covertly.

Let's say that you seek approval of the organisation and the crew members and then you are refused access. You could carry on covertly, in your role as a customer, or

| Definition |
| --- |
| **reactivity:** reaction by research participants to any research intervention that affects data reliability. |

abandon the plan. If you decide to carry on covertly, then those being observed may discover your actions with the consequence that you must explain what they would see as your deceit. It is our view that researchers should not practise deceit at any time as this is a clear violation of the principles of ethical research.

### Causing harm to through unauthorised use of secondary data

It's not just through the collection of primary data that you can cause harm. The collection of secondary data also raises ethical issues. Say, for example, you want to establish a sample of customers from whom you want to collect data on service satisfaction levels. This may involve a study of customer databases to form the sample. From the databases you may have personal details of many individuals who have not consented to you having this information. It's important that you treat this information in the strictest confidence and don't use it in any way that might cause harm to these individuals.

It's also important that you are honest, stick to the declared purpose of your research and not use secondary data in any way other than that which you originally intended.

### Data collection and honesty

Having raised the topic of honesty in the previous sub-section, we touch here upon the most apparent dishonest behaviour in data collection, that of making up the data. This can be blatant, such as completing questionnaires yourself rather than delivering them to intended respondents. On the other hand, it can be more subtle, where you decide to include only responses which suit you for some reason and ignore those that do not suit you. Not only do you have an ethical duty to report your findings honestly, but your data will be unreliable and invalid if you have practised dishonesty in your data collection.

### Ethical issues and data collection using the Internet

The emergence of the Internet has presented many new opportunities for conducting research, including some in the business arena. The main ethical consideration is likely to revolve around the issue of consent. The potential topics here are so varied that it is well to check with your university's research ethics guidelines if you think that your research topic may breach any ethical guidelines. An example of the sort of topic which may be involved is shown in Research in practice 3.3.

### Research in practice 3.3

#### Ethical issues in research

Most organisations play an active part in helping the environment by making the decision to go green. One of the most visible ways of doing this is through an office recycling programme through which employees can help reduce environmental waste by recycling office paper, cans, bottles and other materials.

Many organisations go beyond these basic recycling initiatives and encourage employees to find other ways to save energy. Such initiatives may include such things as car-sharing for travel to work journeys, negotiation of deals with local motor suppliers to supply cars with hybrid engines and the consumption of vegan food in the company restaurant.

Ronnie was very enthusiastic about the green movement. It permeated many aspects of her everyday life. So it was natural that she wanted to make this the subject of her undergraduate research project. Ronnie had read that a leading maker of computers of all sizes had told its employees that turning off their computers for one hour each day could save the company $1 million per year in energy costs as well as help the environment. So she concluded that ensuring that all office computers were switched off at night, when typically they would not be in use, would be similarly environmentally friendly.

Ronnie was doing her student placement in a large pharmaceutical company. The company had a sophisticated corporate responsibility policy which included a well-developed section on environmental action. The policy urged employees to switch off their computers when they finished work at the end of the day. Consequently, Ronnie devised a research design that involved discovering the extent to which employees were committed to such an initiative and the degree to which the level of commitment was translated in action.

The executive to whom Ronnie spoke about the matter was quite willing to offer help, although she expressed some concern about the potential for 'snooping' which such research may entail. She was in agreement with the testing of employee attitudes but unhappy with the notion of 'checking up'. Ronnie understood this concern but felt that simply establishing employee attitudes to computers being switched off at night was not enough: it was the sort of issue about which most people would indicate agreement that it was 'a good thing to do'. But Ronnie was keen to discover whether such agreement led to action; this, she thought, would be the true measure of commitment.

Ronnie explained this stumbling block to her research supervisor, who agreed with her point about the potential difference between words and action, but he too sympathised with the company executive's view about the potential for 'snooping' that such research may involve. Checking whether computers were switched off at night may well breach the university's code of research ethics which stated that 'participants in a research study have the right to give their informed consent before participating.'

Ronnie thought hard and long about her supervisor's strong recommendation to think of another research design which would receive the company's blessing and not fall foul of the university research ethics committee. She was still committed to research on an environmental topic, but reluctantly agreed to think of another research design which would be consistent with ethical principles.

## Compliance with the data protection legislation

If you are studying at a UK university, the principles of the Data Protection Act 1988 have implications for your research project if it involves the processing and storage of personal data. If you are studying elsewhere, it is likely that similar data protection legislation will exist that will have implications for your research project. It is therefore as well to be aware of these before you reach this stage of your research project. In the United Kingdom, the principles mean that anyone collecting personal information must:

- fairly and lawfully process it;
- process it only for limited, specifically stated purposes;
- use the information in a way that is adequate, relevant and not excessive;
- use the information accurately;
- keep the information on file no longer than absolutely necessary;
- process the information in accordance with your legal rights;
- keep the information secure;
- never transfer the information outside the EEC without adequate protection.

*Source:* Gov.UK (2015).

## What are the ethical questions you should consider at the reporting stage?

### Confidentiality and anonymity at the reporting stage

Earlier in this section we mentioned how organisational gatekeepers are often very reluctant to allow the organisation to be named in anything you write as a result of your research. You can overcome this by referring to the organisation as, for example, 'Organisation A', etc. But sometimes organisations are not so sensitive. If the research topic is not controversial in any way, then confidentiality may not be an issue, and the organisation can be named. If the organisation is particularly sensitive about being identified, you must ensure there are no 'clues' in anything you write, so you will need to conceal details such as the organisation's location, products and market if these details are likely to allow readers to guess the organisation's identity.

If the organisation is named in your report, then it is almost certain that you will need to let them read your work to understand the context within which they will be named. Indeed, even if the organisation is made anonymous, managers still may want to see the report to ensure that you have honoured any promise of confidentiality.

As well as the organisation, you have an ethical responsibility to protect individual respondents' right to anonymity in your project report, unless, of course, you have their explicit permission to do otherwise.

### Your ethical obligation not to report conclusions that would be harmful to your participants

Earlier in this section we commented upon the ethical obligation you have to use the time you have been granted by the organisation's managers in a way that is of benefit to the organisation.

Another ethical consideration is the use that may be made of the conclusions you draw in your project report. Clearly you face a dilemma if information you have been given freely by cooperative respondents is reported by you in such a way that it can be used to harm them. This is particularly the case if you have their permission to name them in your report. It may be less problematic if your respondents are made anonymous. If you feel at the beginning of the data collection stage that your results may point to conclusions that could result in actions which disadvantage your respondents, then it will be more honest to tell them this. It may mean that you are not given access to all the data you wish for, but at least you will be behaving honestly.

**Table 3.6** Guidelines for action to ensure you observe correct ethical standards

---

- Use your university's, or professional body's, research ethics code of practice as a guide at all stages of your research.
- Anticipate potential ethical issues that will affect your proposed research and plan to overcome problems.
- Always get informed consent from your participants and respondents through the use of openness and honesty at all times.
- Don't make dishonest promises about the likely benefits of your research.
- Respect your participants' and respondents' rights to privacy at all stages of your research project.
- Be honest and objective about your data, both in the way you collect them and their analysis.
- Consider how you will use secondary data in order to protect the identities of those who contributed to their collection or who are named within them.
- Don't forget that interviews mean that there is greater scope for ethical issues to arise.
- Don't refer to information gained from a particular participant when talking to other participants, as this may allow identification of the individual with possibly harmful consequences to that individual.
- Be very careful about the conduct of covert research and consider its ethical implications.
- Make sure that you honour the promises you give to all participants and respondents regarding the confidentiality of the data obtained and their anonymity.
- Ensure you comply with all of the data protection legal requirements.
- Be aware of the complex ethical considerations in using the Internet and email to ensure high ethical standards are maintained.
- Make sure you preserve the anonymity of your participants and respondents in your project report unless you have their permission to do otherwise.

---

## Summary

- Organisations are less likely to grant you research access if you are from outside the organisation.
- If you are from inside the organisation and wish to do research in that organisation, you will face other problems such as those concerned with status.
- There are strategies you can adopt to ease the process of gaining access to organisations to do research. These include using existing contacts; anticipating the responses of the organisation's gatekeeper; ensuring you have sufficient time to accommodate the inevitable delays; presenting a professional written request and boosting your credibility through reducing concerns of the organisation.
- Strategies for managing yourself through the research process include managing your time; maintaining your motivation and keeping in touch with individuals who can help.

- Strategies for managing your supervisor through the research process include being clear about your expectations from your supervisor and what your supervisor should expect from you.

- Managing your relationship with your university involves being clear about the standards expected from you, particularly the academic standards in the final written report.

- You must be very conscious of your ethical responsibilities while conducting your research.

- The key ethical principles you should adopt are: not causing harm to research participants and respondents; ensuring people are not coerced into participating in your research; seeking the consent of participants and respondents; maintaining high standards of honesty and preserving confidentiality.

- Awareness of your ethical responsibilities applies to all stages of the research process.

## Thinking about your research process

→ Think about the data you will need to answer your research question(s) and meet your objectives. Assuming you need access to an organisation to get some or all of these data, make a list of possible obstacles to gaining access. Then, using the checklist of points to follow to increase your chances of getting access in Table 3.1, plan how these obstacles might be overcome.

→ Draft a request for research access to be sent to your research organisation's gatekeeper. Your request should focus upon the purpose of your research, the demands being made of the participant and what you will do with the information you obtain.

→ Draw up a 'contract' to discuss with your supervisor which should include the expectations you have of your supervisor and the expectations you think your supervisor should have of you.

→ Get hold of a copy of your university's code of research ethics. Note those aspects of the code you that you feel are relevant to your research and list the implications for action you need to take to ensure the code is followed.

## References

Gov.UK (2015) *Data protection*. Available at: https://www.gov.uk/data-protection/the-data-protection-act [Accessed 15 June 2016].

Oxford Brookes University (2016) *Ethical Standards for Research Involving Human Participants: Code of Practice*. Available at: https://www.brookes.ac.uk/Documents/Research/Policies-and-codes-of-practice/ethics_codeofpractice/ [Accessed 11 November 2016].

Henley, J. (2016) Sweden leads the race to become cashless society. *The Guardian*, 4 June 2016.

University of Plymouth (2016) School of Marine Science and Engineering, Project Marking Scheme. Available at: http://www.tech.plym.ac.uk/sme/mingproject/MScheme910.pdf [Accessed 12 June 2016].

# Chapter 4

# Using secondary data

## 4.1 Why you should read this chapter

When you started to think about how you would obtain the data to answer your research question, you probably began by considering how to design your own questionnaire or the people you were going to interview. While this is not unusual, it is a great shame, as it meant you implicitly ignored the vast amount of data that have already been collected by other people for other purposes, which could also be useful in answering your research question. In this chapter, we look at using data that were originally collected for some other purpose, termed **secondary data**, for your own research. Such secondary data can be contrasted with **primary data**, which are data you collect specifically for your research project. We talk about this in Chapter 6.

The number of sources of potential secondary data and the ease of getting access to them continues to expand rapidly alongside the growth of the Internet. Increasingly, university business schools have subscriptions to online market and financial databases providing access to a wealth of data that have already been collected and collated from multiple sources. Many national governments, non-governmental agencies and other organisations allow open access to the data they have collected, making it available for anyone to use on the Internet. Such data include the results from large-scale surveys such as national censuses as well as more specific surveys and research reports. They include numeric data such as official statistics (often in the form of downloadable tables) and non-numeric data such as government reports, interviews, documents, photographs and conversations. You can also find such data reproduced in varying levels of detail in other published sources such as quality newspapers as well as on associated websites. Quality newspapers, for example, contain a wealth of data on organisations and business and management issues in both numeric and non-numeric forms. You can

> **Definitions**
>
> **secondary data:** data used for a research project that were originally collected for some other purpose.
>
> **primary data:** data collected specifically for the research project being undertaken.

easily obtain up-to-date statistics such as share prices. They also sometimes contain transcripts of interviews with business leaders and politicians (along with commentaries on the content of the actual interview). When you re-analyse data reported in such media, you are using them as secondary data, the media being the source where you found your data.

We believe that such secondary data can provide you with fantastic research opportunities, which would otherwise be outside your reach. For example, it is extremely unlikely that you will have either the time or the financial resources to design and distribute a questionnaire to thousands of potential respondents to collect data for your research project. Similarly, you're unlikely to be granted access to interview the chief executive of a large multinational company. However, through using secondary data such as that already collected through an existing large-scale survey or in the form of a published interview with a chief executive, you will still be able to gain insights for your own research.

In this chapter, we begin by exploring the questions 'What forms does secondary data take?' and 'Why should you use secondary data?' We then discuss the pitfalls of using secondary data and offer advice on how to assess the suitability of secondary data for your research project. We finish with suggestions of where and how to find secondary data. However, before you decide to use secondary data for a research project, we would urge you to check your research project assessment regulations very carefully. For some research projects your university may expect you to use only secondary data. For other projects you may be required to collect primary data or use a combination of both primary and secondary data.

## 4.2    Forms secondary data can take

Secondary data comes in many forms. As we hinted in the introduction, these include both **quantitative data**, consisting of numbers such as tables of figures, and **qualitative (non-numerical) data** types. The latter include text materials such as organisations' policies or minutes of meetings, and non-text materials such as video and voice recordings, and images such as photographs. Secondary data can include **raw data** that have not been processed, such as actual responses to questionnaires available from a data archive or the transcript of a television programme interview available on the television company's website. These will have been originally collected and used for some other purpose. Here the source of the data is the data archive or the television company's website. Secondary data can also include as **compiled data**, where the data

---

**Definitions**

**quantitative data:** data consisting of numbers or data that have been quantified, such as tables of figures.

**qualitative data:** non-numerical data or data that have not been quantified, such as text materials, and non-text materials such as videos, voice recordings and images.

**raw data:** data for which no processing has taken place.

**compiled data:** data that have been processed, such as through some form of summarising or selection.

presented have either been selected or summarised from the raw data such as a table of data in a journal article. Here the table contains the secondary data and its source is the journal article. We find it useful to group the forms of secondary data into three broad types: survey, documentary (in some form) and multiple source (Saunders et al., 2016), which are summarised along with examples in Figure 4.1.

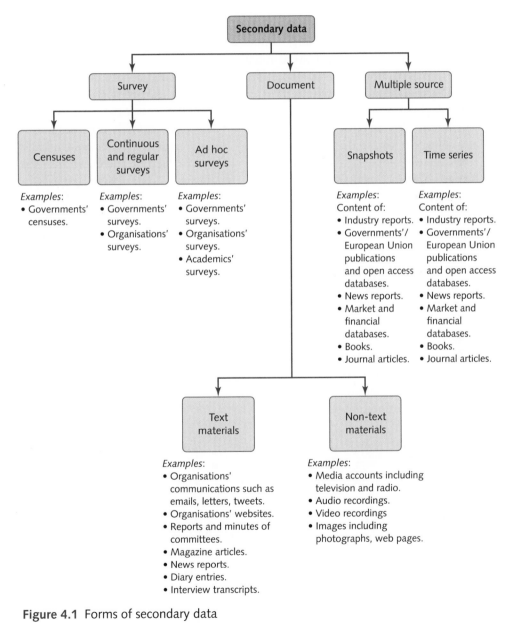

**Figure 4.1** Forms of secondary data
*Source:* Developed from Saunders et al. (2016).

## Survey secondary data

Our first form of secondary data was originally obtained through a survey strategy, usually a questionnaire. Such data are often made freely available (particularly by public authorities) either as compiled data tables or, more frequently, as data sets which can be downloaded and opened in a spreadsheet. Not surprisingly, such data sets are predominantly quantitative, and so you will need to analyse them using statistics and graphs (section 7.3). These data will have already been obtained using one of three types of survey strategy:

- *Censuses* are official counts usually conducted by a government or on behalf of a government to meet the needs of government departments, with the aim of collecting data from every household in a country. Many governments have collected data about their entire populations for more than a hundred years through a census: for example, the United Kingdom's decennial *Census of Population*, the most recent of which took place in 2011. Because they are official, participation in censuses is usually obligatory and so the level of response is usually high. Census data are usually collected using some form of questionnaire; the precise method and questions used being clearly documented. You will find such data are widely available and easy to obtain online and in printed reports.

- *Continuous or regular surveys* are those, other than censuses, that are repeated over time but do not collect data from an entire population. They include surveys where data have been collected both on behalf of governments and by non-governmental bodies such as private organisations throughout the year or annually, often using a questionnaire or structured interview. You will find that data collected by some of these surveys, particularly those undertaken by or for government organisations, are available online. Alternatively reports and associated presentations may be available (Research in practice 4.1). However, where data have been collected for a commercial purpose, or is of a sensitive nature, they are unlikely to be so easy to obtain. For example, although many organisations conduct ongoing surveys of their customers' satisfaction as well as employee attitude surveys, it is unlikely you will find, or be allowed access to, more than a brief summary of the associated findings to support your research project.

- *Ad hoc or 'one off' surveys*, as their name suggests, are one-off surveys. Like continuous or regular surveys, these surveys do not collect data from an entire population. Ad hoc surveys are likely to be far more specific than the other forms of survey in their subject matter. They include questionnaires and structured interviews undertaken by organisations and by independent researchers such as your lecturers for a specific purpose. However, invariably because of their ad hoc nature, it is much more difficult for you to locate such surveys, let alone gain access to the associated data. At best, you're likely to be reliant on an associated summary report or journal article.

## Research in practice 4.1

### Private organisation's regular survey

Jemma's research objective was to explore the influence of trust and distrust on people's behaviours regarding companies. In particular, she was interested in the extent to which Millennials' (people born between 1980 and 1995 (Pricewaterhouse Coopers, 2013)) behaviours differed between companies they trusted and companies they distrusted. When reviewing the literature, she had discovered that a number of authors had referred to the *Edelman Trust Barometer* so she had searched for it using Google. Her search had revealed that the *Barometer* was based on a regular survey conducted annually by the PR company Edelman. Edelman's website included links to an archive of summary reports dating back to 2001 as well to a 70-slide presentation of the global results for the 2016 survey (Edelman, 2016). Conducted in October and November 2015, the research surveyed over 33,000 respondents aged 25–64, asking questions about trust and credibility. The global results slides included data about the percentage of people engaging in specified behaviours with companies they trusted and companies they distrusted. These percentages formed part of the secondary data for Jemma's research project:

|  | Behaviour with distrusted companies | Behaviour with trusted companies |
|---|---|---|
| Refused/**chose** to buy products/services | 48% | 68% |
| Criticised/**recommended** companies to a friend/colleague | 42% | 59% |
| Shared *negative*/**positive** opinions | 26% | 41% |
| Disagreed with others/**Defended the company** | 35% | 38% |
| Paid more than wanted to buy products/services/**paid more** | 20% | 37% |
| Sold shares/**bought shares** | 12% | 18% |

Behaviour relating to distrusted companies is in *italics*; behaviour relating to trusted companies is in **bold**.

*Source:* Edelman (2016).

Jemma combined these regular survey data with reports from quality newspapers about the changing levels of trust in companies. Using these data and research findings reported in the academic literature, she was able to argue that there were significant differences in people's behaviours when they trusted companies and when they distrusted companies.

## Documentary secondary data

Documentary secondary data consist of both text and non-text materials that were originally collected for some other purpose. As with survey secondary data, it is relatively easy for you to access such data online. This can be done particularly through the websites of public bodies such as government departments and media corporations such as the BBC and Sky as well as from video-sharing websites like YouTube®. Indeed, although individuals upload much of the video content on YouTube, many organisations also upload material on this site. Whether or not such materials are considered secondary data is dependent upon how you use them.

When you analyse such 'documents' directly as part of your research, you're using them as secondary data. However, you're more likely to be simply using them as a place to find secondary data. Let's take an example of a BBC news report uploaded on YouTube. If you want to use this to explore the media's attitude to the government and in particular how they have reported government policies, then the BBC news report on YouTube is your secondary data. This is because the video clip itself is the subject of your analysis. However, if you're using this YouTube video clip as a place to find secondary data, say, a record of government figures for the number of people who are unemployed and seeking work, the video clip is only the source of your secondary data. Your secondary data are the number of people who are unemployed and seeking work. This is because you are treating the data which have been reported in the video clip as the subject of your analysis, rather that the video clip itself. In other words, the YouTube news report is simply where you found these data. It is a source in which the secondary data on government figures for the number of people who are unemployed and seeking work you're using have been recorded subsequent to their being collected. Once obtained, you can analyse secondary data using either or both quantitative and qualitative techniques (Chapter 7).

Documentary secondary data will have originally been collected as text, materials, non-text materials or a combination (Research in practice 4.2):

- *Text materials.* This form of secondary data consists of a wide range of textual secondary data, including those documents held as administrative and public records such as reports and minutes of meetings as well as diaries and transcripts of interviews (including those originally broadcast on radio and television). Books and journal articles are considered to be secondary data only when you are analysing them directly as part of your research.

- *Non-text materials.* Non-text documentary secondary data include video and voice recordings, podcasts, films, radio and television programmes, images such as photographs and drawings as well as materials stored in organisations' databases. As before, it is the video or photograph rather than its source (e.g. YouTube) that are the secondary data.

### Research in practice 4.2

### Using social networking sites

Han's research was concerned with the impact of social media on brand awareness. He was aware from the academic literature that social media was important in marketing and could influence consumers' perceptions of different festivals as brands (Hudson et al., 2015). Aspects such as a festival's image and atmosphere were particularly important to festival brand loyalty and equity (Leenders, 2010). Based on the academic literature on branding and social media, Hans argued that, to use social media most effectively, festivals needed to follow a three-stage process of providing material of interest, engaging people and using them as advocates for their festival.

Along with many other festivalgoers, Hans had 'liked' the Facebook pages of the festivals he attended. These pages often contained festival organisers' posts about the festival as well as comments and other posts from festivalgoers comprising both text and non-text materials. Although the data in these posts were not originally intended for Han's research, he considered they would provide data about the effective use of social networking sites for festival marketing. Because many fesitvals' Facebook pages were open to everyone, Hans considered that the information was in the public domain so he could use it for his research without seeking consent.

## Multiple source secondary data

Our final type of secondary data, multiple source, consists of different data sets that have been combined to form a new data set prior to your accessing the data. Such secondary data can be based entirely on documentary or survey secondary data, or a combination of the two. You almost certainly come across such data on a daily basis as tables and listings in quality newspapers such as the *Financial Times* (and associated websites). These are compiled from a variety of sources, an example that appears in the *Financial Times* and on its associated website (http://www.ft.com) being the FT Global 500. This provides a snapshot of the world's top 500 companies for that year, bringing together data from different sources, to record their market capitalisation, sector, turnover, net income, total assets and number of employees. Such data can provide you with extremely useful background material for your project when, for example, researching a particular market sector.

Data are combined into a multiple source secondary data sets in one of two forms: either as a snapshot or longitudinally as a time series.

### Snapshot

Snapshot multiple source secondary data consist of data drawn from more than one source which relates to a single time, much of it being accessible online. You will find that these data are often combined geographically in country or region reports such as the European Union's *Eurostat Yearbook* and *Eurostat Regional Yearbook* (Eurostat, no date). These online-only publications are updated on a rolling basis, each article being updated as new data, both quantitative and qualitative, become available. Data may also be combined for a particular industry or sector to create a snapshot. Many university libraries have online subscriptions allowing online access to business intelligence companies' reports and data. Key Note, for example, provides downloadable market insights and analysis reports covering over 30 different industry sectors for UK, European and international markets. For those sources where your university does not have a subscription, you may well find the price prohibitive, although very occasionally a reference copy may be held in your university library.

## *Time series*

**Time-series** multiple source secondary data are created by combining comparable variables (we defined these in section 1.7) collected through different surveys at different times, or through the same survey that has been repeated over time. These include series of data such as number of people out of work, manufacturing output and, as illustrated in Research in practice 4.3, change in retail sales. You can also combine different

---

**Definition**

**time-series data:** data recorded over time for the same variable or variables, usually at regular intervals.

---

**Research in practice 4.3**

### UK government longitudinal data

As part of his research project examining trends in the retail industry over the past five years, Muhammad was interested in how UK retail sales had altered. Searching the

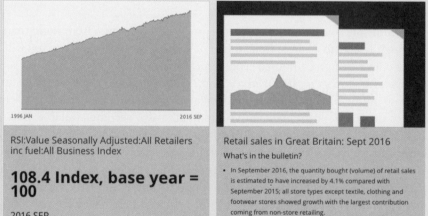

## Retail industry

Sales by retailers in Great Britain directly to end consumers, including spending on goods (in store and online) (Retail Sales Index) and spending on services (Index of Services). The industry as a whole is used as an indicator of how the wider economy is performing and the strength of consumer spending.

On this page:

Time series | Dataset | Publications

View all content related to this topic:

All data | All publications

**Highlights**

RSI:Value Seasonally Adjusted:All Retailers inc fuel:All Business Index

1996 JAN    2016 SEP

### 108.4 Index, base year = 100

2016 SEP

Retail sales in Great Britain: Sept 2016

What's in the bulletin?

• In September 2016, the quantity bought (volume) of retail sales is estimated to have increased by 4.1% compared with September 2015; all store types except textile, clothing and footwear stores showed growth with the largest contribution coming from non-store retailing.

*Source*: © Office for National Statistics (2016). Contains public sector information licensed under the Open Government Licence v3.0.

UK Office for National Statistics website www.ons.gov.uk, he initially found a graph of retail sales for the period January 1996 to September 2016 with hyperlinks to both downloadable publications and data sets. Muhammad clicked on the hyperlink to the bulletin *Retail Sales in Great Britain: September 2016* and read it carefully. The hyperlink 'Data set' linked to a downloadable spreadsheet comprising 27 tables of retail sales data, for the period 2010 to September 2016. Muhammad subsequently reanalysed these data as part of his research project.

secondary data sets to create time-series data, such as changing attitudes to gender discrimination. For many research projects, this will be the only way in which you will be able to obtain longitudinal data because of the time constraints set by the research process.

## 4.3   The potential of secondary data

We've already mentioned the potential of secondary data in terms of saving you time and money by allowing you access to larger data sets than you could ever hope to collect yourself. This huge variety of large, often high-quality data sets that are readily available at no cost is one of the major opportunities offered by secondary data; as Mark says to his students, 'If someone else has already collected suitable high-quality data which you're allowed to use, why bother to collect the data yourself?' The use of such data also allows you to show that you can find and integrate valuable material into your arguments, giving your project an air of authority. However, in addition to access to larger data sets than you could collect yourself, the authority such data sets can provide and time and money savings, there are a number of other reasons for using secondary data in your research project. These are listed in the following sub-sections.

### Data are often already in the public domain

For many researchers, a key advantage of using secondary data is that much of these data are already in the public domain. This means you do not need to negotiate access to research participants (Chapter 3) or obtain permission to use the data. Indeed, many public authorities include a statement explicitly granting all users permission in the form of a licence to use the data, usually providing that you acknowledge the source with an appropriate attribution statement such as 'Contains public sector information licensed under the Open Government Licence v3.0' (Research in practice 4.3). However, for data that are not in the public domain, such as that contained in organisations' databases or administrative records, you will still need to obtain permission.

### Data are often available in software compatible formats

While secondary data are available in many forms (section 4.2), they are increasingly available using the Internet in formats that can be read directly into spreadsheets and other analysis software such as IBM SPSS Statistics (Research in practice 4.4). Some public authority data sets also allow you to select and download the precise data you require rather than downloading a large data set, much of which you will not need. This means you can focus on what data you actually need while also saving considerable time by not having to type your data into, for example, spreadsheets.

## It is an unobtrusive method

Not surprisingly, as secondary data have already been collected, you will not need to ask your potential respondents if you can collect the data from them! This means you will be respecting their privacy and rights as individuals to be left alone. You will also not be taking up any of their time in either seeking permission (where data are in the public domain) or actually collecting data. Issues relating to confidentiality of participants are also reduced or avoided as the data have already been anonymised as part of the original collection process. This means you're unlikely to risk breaching your university's code of ethical practice (Chapter 3). However, if you intend to use data held by a particular organisation, such as one for which you work, you will need to ensure the anonymity of that organisation is preserved and to obtain written permission to use their data for your research project.

## Data sets can be readily combined

Data from a range of secondary sources, such as different surveys, can be combined to create one new data set. You will find this particularly helpful if you wish to undertake a longitudinal study. For such studies, you can combine data from a series of surveys where the same questions have been asked into one data set. Indeed, for many public authority data sets, aggregation of variables or the combining of data from different surveys has already been undertaken before the data are made available (Research in practice 4.3 and 4.4). However, as you can see in Research in practice 4.4, to fully understand such data, you need to be clear about the precise definitions used for each variable. You can also combine data sets from different geographical areas such as countries or regions to make comparisons between countries or regions. This can be useful if, for example, you're comparing changes in manufacturing output between two countries.

### Research in practice 4.4

#### Eurostat (European Union) downloadable data

Jasvinder had decided to pursue a research project on tourism and, in particular, why some European Countries were more popular with tourists than others. She noticed the European Union's Eurostat website included a link to the Main Tables for Tourism data (Eurostat, 2016).

*Source:* Eurostat (2016) Copyright European Communities, 2016. Reproduced with permission.

This had a series of further links to downloadable tables, including four providing data for each member state, which he felt could be most useful:

- Nights spent at tourist accommodation establishments
- Nights spent at hotels and similar accommodation
- Nights spent at holiday and other short-stay accommodation
- Nights spent at camping grounds, recreational vehicle parks and trailer parks

These tables presented data collected from 2006 to 2015, highlighting massive differences in the number of nights spent at tourist accommodation establishments between member states, the highest number of nights in 2015 being recorded for Germany, Spain, France and Italy; data for the UK not being available for that year. The data also indicated that certain forms of accommodation were used far more in some member states; for example, more nights were spent at camping grounds, recreational vehicle parks and trailer parks in France than any other member states.

However, before using these data, Jasvinder needed to be sure she understood precisely what the data meant. She therefore clicked on the hyperlink to the 'Manuals and Guidelines' web pages and then downloaded the *Methodological Manual for Tourism Statistics* (Eurostat, 2014). This defined each of the types of tourism accommodation in considerable detail, outlying what each type included and excluded. For example, camping grounds, recreational vehicle parks and trailer parks included 'provision of accommodation in campgrounds, trailer parks, recreational camps and fishing and hunting camps for short stay visitors, provision of space and facilities for recreational vehicles . . . but excludes mountain refuge, cabins and hostels' (Eurostat, 2014: 59).

## Data are more open to public scrutiny

Choosing to use secondary data can provide you with access to data of very high quality. For example, the surveys conducted by professional researchers working in government departments or private survey organisations have to meet exacting scrutiny standards in terms of rigour of the research method used. These data sets are therefore likely to be larger and of better quality than any survey you can design and deliver yourself. The majority of them, in addition to the data collected, provide you with information about precisely how the data were collected, including sample size and selection, response rates, a copy of the data collection instrument used (such as a questionnaire) and an assessment of how representative the data are. This information can be used by you and other users to judge the quality of the data and can, as we outline in section 4.4, also help you to assess the suitability of the secondary data for your research.

### Data can provide contextual background

If you're collecting your own data, it is often useful to set the findings from your own data within a broader context. For example, if you have collected data for your research project through interviews with a particular service organisation's potential customers, you can use secondary data such as a market research report for that service to locate your findings in the broader context of that particular industry. Alternatively, you might wish to use recent government population estimates to assess the generalisability of your findings by assessing whether your participants were representative, being present in the same proportions for each age group as in that population.

## 4.4  Possible pitfalls of using secondary data

As you will have gathered from reading this chapter so far, we are fans of using secondary data in research. However, our enthusiasm, and hopefully yours, needs to be tempered with realism. While secondary data offers considerable potential for many research projects, its very nature means that it is open to a variety of often valid criticisms. As our definition of secondary data indicates, it was collected for a different purpose. This means the data may not meet your research needs fully, and it may have been manipulated in some way. You will not have undertaken data collection. You're therefore very unlikely to know precisely how the data were collected or the impact this will have on the actual data you are now going to use. Finally, although public authorities make their data available free of charge, do keep in mind that the cost of actually obtaining such data is high. For this reason, other organisations (such as market research companies) may ask you to pay for it. In addition, the commercial sensitivity of some data means organisations may refuse to allow you to use their data even if they employ you. These criticisms represent potential pitfalls about which you need to be aware and which we will now discuss in more detail.

### Only meets the research needs partially

Unlike data you collect yourself to answer your research question, secondary data are unlikely to have been collected for that same purpose. This means the data may be inappropriate for your research question or, as is more likely, only partially relevant.

Reasons for this vary but include the data not being current, problems with definitions used for particular secondary data variables, the way in which data have been aggregated not matching your needs and because the data contain clear errors.

Most quantitative secondary data are still only available in aggregated tabular form (Research in practice 4.1 and 4.4). Where the tables into which data have been aggregated do not meet your needs, perhaps due to the categories used being too broad, this may cause problems. Similarly, it is also likely to be problematic where definitions used for the data variables (Research in practice 4.4) in these tables differ from those in other tables or are unclear. Invariably, the solution here depends upon the extent to which you judge the secondary data to be inappropriate for your own research. Where the data do not meet your needs at all, your only solution is to find alternative data. However, where the data meet your needs partially, you will need to adapt and compromise. The extent to which you compromise will depend upon what other secondary data are available and whether you're able to collect appropriate data yourself. If you do decide to compromise, you will need to explain in your project report your concerns and the compromises you have made, and why you still feel able to use these secondary data. For example, if you're comparing data on satellite TV subscribers between countries in Europe, the most recent data you will be able to obtain is likely to be available only for some countries and at least a few years out of date. In your project report, therefore, you need to make clear these omissions and when the data were collected, explaining it is the most recent data available.

## Data are not always value-neutral

The original purpose for which secondary data were collected is invariably reflected in the way they are presented and the interpretations of those who produced them. Data are often used to support an argument or make a particular point and so may be presented in the way that best supports that argument. This is often apparent if you compare the data presented about the same topic by two newspapers with different political affiliations. When you do, you will probably see that, although some of the data used are the same, different data from the same original data set will also have been quoted selectively by each newspaper to support their different interpretations.

Definitions used can also change within a single data set over time, impacting on the meanings attributed to the data. For example, between 1979 and 1994, there were nine significant changes in the calculation method used for the United Kingdom's monthly count of unemployment claimants, resulting in the overall number of claimants being reduced by 481,000 (Fenwick and Denman, 1995). Not surprisingly, the claimant count became widely criticised as a data source because it 'seriously underestimated' the number of people out of work, the definitional changes making any serious estimation of changes in the unemployment rate over time 'virtually useless' (Levitas, 1996: 46). It is therefore important that you remember secondary data may have been manipulated by people to serve their own purposes, and therefore assess the likely impact of this on actual data values. In particular, you should not accept any secondary data without first understanding the precise definitions used and, for longitudinal data, whether these have been altered over time.

### Unlikely to know precisely how the data were collected

When using secondary data, you have no control over the quality of the data. You therefore have to infer the likely quality from other information provided. Researchers should always provide clear information about the method of data collection and the variables about which questions were asked. This should be in sufficient detail for you to infer the quality of the data in both reports and articles as well as for actual data sets. Despite this, it is unlikely as a user of secondary data that you will ever know the precise context in which each of a series of interviews took place or the nuances of the relationship between an interviewer and the participant. Whatever the level of detail provided about the method, you will obviously know less than if you had collected the data yourself. For some secondary data sets, no information will be provided about how they were collected. It is best to treat these data with caution, as often this information is not provided because it would indicate that there are problems with these data. However, this is not always the case. A number of excellent market research companies provide very limited information about their data collection methods as they consider such details commercially sensitive.

### Can be costly to obtain

Where data have been collected for commercial reasons, you're likely to find access both difficult and costly. Market research reports such as those produced by the Mintel International Group, although easy to identify and locate online, are expensive to purchase. This means, if they are not available in your university library or at another library you can visit, you will be unable to access the data such reports contain.

## 4.5    Assessing the suitability of secondary data

When deciding whether to use secondary data, there are a number of things you need to think about. Like many students, you may think that using secondary data is easy because you do not need to design a data collection method or collect the data yourself. This is not the case. The time you have saved will be used in ensuring you have access to the data and that the data will enable you to answer your research question. Fortunately, because the data already exist, you can assess their suitability before you begin your analysis. Inevitably, the suitability is dependent upon the data being relevant to your own research. However, if the data are relevant, suitability will also depend on the purpose for which the data were originally collected and the method that was used. Let's now discuss these in more detail.

### The relevance of the data

The most important criterion regarding the suitability to you of any data set is that it provides you with the information you need to answer your research question. This means that the data collected, and the definitions used for the variables in which you're interested, must be a close match to the data you ideally require. Often you will find that the data available and the definitions that were used are not exactly as you would wish for in an ideal world. For example, you may ideally require data on the purchasing power of children, defined as the under-18 demographic group. If the secondary data defines this group as less than 17 years of age, these data will not match your requirements exactly. However, the world of secondary data is not perfect. You may therefore decide to use these data and state in your project report that they do not include 17-year-olds, offering an indication of the likely impact of this on your subsequent analysis. In doing this, you're offering both an assessment of the suitability of these data to answering your research question and ensuring that those who read your project report are aware of possible limitations and their likely implications.

When using secondary data, you will need to exclude those data that are not relevant to your research question. Data on the United Kingdom will need to be excluded if your research is only concerned with a post-Brexit European Union. Alternatively, some secondary data sources, in particular those collected by government surveys, may not include all the data variables you would ideally require for your analysis. You will need to make an assessment as to whether these missing variables are essential to answering your research question. If they are, then the data that are available are not suitable, and you need to look elsewhere.

## The original reasons for collecting data

Assuming you have found what appears to be suitable secondary data, you need to look in more detail regarding the reasons why the data were originally collected. A good place to start when trying to establish the original purpose is to look for the objectives or research questions. For research reports and articles, these are often stated in the introductory section or, for data accessed online, in the accompanying documentation or notes. Alternatively, you can look at who commissioned the research. For example: were data collected for a public authority such as a government department, or by a private organisation that employed a market research company or perhaps an academic to collect the data? The answers to such questions will give you an idea of the original motivations behind collecting these data and, as a consequence, your analysis and interpretation. If, for example, the research was undertaken for a trades union, it is likely that the focus of the data collected and the associated report will be different than if it was undertaken for an employer or employers' organisation. You may consider the original focus of the research too narrow in relation to your own research question, highlighting the need either to find additional secondary data or to collect your own primary data. Alternatively, you may feel that the data, although useful, needs to be treated with caution because of the potential for bias caused by the original purpose of the research. Whatever you decide, it is important that you explain the reasons for your decision clearly in your project report.

## The method used

Assessment of the method used is concerned with how the data were collected, including the actual questions used to obtain the data. When assessing the method, you need to establish precisely how data were collected, including any personal interaction between participants and the person collecting the data. Data collected using an Internet questionnaire will inevitably constrain those who participate (and therefore the data collected) to people who have Internet access and, in most cases, an email address. Similarly, data collected using a telephone interview will restrict those who participate to people who have access to a telephone. In both examples, the people who respond may not be representative of the population as a whole or those you wish to research. You therefore need to treat the data with care. Data collected using structured interviews conducted by a professional interviewer either by telephone or face to face are likely to have followed a set and detailed script, meaning that all participants are likely to have been asked exactly the same questions in the same way. In contrast, questions asked by amateur interviewers might unwittingly have been reworded for some participants, prompting a different response indicating that perhaps the data quality is more variable. You therefore need to pay particularly careful attention to who conducted the interview.

## The questions used

For data collected originally using interviews or questionnaires, question phrasing is crucial. For large-scale questionnaire surveys, organisations spend a vast amount of resources in trying to ensure that the questions asked would not be misinterpreted and are neither biased nor leading. Despite this, it is still worthwhile examining carefully the questions asked to ensure that the data collected is relevant to your own research and, of equal importance, that you do not misinterpret responses in these data.

## 4.6  Where and how to find secondary data

The breadth of forms of secondary data we've discussed in this chapter serve also to emphasise the variety of places where you may find secondary data. Despite the Internet and availability of general search engines such as Google and Bing, finding suitable data still depends in part on your awareness of **information gateways** and potentially useful secondary data sites. It is also important to recognise that not all secondary data will be in electronic form or accessible online. Some will be paper-based and listed in your own university library's catalogue. Other paper-based secondary data will be in reports that are held only in specialist libraries or organisations. The latter of these will be the most difficult to locate and may involve you visiting a specialist library or, if permission is granted, an organisation to browse through publications or reports. Remember, even if you intend to use data you know is held by an organisation for which

---

**Definition**

**information gateway:** website that provides access to specific websites and pages, each site having been evaluated prior to being added to the gateway.

you work, you will still need to seek written permission to reuse these data for your research project.

For secondary data published by governments, finding the data online is relatively easy compared to other sources. Precise references to particular government sources are often given in journal articles and books, although often the associated web addresses will have changed. Some governments and government departments provide guides or lists of statistics they make available. However, like the majority of other secondary providers, most governments expect you to use either a combination of menus and web links or the search engines within their own information gateway to find data that are available. It is therefore important that you have a reasonable idea of the sort of data you're looking for and the search terms and phrases that are likely to have been used to describe it. Providing you then know the web address of an appropriate information gateway (Table 4.1), it is relatively straightforward to search for specific secondary data published by governments.

You will find data held by non-governmental organisations more difficult to locate. For data that are available online, there are a number of other information gateways that are of use (Table 4.1). If you find that these do not eventually produce useful data, general search engines such as Google, Bing and Yahoo can help you locate potential data sources. In some cases, these data will be held in reports that can be downloaded from sites hosted by professional and trade associations. In others, there will be only a reference to an internal report for a private company, and it will be necessary for you to request the document and seek written permission before the data can be used.

**Table 4.1** Selected information gateways to secondary data sources

| Name | Internet address | Content |
| --- | --- | --- |
| UK Office for National Statistics | http://www.ons.gov.uk/ | UK national statistics |
| Direct.gov | http://www.gov.uk/ | UK government information service |
| Eurostat | http://ec.europa.eu/eurostat | European Union and member states statistics |
| Europa | http://europa.eu | European Union information service |
| Morningstar | http://www.morningstar.co.uk/ | Financial information on companies, trusts and markets |
| USA.gov | http://www.usa.gov/ | USA government information service |

## Summary

- Secondary data are data that were originally collected for some other purpose. They can be contrasted with primary data, which are collected for the specified research purpose.

- Secondary data comes in many forms including both quantitative (numerical) data and qualitative (non-numerical) data. These can be grouped using the actual source or sources of the data into survey, documentary and multiple-source secondary data.

- Secondary data can provide you with fantastic research opportunities that would otherwise be outside your reach, by allowing you access to larger data sets than you could ever hope to collect yourself and by saving you time and money.

- Other reasons for you using secondary data include:
  - the data are already in the public domain, thereby often avoiding concerns about access and permission to use the data;
  - the data are often available in software-compatible formats, allowing easy analysis;
  - the data provide an unobtrusive method, respecting individuals' rights to privacy and being left alone;
  - the data can be readily combined with other data sets, allowing, for example, longitudinal studies;
  - the data can provide contextual background to a research project.

- However, using secondary data has a number of possible pitfalls, including:
  - the data may only meet your research needs partially;
  - the data may have been manipulated in some way and so not be value-neutral;
  - the definitions used within the data may have changed over time;
  - the data can be costly to obtain.

- The suitability of secondary data to your research project is dependent upon:
  - the relevance of the actual data to your research question;
  - the original reason for collecting the data;
  - the methods used to collect the data and the actual questions asked.

- Increasing provision of online open-access data by governments has increased the availability of secondary data considerably.

- Not all secondary data will be available online. Some will be paper-based and available in your own university's library. Other secondary data will be in reports that are held only in specialist libraries or organisations.

## Thinking about using secondary data

→ Think about how you might use secondary data to answer your research question(s) and meet your objectives. If you consider secondary data would be helpful, or its use is a criterion for your assessment, make a list of the data variables you think you're likely to require, being as precise as possible in the terms you use.

→ Initially, use the information gateways listed in Table 4.1 to search the Internet for secondary data information sources that contain these variables. If these result in no suitable data, try using general search engines such as Google, Bing or Yahoo, or other sources.

→ Evaluate the relevance of the data variables in each of these sources against the data variables you require (section 4.5). Remember, it is unlikely that you will find secondary data that matches your requirements exactly.

→ Evaluate the suitability of each secondary data source by considering the original purpose of the research, the methods used and the questions used as outlined in section 4.5.

→ If the data are suitable, where appropriate seek and gain permission to use the data before obtaining a copy.

## References

Edelman (2016) *2016 Edelman Trust Barometer Global Report*. Available at: http://www.edelman.com/insights/intellectual-property/2016-edelman-trust-barometer/global-results/ [Accessed 28 October 2016].

Eurostat (no date) *Europe in Figures*. Available at: http://ec.europa.eu/eurostat/statistics-explained/index.php/Europe_in_figures_-_Eurostat_yearbook [Accessed 1 November 2016].

Eurostat (2014) *Methodological Manual for Tourism Statistics Version 3.1*. Luxembourg: Publications Office of the European Union.

Eurostat (2016) *Tourism: Main Tables*. Available at: http://ec.europa.eu/eurostat/web/tourism/data/main-tables [Accessed 1 November 2016].

Fenwick, D. and Denman, J. (1995) The monthly unemployment count: change and consistency, *Labour Market Trends,* November, 397–400.

Hudson, S., Roth, M.S., Madden, J.T. and Hudson, R. (2015) The effect of social media on emotions, brand relationship quality and word of mouth: An empirical study of music festival attendees. *Tourism Management*, 47(1), 68–76.

Leenders, M.A.A.M, (2010) The relative importance of the brand of music festivals: a customer equity perspective. *Journal of Strategic Marketing*, 18(4), 291–301.

Levitas, R. (1996) *Interpreting Official Statistics*. London: Routledge.

Office for National Statistics (2016) *Retail Industry*. Available at: http://www.ons.gov.uk/businessindustryandtrade/retailindustry#datasets4 [Accessed 31 October 2016].

Pricewaterhouse Coopers, University of Southern California and the London Business School (2013) *PwC's NextGen: A Global Generational Study*. Available at: http://www.pwc.com/us/en/people-management/publications/nextgen-global-generational-study.html [Accessed 27 October 2016].

Saunders, M., Lewis, P. and Thornhill, A. (2016) *Research Methods for Business Students* (7th ed.). Harlow: Pearson.

# Chapter 5

# Choosing your research design

## 5.1 Why you should read this chapter

Perhaps when you first started thinking about your research project, you thought about collecting the data, maybe through a questionnaire. This is perfectly normal, as it is an exciting part of any research project. But as on any journey, the research journey may take a number of routes and be accomplished by a variety of methods. The most obvious option is not always the best, whether deciding which route to use when travelling from one city to another or on the method for researching the reasons why consumers prefer recording television programmes rather than watching them live. So it will not surprise you to learn that you have many options when designing your research project. What will be a major factor in determining the quality of your research proposal is the extent to which you have considered these various options, and the clarity of thought which you have displayed in coming to a decision as to which design to adopt. The main part of this chapter is concerned with the different options you face when designing your research. We examine the differing purposes of projects which we call exploratory, descriptive and explanatory research. These project purposes may be thought of as the overall umbrella under which more detailed research strategies shelter. We then go on to detail these research strategies: the general ways in which to set about answering the research questions, the writing of which we examined in Chapter 1. There is a choice to be made regarding the use of quantitative and/or qualitative methods in a research design. Consequently, we consider the methodological choices of using one or more quantitative methods, one or more qualitative methods or combining them in a so-called mixed-method design. Our practical examination of research design and strategies ends with a consideration of the time frame applying to the research. It may be that the research questions you have set dictate that the research be carried out over an extended period of time. Alternatively, a snapshot may be perfectly acceptable.

The chapter begins and ends with two other issues which impart quality to your research design. The first of these is the subject of research philosophy. A consideration of your own research philosophy helps you to examine your fundamental ideas about research: those ideas that will underpin your research and which you may not have even thought about! In other words, it starts you thinking about your thinking. The second research issue is that of research credibility. Here we address the question of whether you have taken the steps in your research design to ensure that your findings and conclusions are believable. Obviously, this is crucially important. If the reader has doubts about the credibility of your research, then you may have wasted your time and that of others. In addition, you may suffer practical consequences such as failing the research module!

## The research onion

At this point, let us introduce our research onion (Figure 5.1). This serves as a route map to chart our way through this chapter. In addition, the onion is a metaphor for describing the layers of the research process. The outer two layers of the onion contain thinking about research philosophies and approaches to developing theory. The next three (central) layers reflect the need to consider methodological choices, research strategies and the time horizon. The centre of the onion, data collection and analysis, are the subjects of Chapters 6 and 7, respectively.

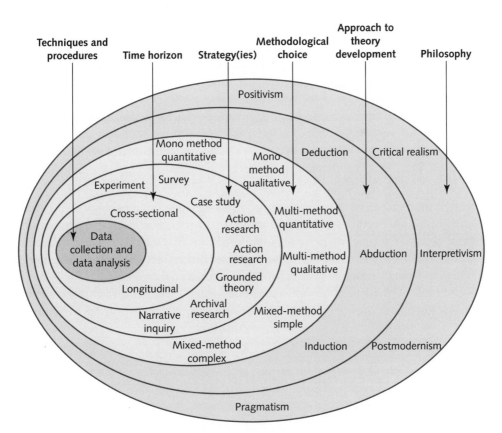

**Figure 5.1** The research onion here
*Source:* © 2015 Mark Saunders, Philip Lewis and Adrian Thornhill.

## 5.2    The importance of research philosophy

### What is meant by the term 'research philosophy'?

The term **research philosophy** refers to a system of beliefs and assumptions about the development and nature of knowledge. This sounds rather profound, but that's just what you will be doing when you conduct your research; developing knowledge in a particular field. Your knowledge development may not be as fundamental as changing the way we think about how organisations develop, but even establishing why customers prefer ice-cream cones to wafers from a particular ice-cream vendor is developing new knowledge.

You almost certainly won't think about your research philosophy at every stage in your research, but you will make a number of types of assumptions which will influence the way in which you set about your research. These assumptions fall into three main categories, which are called ontological assumptions, epistemological assumptions and axiological assumptions. Let's have a look at what these mean and the implications they have for your research.

Ontological assumptions are about the nature of reality. Your ontological assumptions shape the way in which you see and study your research objects. In business and management these objects include organisations, management, individuals' working lives and particular organisational events. Your ontology, therefore, determines how you see the world of business and management and, therefore, the direction your research project will take.

For example, take the case of organisational change, in particular resistance to that change. Traditionally, the ontological assumption made by managers and researchers has been that resistance to change hinders the change process. So the focus of research has usually been on how resistance to change could be eliminated. The emphasis has been on the sources of that resistance, the reasons for it and how it may be overcome. But recently, some practitioners' and researchers' ontological assumptions about change have altered. They have begun to think about resistance to change as inevitable – something that happens all the time whenever organisational change is initiated. Indeed, resistance can be seen as beneficial as it can highlight problematic aspects of change programmes and help to generate different ways of solving organisational problems.

Epistemological assumptions are about knowledge – what constitutes acceptable, valid and legitimate knowledge, and how we can communicate knowledge to others. In business and management a wide range of knowledge sources may be relevant. These may include numerical data, written texts, visual data (e.g. photos and videos) and personal diaries. These can all be considered legitimate. Consequently, your choice of research methods may be heavily influenced by your epistemological assumptions. For

> **Definition**
>
> **research philosophy:** overall term that relates to the development of knowledge and the nature of that knowledge in relation to research.

example, the positivist (see the next section) assumption that objective facts offer the best scientific evidence is likely to result in the choice of quantitative research methods, leading to research findings which are likely to be considered objective and generalisable. But, for a person with a different epistemological view, such as an interpretivist, such methods are less likely to offer a rich and nuanced view of organisational life.

Axiological assumptions emphasise the importance of values and ethics within the research process. The values that we are referring to here are our own as researchers, and those of our research participants. There is no doubt our values play a tremendously important part in what research project we choose and the way in which we go about collecting our data. For example, choosing to collect data by interview suggests that you place greater value in personal interaction with your respondents than were you to decide to collect their views through an Internet questionnaire.

You may find it helpful to write your own statement of personal values in relation to the topic you are studying. For example, if you are studying an organisation's policy on corporate social responsibility, your own values may have had a telling influence on the choice of this topic and the way in which you design your research. In addition, reference to your statement of personal values will help heighten your awareness of the value judgements you are making in drawing conclusions from your data. It would be perfectly normal had you not considered your own beliefs about the nature of the world around you, what constitutes acceptable and desirable knowledge or the extent to you which your values influence your choice of research topic and data collection techniques. But as a researcher, it's very helpful to develop the skill of reflecting upon such issues. Many examiners will want to understand why you decided to go down a particular route.

We now turn our attention to the five research philosophies that form the outer layer of our research onion.

## Five research philosophies

### Positivism

**Positivism** relates to the philosophical stance of the natural scientist. Here you study observable social realities (e.g. organisations, managers) to produce law-like generalisations. Positivism promises unambiguous and accurate knowledge using methods designed to yield pure data and facts uninfluenced by human interpretation or bias.

If you were to adopt an extreme positivist position, you would:

- see the social realities you are studying as real in the same way as physical objects and natural phenomena are real;

- focus on discovering observable and measurable facts and regularities, and only phenomena that you can observe and measure would lead to the production of credible and meaningful data;

| Definition |

**positivism:** a research philosophy similar to those used in the physical and natural sciences. Highly structured methods are employed to facilitate replication, resulting in law-like generalisations.

- look for causal relationships in your data to create law-like generalisations similar to those produced by scientists;
- use these universal rules and laws to help you to explain and predict behaviour and events in organisations.

In adopting a positivist philosophy, you may well use existing theory to develop hypotheses. You would test these hypotheses in the expectation that they would be confirmed, in whole or part, or refuted, leading to the further development of theory that could then be tested by further research. But it doesn't necessarily mean that, as a positivist, you have to start with existing theory. You could develop hypotheses which would lead to the gathering of facts (rather than impressions), which would provide the basis for subsequent hypothesis testing. As a positivist, you would also try to remain neutral and detached from your research and data in order to avoid influencing your findings. This means that you would undertake research, as far as possible, in a value-free way. Positivists claim to be external to the process of data collection as there is little that can be done to alter the substance of the data collected. Positivist researchers are likely to use a highly structured methodology, such as questionnaires or structured observation, in order to facilitate replication. Furthermore, the emphasis will be on quantifiable data that lend themselves to statistical analysis.

### (Critical) realism

Like positivism, realism relates to scientific inquiry. It has two distinct strands. That which concerns us most as business and management researchers is called critical realism. But first, let's clarify what is a more extreme form of realism, termed direct realism. Put simply, direct realism says that what you see is what you get: what we experience through our senses portrays the world accurately. By contrast, the philosophy of **critical realism** focuses on explaining what we see and experience, in terms of the underlying structures of reality that shape the observable events. Critical realists argue that we experience the world in two stages. First, there is the object itself and the sensations conveyed by the object. Second, there is the subjective processing that is present in our minds after that sensation meets our senses. Direct realists hold that the first step of processing is sufficient.

Once again, we can hear you saying 'What has all this to do with business and management research?' The answer is that the distinction between direct and critical realism is important for much business and management research. We are often concerned with first describing complex business situations in order to understand what is going on. So we need to study not only what is immediately apparent but also what lies behind what is immediately apparent. We need to understand the deeper structures and

---

| Definition |
| --- |
| **critical realism:** a philosophy which focuses on explaining what we see and experience with the emphasis on understanding the underlying structures of reality that shape the observable events. |

relations that are not directly observable but lie beneath the surface of social reality. Let's say you had to study a major organisational problem, such as that faced by Samsung when the battery caught fire in its new Galaxy Note 7 mobile phone shortly after its introduction in 2016. In order to arrive at a conclusion for the causes of such a debacle from which others may learn, you would need to understand a good deal about the context of the event. For example, you would need to know about the relationship between product marketing managers and technical executives. Presumably the marketeers would wish the product to get to market with the minimum of delay, whereas the technicians would be more concerned with getting the product right. Such a tension would not be immediately apparent to the researcher but would necessitate understanding the structures and relationships that were beneath the surface of what was immediately evident.

## Interpretivism

The concern of the critical realist with greater organisational complexity points the way towards **interpretivism**. Interpretivism relates to the study of social phenomena in their natural environment. So a wish to understand what is going on in a work organisation, for example, would make it necessary to conduct research in that organisation among its 'social actors'. The term 'social actors' suggests the metaphor of a theatre. As humans, we play a part on the stage of social life. Theatre actors have specific roles which they each interpret in a particular way (it may be their own or that of the director), playing these roles in accordance with their interpretations. Similarly, as social actors we interpret our everyday social roles in accordance with the meaning we give to these roles. The way in which you quickly have to move from the role of student to that of employee means a process of social adaptation on your part, which reflects your interpretation of which behaviours are appropriate for this new role. If we interpret the roles that we play according to our definition of what is appropriate, then we also interpret the social roles of others in accordance with our definition. This suggests that, as researchers, our values play a part in the research process. This is inevitable. It would be naive to think that our own personal values play no part in our research. Even the choice of research topic, as well as the decision about the research methods to adopt, reflects our values. Clearly, the skilled researcher needs to be wary of this. Understanding the social world of our research subjects from their point of view is the key here.

For business and management research, the interpretivist perspective is very relevant, particularly in such fields as organisational behaviour, marketing and human resource management. Not only are business situations complex, but they are also unique. They represent a particular set of circumstances and individuals coming together at a specific time to create a unique social phenomenon.

---

Definition

**interpretivism:** a philosophy which advocates the necessity to understand differences between humans in their role as social actors.

### Postmodernism

**Postmodernism** emphasises the role of language and power relations, seeking to question accepted ways of thinking and to give voice to alternative marginalised views. Postmodernists go even further than interpretivists in their critique of positivism, attributing even more importance to the role of language. Postmodernist business and management researchers emphasise the importance of flux and change in organisational life. They believe that any sense of order is provisional and without foundation, and can only be brought about through our language with its categories and classifications. At the same time, they recognise that language is always partial and inadequate. In particular, it marginalises and excludes aspects of what it claims to describe, whilst prioritising and emphasising other aspects.

Postmodernists argue that what is generally considered to be 'right' and 'true' is decided collectively by powerful alliances in organisations. For example, in some organisations, what is right may be decided by accountants whose power derives from the dominance of the organisation's financial resources. This does not mean that, in this example, the accountants' way of thinking is necessarily the 'best' – only that it is seen as such at a particular point in time by particular groups, such as shareholders. Other perspectives that are suppressed are potentially just as valuable and have the power to create alternative 'truths'.

Postmodernist researchers seek to expose and question the power relations that sustain such dominant realities. The goal of postmodern research is therefore to radically challenge the established ways of thinking and to give voice and legitimacy to the suppressed and marginalised ways of perceiving issues that have been previously excluded. Let us look at another example. As a postmodernist researcher, you would, instead of accepting the concept of 'management' as a given, focus on the ongoing processes of managing. You would challenge the accepted concepts and theory of management and try to demonstrate what perspectives and realities they exclude and leave silent, and whose interests they serve. This is likely to be the position of the trade union researcher, who will see management, ideally, as a collective process involving employees as well as managers, both parties having a legitimate role to play in the process of management. As a postmodernist, you would be using all forms of data – texts, images, conversations, voices and numbers – and similar to interpretivists, you would undertake in-depth investigations of phenomena. A vital part of postmodernist research is the recognition that power relations between the researcher and research subjects shape the knowledge created as part of the research process.

---

> **Definition**
>
> **postmodernism:** a philosophy which emphasises the role of language and power relations that seeks to challenge accepted ways of thinking and give voice to alternative views.

## Pragmatism

Although our choice of research methods may reflect our values, it would be wrong to think that the differing philosophies we have outlined above should be thought of as a 'shopping list' from which to choose a philosophy. In practice, you are far more likely to be guided by what is possible. Indeed, if a research problem does not suggest unambiguously that one particular type of knowledge or method should be adopted, this only confirms the pragmatist's view that it is perfectly possible to work with different types of knowledge and methods. This is the pragmatist's position. **Pragmatists** considers that the most important determinants of the research philosophy you adopt are your research question(s) and objectives. Often, the pragmatist researcher starts with a problem, their research aiming to contribute practical solutions that inform future practice. The pragmatist would argue that it is quite possible to work with methods that indicate, for example, a quantitative approach, say a questionnaire, alongside a more qualitative stance, through interviewing the key participants at meetings about their interactions. This echoes an argument that runs throughout this text: that mixing methods, both qualitative and quantitative, are possible, and may be highly appropriate, within one study.

---

**Definition**

**pragmatism:** a philosophy which argues that the most important determinant of the research design adopted are the research question(s) and objectives, the aim often being to contribute practical solutions.

---

## 5.3  Differing approaches to theory development: deduction, induction and abduction

We now move to the next layer of the onion to examine three different approaches to theory development: deduction, induction and abduction. We mentioned the topic of theory in Chapter 1, and you will remember that theory is broadly defined as an explanation of the relationship between two or more concepts or variables. The role of theory will loom large in your study, as all research projects will need to link to theory in some way. The most likely link will be to an existing theory explained in the literature relevant to your research topic. For example, you may wish to explore the theory in a different context, say, in your own employing organization or in a different cultural context. The purpose will be to explore the extent to which the theory applies or to suggest a modification to the theory based on your own findings and conclusions.

The distinction between deduction and induction in particular takes us back a stage to the development of the theory which you may be using from the literature. Although, as we said, you may be using existing theory, it is useful to see how that theory may have been developed.

## ● Deduction: clarifying theory at the beginning of the study

**Deduction** is a research approach which involves the testing of a theoretical proposition by using a research strategy designed to perform this test. There are five sequential stages in deductive research. These are:

1  defining research questions from the general theory that exists;

2  operationalising these questions in a way that enables what is occurring to be established (i.e. specifying the way in which the questions may be answered). This may be in the form of a testable proposition (hypothesis) about the relationship between two or more concepts or variables, or set of hypotheses, to form a theory;

3  collecting data to answer the operationalized questions or test the hypotheses;

4  analysing the data collected to determine whether it supports the existing general theory or suggests the need for its modification;

5  confirming the initial general theory or modifying it if the findings do not confirm the existing general theory. (In the event of step 5 resulting in a modified theory, the five sequential stages can be repeated to test the new theory.)

The key characteristics of deduction are, first, to explain causal relationships between variables. For example, you may wish to establish the reasons for too many errors being made by call centre operatives in giving information to customers. Having studied the error patterns, it seems to you that there may be a relationship between the number of errors and the length of the initial training programme received by operatives. You define your research questions (stage 1) which explore the proposition that those operatives receiving the shorter version of the initial training programme are more error-prone than those who undergo the longer version. Secondly, you need to operationalise the questions as testable propositions (stage 2). These questions, therefore, need to be expressed in a way that enables what is occurring to be established. In the call centre example mentioned earlier, the two key concepts in the questions are error levels and training-programme length. The second concept may be more straightforward than the first. For example, you would need to be clear about what constitutes an error and distinguish between the seriousness of errors. The third characteristic of deduction is the need to collect and analyse data to answer the research questions (stages 3 and 4) and to see whether or not the existing theory is confirmed (stage 5). The fourth characteristic is the use of a clearly structured methodology to facilitate replication. This is important to achieve reliability, as we see later in this chapter.

---

**Definition**

**deduction:** a research approach which involves the testing of a theoretical proposition by using a research strategy specifically designed to collect data for the purpose of its testing.

## Induction: conducting and developing theory from the explanations that arise

If deduction has a 'top-down' flavour, then **induction** suggests a 'bottom-up' approach to theory development. Inductive reasoning moves from specific observations to broader generalisations and theories. With inductive reasoning, we begin with specific observations and measures, by observing patterns and repeated occurrences of phenomena and formulating some speculative hypotheses or propositions from what has been observed which can be investigated. All this is with a view to developing some general conclusions or theories.

When using the inductive approach, you are often trying to gain an understanding of the meanings humans attach to events. Let's consider again the example of the error-prone call centre operatives. An important impression you would want to gain is whether the operatives actually like their jobs. The literature on call centres you have reviewed suggests that it is possible to distinguish between those jobs that are intrinsically interesting and those that are simply dead boring! Some jobs may be more demanding and stressful than others. Some operatives may simply not be cut out for this type of work. Already you can see that alternative explanations are beginning to form for the differential levels of operative errors. It may be that the explanation is more complex than the amount of training that the operatives receive.

With induction, the emphasis is on a close understanding of the research context. We raised the point earlier about the necessity to conduct research in more than one call centre in the ability to generalise a theory across all call centres. From an inductive stance, we are more likely to want to get a detailed picture of the experience of working in one, or perhaps two call centres that have different environmental characteristics.

Induction possesses a more flexible structure to permit changes of research emphasis as the research progresses. It may be that the stress in the call centre operatives you are studying becomes a major issue in your data collection. This may present itself as an alternative explanation for high error levels to that suggested by insufficient training. In that case, it may be sensible to build much more attention to stress experience into your research questions.

## Abduction: combining deduction and induction

Instead of moving from theory to data (as in deduction) or from data to theory (as in induction), an abductive approach moves back and forth, in effect combining deduction and induction. In essence, this matches what many business and management researchers actually do. **Abduction** begins with the observation of an unexpected

---

**Definitions**

**induction:** a research approach which involves the building of theory from analysing data already collected.

**abduction:** approach to theory development involving the collection of data to explore a phenomenon, identify themes and explain patterns to generate a new – or modify an existing – theory which is subsequently tested.

occurrence and then works out a plausible theory of how this could have occurred. Some plausible theories can account for what is observed better than others (Van Maanen et al., 2007), and it is these theories that will help uncover more unexpected observations. Surprising discoveries can occur at any stage in the research process, including when writing your project report!

Using an abductive approach to our research on the reasons for too many errors being made by call centre operatives would mean obtaining data that were sufficiently detailed and rich to allow us to explore the phenomenon and identify and explain themes and patterns regarding error incidence. We would then try to integrate these explanations in an overall conceptual framework, thereby building up a theory of error rate explanation. This we would test using evidence provided by existing data and new data modifying our theory as necessary.

## ● Combining research approaches

In the discussion of induction and deduction, you have probably gained the impression that there are rigid divisions between deduction and induction. This is not so. As we have seen in our discussion of abduction, is it possible to combine deduction and induction within the same piece of research. It is also, in our experience, often advantageous to do so although often one approach or another is dominant. It would be quite usual, for example, to start with an exploratory study in order to arrive at a tentative theory inductively before testing that theory in a deductive piece of quantitative work. In our example of error-prone call centre operatives, a few focus groups may give some clear indications as to the reason for some staff making more errors than others. These indications may then form the basis for questionnaire design and administration. We cover mixed-methods research later in the chapter.

Whether your reasoning will be predominantly deductive, inductive or abductive depends on a number of factors – in particular, the emphasis of the research and the nature of the research topic. If your topic enjoys the support of a lot of literature from which you can define a theoretical framework, then it may be more suitable for a deductive approach. For a new topic about which there is little existing literature, it may be more appropriate to adopt an inductive approach by collecting and analysing data and reflecting upon what theoretical themes the data suggest. Alternatively, if your topic is rich in information in one context but in the context in which you are researching there is little information, this may persuade you to adopt an abductive approach, enabling you to modify an existing theory.

In addition, the time available to you may influence your decision about which approach to adopt. The timescale for a piece of deductive research can be shorter, although time will be needed to set up the study prior to data collection and analysis. As data collection is often based on 'one take', it should be possible to predict the timescale. But inductive and abductive research can take much longer, and the timescale can be more difficult to predict as the ideas have to emerge gradually.

Two other factors may determine which research approach you adopt. First is the extent to which you are prepared to indulge in risk. Deduction can be a lower-risk strategy, but with induction and abduction you have to live with the fear that no useful data patterns and theory will emerge. Second, you have to consider your audience. Most managers are familiar with deductive research methods and may doubt the reliability of data collected inductively.

| 5.4 | Differing purposes: exploratory, descriptive and explanatory studies |
|---|---|

## Exploratory studies

Exploratory research is about discovering information about a topic that is not understood clearly by the researcher. This lends itself particularly well to new phenomena where you may not be prepared to launch into a piece of full-scale research but want to gain some insights that will inform your research design. The marketeer, for example, may be aware that there is a change in the consumers' preference away from organic food after the initial enthusiasm for such food. But the marketeer may not fully appreciate what form that preference is taking and why the phenomenon is happening. An **exploratory study** may well provide tentative answers to these initial questions, which need to be followed up with more detailed research to provide more dependable answers.

The most usual ways of conducting exploratory research are:

- searching the academic literature;
- using unstructured observations;
- using semi- and unstructured interviews.

The Internet is particularly useful for doing some basic literature search work in an exploratory study. This may help in pointing you towards relevant academic journal articles to be found on academic journal databases in your library such as Emerald Insight and Business Source Premier. Of course, non-academic articles from the Internet, such as those in newspapers or produced by commercial enterprises, should not be thought of as an alternative to academic articles.

As well as literature searching, exploratory studies are well suited to qualitative methods such as semi- and unstructured interviewing or unstructured observation. For example, informal discussions with consumers, organic food growers and supermarket executives may provide useful insights into changing preferences for organic food. Consumer focus groups are a well-known method of establishing consumer views which may be valuable as a piece of exploratory research. Case studies of families' food consumption may be helpful in an explanatory study, as may small-scale pilot studies.

> **Definition**
>
> **exploratory study:** research that aims to seek new insights, ask new questions and assess topics in a new light.

Although the methods used in exploratory research indicate a good deal of flexibility, they do not mean absence of direction to the inquiry. It means that the focus is initially broad and becomes progressively narrower as the research progresses.

While exploratory research provides insights into, and a fuller understanding of, an issue or situation, definitive conclusions should be drawn only with extreme caution. Yet it is very valuable in helping you to decide the best research design, data collection method and selection of subjects. Of course, it may point to the fact that the issue which you thought was of great importance is in fact a non-issue. In that case, you will have saved yourself going up a blind alley and delivering a meaningless piece of research!

## Descriptive studies

You may have received comments on your assessed assignments from lecturers, which say something like, 'It's good as far as it goes, but it tends to be too descriptive'. This means that they wanted you to analyse and explain what was going on with a given topic. The question 'Why did the situation occur?' is the question to which they wanted the answer – not the answer you supplied, which was likely to have been a description of the situation. However good your description, the point remains that describing a phenomenon is much easier than explaining why it occurred. That said, descriptive research certainly has an important role to play, often as the forerunner of explanatory research.

**Descriptive study** or research seeks to describe accurately persons, events or situations. It is appropriate for asking such 'what', 'when', 'who', 'where' and 'how' questions as:

- What is the employee absentee rate in particular departments?
- When are employees most likely to be absent in those same departments?
- Who are the employees who are most frequently absent?

Look again at the three questions above. You will note that they each require responses than can be quantified. They each involve the collection of measurable, quantifiable data. So, the data collection methods typically used in descriptive research are:

- questionnaires;
- structured interviews;
- structured observation;
- reanalysis of secondary data.

Descriptive research should be thought of as a means to an end rather than an end in itself. This means that if your research project utilises description, it is likely to be a forerunner to explanation. However, descriptive research can tell us a lot about the world around us, which is very valuable in its own right, as the example in Research in practice 5.1 indicates.

> **Definition**
>
> **descriptive study:** research designed to produce an accurate representation of persons, events or situations.

**Research in practice 5.1**

### The emergence of shopping 'serial returners' hinders growth of UK businesses

Research in 2016 from payments company Barclaycard reveals that consumer demand for free and easy returns when shopping online is placing increased pressure on retailers and impacting their bottom line. The report notes the emergence of the 'serial returner' – the online shopper who habitually over-orders and takes advantage of free returns.

Barclaycard found that:

- Six in 10 retailers report that they are negatively impacted by consumers' propensity to return unwanted items.
- Online-only businesses are hardest hit as three in 10 say managing returns is affecting profit margins.
- One in five businesses have increased price of items to cover the cost of managing and processing customer returns.
- Four in 10 shoppers say standardising clothing and shoe sizes could help retailers reduce their level of returns.

The findings indicate that in the previous 12 months, the increasing rate of returns has presented a number of challenges for online retailers, with 31% claiming that managing the returns process has an impact on their profit margin. This comes as online shopping continues to grow in popularity, with spending in digital channels rising 14.1% year-on-year in 2015, compared to just 1.1% in-store.

'Serial returners' regularly order more than they need with no intention of keeping every item. Three in ten shoppers deliberately over-purchase and subsequently return unwanted items, with 19% admitting to ordering multiple versions of the same item to make up their mind at home – safe in the knowledge they can choose from the ever-growing number of ways to quickly and easily send items back, such as hourly courier services and local drop-off points.

Six shoppers in ten say a retailer's returns policy impacts their decision to make a purchase online, and almost half (47%) of these would not order an item if they had to fund the cost of sending it back from their own pocket. Consequently, web-based retailers are caught between trying to attract customers and remaining competitive while also ensuring they protect their bottom line.

Fifty-seven per cent of retailers say that dealing with returns has a negative impact on the day-to-day running of their business, leaving many with no choice but to find another way to recover the cost incurred. A third of online retailers offer free returns but offset the balance by charging for delivery, while one in five increase the price of items to cover the cost of returns.

Concern about being able to afford the costs of managing the delivery and returns process led to 22% of bricks-and-mortar retailers choosing not to sell online.

Thirty-eight per cent of returners said they would send back fewer purchases if businesses were to standardise clothing and shoe sizes, which can vary between and even within retailers. Eighteen per cent said a better in-store experience, such as shortened queues for clothing store fitting rooms so they can try on sizes without the wait, would

→

also reduce the number of returns they make. In addition, 18% said they would like retailers to introduce technology to help them better visualise an item when shopping online, such as the ability to 'try on' clothing after uploading an image of themselves.

*Source:* Barclaycard (2016).

The data in Research in practice 5.1 is valuable to online retailers in particular in giving them an idea of the scale of a problem. It also points to an explanation of why the phenomenon may be occurring. But the strength of this piece of research is giving retailers the basis upon which to formulate action to solve the problem of returns while still retaining the goodwill of their customers and trading within the restrictions of consumer law.

## Explanatory studies

**Explanatory studies** takes descriptive research a stage further by looking for an explanation behind a particular occurrence through the discovery of causal relationships between key variables. As we saw in Research in practice 5.1, the question moves from just 'to what extent do customers return goods to retailers?' to include 'and why this is happening?' Answering such questions can use quantitative, qualitative or both types of data. The methods you use to collect your data, therefore, depend to a large extent on the focus of the research.

The methods typically used in explanatory research can typically include:

- questionnaires;
- interviews;
- observations;
- reanalysis of secondary data.

If the focus is on explaining the impact of different factors, such as the ease with which returns can be made, quantitative values can be attached to the variables, and they can be subjected to statistical tests such as correlation in order to get a clearer view of the relationship (section 7.3). Alternatively, the focus may be on other possible explanatory factors, such as the reasons why product returns may vary by customer age and location. Much of the explanation may centre upon differing attitudes or beliefs of customers which may be difficult to quantify (section 7.4). Even if your feeling is that qualitative research may be appropriate for your research questions and objectives, remember, qualitative research may benefit at some stage from an element of quantitative processing of data.

### Definition

**explanatory study:** research that focuses on studying a situation or a problem in order to explain the relationships between variables.

## 5.5  Differing strategies

Now we concentrate on the research strategies you may use. Let's make it clear at the beginning of this section that the label that is attached to a particular strategy is relatively unimportant. What is important is that the strategy you choose will enable you to answer your particular research question(s) and meet your research objectives. Nonetheless, the labels are a useful way of categorising the different strategies available to you.

Each of the strategies can be used for exploratory, descriptive and explanatory research. Some of these more clearly belong more closely to the deductive approach, others to an inductive or abductive approach. But, as with the attachment of labels, it is not helpful to allocate strategies to one approach or the other. We emphasise that your research strategy will be guided by your research question(s) and objectives as well as the extent of your existing knowledge, the amount of time and other resources you have available, as well as your own philosophical leanings. Finally, we must point out that these strategies are not mutually exclusive. So, for example, a case study may include a survey and archival research.

The order in which we explain the strategies below is simply that which they appear in the research onion (Figure 5.1). It does not imply that those explained earlier are any more important than those below them in the list.

### ⬤ Experiment

The purpose of an **experiment** is to study causal links between variables; to establish whether a change in one independent variable (e.g. the running of a sales promotion) produces a change in another dependent variable (e.g. the level of sales). The essential components of an experiment are the following:

1  Manipulating the independent variable. To assess the effect of a sales promotion on the level of sales, the sales promotion may be manipulated by differentiating the offer, altering the time period over which it runs or changing the level of advertising.

2  Controlling the experiment by holding all other independent variables constant. Therefore, the sales experiment would be held at the same time of year, in the same (or similar) location.

3  Observing the effect of the manipulation of the independent variable on the dependent variable.

4  Predicting the events that will occur in the experimental setting.

---

**Definition**

**experiment:** a research strategy that involves the definition of a theoretical hypothesis; the selection of samples of individuals from known populations; the allocation of samples to different experimental conditions; the introduction of planned change on one or more of the variables; and measurement on a small number of variables and control of other variables.

The steps in the experiment are the following:

1  Identify and define the issue that is to be studied (e.g. the effect upon sales of promotions).

2  Formulate research hypotheses (e.g. the sales revenue of yogurt will double when a 'Buy 2, get 1 free' offer is run).

3  Design the experiment by:

   (a)  selecting the relevant product and sales promotion;

   (b)  identifying and controlling the factors which may affect the outcomes (e.g. time, location);

   (c)  choosing the way in which the outcomes will be measured;

   (d)  conducting a pilot study to test the effectiveness of the experiment and predict any problems which may be overcome by adjusting the experiment design.

4  Run the experiment and collect the data.

5  Assemble the data and apply relevant tests to ensure statistical significance of the findings.

Although our sales promotion example is a situation where an experimental strategy may apply in business, the strategy is not applicable to many business and management research questions. This may be for a number of practical reasons. For example, it may be seen as unfair to apply certain disadvantageous working conditions to one group of employees and not the other. Moreover, it would be unethical if the disadvantaged employees were not told of the experiment and the way it would involve them. Seeking volunteers may be problematic, as some people are unwilling to participate in experiments and so those who volunteer may not be representative of the population you wish to study. This is why the experiment strategy is often used only on captive populations such as university students! In addition, if the results are to be statistically valid, then an experiment that involves a large group of subjects may be necessary with all this implies in terms of cost and complexity.

## Survey

When you mention the term 'research' to most people, it is often the **survey** strategy, usually using a questionnaire, that springs most readily to mind. Few days pass without the news reporting the results of a new 'survey' that indicates a snapshot of social and economic life. Indeed, the notion of the researcher selecting a sample of respondents from a population and administering a standardised questionnaire is the image with which you may be most familiar. The survey strategy is popular in business and management research.

---

**Definition**

**survey:** a research strategy which involves the structured collection of data from a sizeable population. Data collection may take the form of questionnaires or structured interviews.

Because it is so widespread, managers find it easy to understand and place a good deal of faith in the results which flow from surveys. The survey strategy is particularly suitable for asking questions such as: 'Who?' 'What?' 'Where?' 'How much?' and 'How many?' These types of questions make them useful for exploratory and descriptive research. One of the reasons the survey strategy is so popular is that it allows the collection of data about the same things from a large number of people in a cost-effective manner. This is because sampling (section 6.2) makes it possible to generate findings that are representative statistically of the whole population at a lower cost than collecting the data for the whole population.

The most common method for collecting data using a survey strategy is the questionnaire. The questionnaire comprises a set of standardised questions. It may be completed by the respondent or an interviewer in a face-to-face situation. Alternatively, it may be completed online or by telephone. The standardised questions make it possible to easily compare responses across different locations or time frames.

It would be wrong to think that administering a questionnaire is quick and easy. Ensuring that your sample is representative, designing and piloting your data collection instrument and trying to ensure a good response rate are all very time consuming. So is the analysis of the data, even though you will undoubtedly use a spreadsheet or statistical analysis software. But from a practical viewpoint, the survey strategy does offer you certain advantages. These come largely from the feeling of being in control of the process. With more qualitative strategies, for example interviewing, you are often dependent upon others for their time. The fact that you will be more in control of your time schedule in the survey strategy makes it an attractive proposition for students who usually have a set period of time, often an academic year, to complete a piece of research.

One of the drawbacks of the survey is that the data collected are unlikely to be as detailed as those collected by other research strategies. Clearly, it is not advisable to ask a large number of questions of a large number of people, so comprehensiveness is bound to be limited. We have all switched off when faced with the fourth page of a questionnaire, not a reaction which will lead to credible research results! But perhaps the biggest disadvantage with the questionnaire method is the attraction that it seems an easy option. Be warned: designing a questionnaire is very easy; designing a good one is enormously difficult.

It would be misleading if we did not mention that the survey strategy is also associated with structured observation and structured interviews (see Chapter 6), both of which are based on the principle of standardisation.

## Case study

We noted in the previous sub-section that the survey method is suitable for asking questions such as 'Who?' 'What?' 'Where?' 'How much?' and 'How many?' In contrast, the **case study** strategy is more appropriate for asking the question 'Why?' (although the

---

**Definition**

**case study:** a research strategy which involves the investigation of a particular contemporary topic within its real-life context, using multiple sources of evidence (data).

questions 'What?' and 'How?' are also relevant). Consequently, the case study strategy is most often used in exploratory and explanatory research.

Case studies are particularly good at enabling the researcher to get a detailed understanding of the context of the research and the activity taking place within that context. So, if you are concerned with understanding why managers make decisions in certain ways rather than an analysis of the decisions that are made, who makes them, the frequency of decisions and their perceived importance, the case study may be the best choice. The key word, of course, is 'context'. Often the key to explaining social phenomena is context. For example, managerial decisions taken in an environment where senior managers are highly supportive of their managers and reasonably tolerant of their failure are likely to be much more adventurous than in an unsupportive climate.

Data collection techniques used in a case study may be varied and include a combination of interviews, observation and documentary analysis as well as questionnaires. Case studies normally use a variety of methods along with secondary data, so you are likely to need to triangulate multiple sources of data, a principle which we explain in the last section (5.6) of this chapter.

The question arises as to whether a single case or a number of cases is most suitable for your research. As with many other decisions related to strategy, this is likely to be governed by what is ideal as a strategy for answering your research questions and what is possible in terms of practical considerations such as access and resources. Like many students, you may choose the organisation in which you work. This is often going to be a practical option. Yet there are likely to be limitations on the extent to which you can call your organisation typical of all similar organisations. For this reason, a case study strategy can also incorporate more than one case. You may choose to use more than one case if you need to generalise from your findings.

Some criticise the case study strategy because they feel that one case, or even a small number of cases, is no basis for placing faith in the findings. They also argue that close exposure to the study of the case biases the findings. For this reason, they dismiss case study research as useful only as an exploratory tool. But a well-designed and skilfully executed study of real-life issues will yield insights not possible in more descriptive strategies.

## Action research

In one application of the case study strategy, you may be working in one organisation in order to gain insights into an aspect of that organisation's life from which you may draw conclusions. Similarly, with **action research**, you may be working in one organisation. But with the case study, the likelihood is that you are 'on the outside looking in' (although you may be a part of that organisation). With action research, the

---

| Definition |

**action research:** research strategy concerned with the management of a change and involving close collaboration between practitioners and researchers.

emphasis is on you taking an involved role as a participant in teasing out the issues, understanding the organization and the project and acting upon what has been found out (Figure 5.2); you are very much the insider. Here you are conducting experiments and acting upon them by making changes and observing the results. Your role is decidedly active rather than passive.

There are four common themes within action research which make its practical application, and value, much clearer:

1  As noted above, the purpose of the research is to be part of and study research in action rather than to conduct research about action. A typical emphasis for the research may be the change process in an organisation.

2  The joint working of organisational members, for example managers and other key workers, and researchers in the action research project. The researchers may be pursuing academic research, or they may be consultants from within or outside the organisation. So the researcher is part of the organisation and the change process. This contrasts with more normal research or consultancy where participants are objects of study.

3  The cyclical nature of the process of action research which consists of diagnosing, planning action, taking action and evaluating action (see Figure 5.2). The diagnostic stage will begin with the establishment of a clear project purpose and continue with fact-finding and analysis on the situation under study. The core of the cycle involves the planning, implementation and evaluation of the changes themselves.

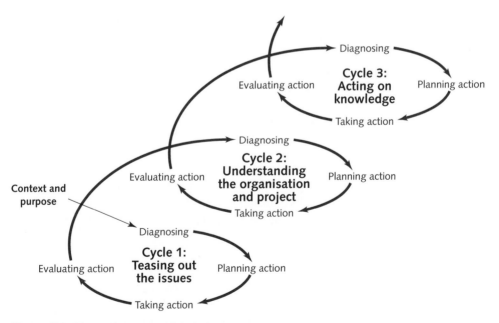

**Figure 5.2** The action research spiral

*Source:* © Saunders et al. (2016), reproduced with permission.

4  The final stage in the cycle is the key one if you are using the action research strategy as an academic project. This is the evaluative stage, where you will draw from the research the lessons which may be learned. These lessons may have a practical dimension (for example, the pitfalls that managers should avoid when introducing a new pay system) or a more theoretical perspective (say, the development of a model of employee behaviours in the pay change process). It is clear here that action research should have implications beyond the immediate project. It must have a wider application.

You will see that action research differs from other research strategies because it is concerned with action, in particular the promotion of organisational change. So it is particularly useful for 'How' questions. A project using action research promises excellent insights into organisational change processes as well as an absorbing project report which, because few student projects use this strategy, will have a distinct novelty value! You may ask why few students pursue action research. The answer is that it is demanding both in terms of hours that need to be devoted to a project, and the length of time needed to progress the action research cycle. It also demands a high level of researcher skill and maturity.

## Grounded theory

**Grounded theory,** usually associated with Corbin and Strauss (2008), belongs principally to the inductive approach to research because you develop theory from data generated by a series of observations or interviews. However, there is an element of deduction (remember – theory to data) in this strategy.

Unlike the deductive approach, data collection starts without the formation of your initial theory, as you would in a deductive approach. Theory is developed from data generated by a series of observations, discussions and interviews. The element of deduction is introduced when these data lead to the generation of predictions which are then tested in further observations. These further observations may confirm, or otherwise, the predictions. A continual process of testing leads to the development of theory.

This all becomes a bit clearer with a practical explanation of how grounded theory works, as you will see in the Research in practice 5.2 example.

## Ethnography

**Ethnography** is concerned with understanding another way of life from the perspective of those pursuing that way of life. Its traditional roots are in the anthropological study of primitive societies. The key concern is learning from people rather than studying them.

---

**Definitions**

**grounded theory:** research strategy in which theory is developed from data generated by a series of observations or interviews principally involving an inductive approach.

**Ethnography:** research strategy that focuses on describing and interpreting the social world through first-hand field study.

## The use of grounded theory in a study of consumer behaviour

Jessica was a full-time marketing student who was doing a placement in a major retail group where she performed a range of different duties. The group was conducting a marketing trial with the objective of generating higher turnover of their more expensive (and more profitable) food items. This was part of a wider strategy to achieve a more exclusive market position for their brand.

One of the activities which formed part of the marketing trial was to offer customers samples of the range of food items (e.g. luxury chocolates) while they were doing their normal shopping. Having sampled the item in question, the customers were then invited to purchase it at a 'special opening offer' price. The range of behaviours exhibited by the customers who sampled the items ranged from indifference, resulting in a refusal to buy, to enthusiasm and a purchase of the offer.

The managers in charge of the marketing trial thought that the difference in sales success level of the trial food items was due to the items themselves, a clear pattern having emerged where some items were more successful than others. However, Jessica was not so sure that this was the sole answer. At university she was particularly interested in consumer behaviour, and she thought that the explanation of the different success levels of the trial items was more complicated than the intrinsic attractiveness of the product. She kept a diary throughout the trial and noted, for example, that some products were received with mild enthusiasm by customers, but nonetheless a sale resulted. On other occasions, an item was received with great keenness but no sale followed.

As the trial progressed, she talked with all the staff involved in sampling the customers and developed her notes to the point where a number of patterns began to emerge. One of these related to consumer decision-making theory, in particular that of impulse buying. As the trial neared its end, Jessica developed a tentative explanation of the differing success levels of the food items based upon the idea that some lent themselves to impulse buying more than others, but just as importantly, some customers were more inclined to make pure impulse purchasing decisions ('Oh, why not?') while others were much more likely to make planned impulse decisions ('I had in mind to buy some of these . . .').

In the final stages of the trial, Jessica took more detailed notes of the behaviour of the customers with her developed theory in mind, and returned to university at the end of the placement with a clear theoretical position to take into the final stages of her project.

Such studies in business research are unusual. But one stands out as one of the most famous of the late twentieth century. It was published in a book called *Working for Ford* by Huw Beynon (1973). Beynon spent much of 1967 in Ford's Halewood plant on Merseyside talking to workers, trade union officials and management. The picture Beynon paints of life on the production line stems largely from the words of the workers themselves: an approach which really brings Beynon's writing to life. Beynon concluded that the work was dull and boring and the whole experience pretty bleak. In his view, Ford was still then run on the principles established by its founder, Henry Ford – principles which emphasised that man is sub-servient to the machine.

Ethnography is obviously very time consuming, since it takes place over an extended time period, so it tends not to be used extensively in business research. Indeed, Beynon started his research in the pursuit of a PhD, but had to abandon the plan simply because he had so much data. He decided to write a book instead.

Although ethnography is time consuming, the grounded theory example in Research in practice 5.2 has some similarities with ethnography. If you are conducting research similar to that in this example, you may wish to look at the ethnographic strategy in more detail.

## Archival research

**Archival research** uses administrative records and documents as the principal source of data. These may, for example, be minutes of meetings, memos or emails containing information or instructions, accounts, contracts or letters. For example, you may wish to study the way in which key messages about company performance are communicated to staff.

Such research concentrates on past events and may allow changes over time to be charted. But the extent to which you use the archival strategy will depend on the availability of key documents. Of course, even if relevant documents exist and you are allowed access to them, they may not meet your precise research needs.

Archival research may not be appropriate for many business research projects as the main research strategy. But it may play a useful supporting role at some stage in many projects if you wish to supplement other data collection methods.

## Narrative inquiry

A **narrative** is a story; a personal account which interprets an event or sequence of events. Qualitative research interviews can involve a participant in 'storytelling'. So the term 'narrative' can be applied to describe the nature or outcome of a qualitative interview. But as a research strategy, narrative inquiry has a more specific meaning and purpose. It may be that your research context leads you to believe that the experiences of your participants are best revealed by collecting and analysing their contributions as complete stories, rather than discrete bits of data that are the result of specific interview questions which you then treat as bits of data in your subsequent analysis.

### Definitions

**archival research:** research strategy which analyses administrative records and documents as the principal source of data.

**narrative:** account of an experience that is told in a sequenced way, indicating a flow of related events that, taken together, are significant for the narrator and which convey meaning to the researcher.

The aim of narrative inquiry is to gain a deeper understanding of organisational realities, closely linked to their members' experiences. As such, the role you, the researcher, adopt in narrative inquiry is that of the listener facilitating the process of storytelling by the participant (or group of participants – it is quite legitimate to have more than one narrator) who is the narrator. The narrative which results may be a short story about a specific event, a more extended story (for example, about a work project) or a career history.

In-depth interviews are the main way of collecting narratives. But there may be other ways: for example, participant observation, autobiographies, authored biographies or diaries. This raises the issue of the narrative researcher adopting the role of narrator in particular circumstances, which we will consider further later.

As with other research strategies, narrative inquiry may be used as the sole research strategy, or it may be used in conjunction with other strategies to lend richness to your data.

## Combining research strategies

We made the point earlier that it is perfectly possible to combine research approaches and strategies within the same study. You may wish to do some preparatory work in an exploratory phase before you firm up your research questions and objectives. This may involve informal discussion or interviews with key personnel. This could be supplemented with an element of scanning of organisational documentation. The exploratory strategy could then be continued with survey work using both questionnaire and structured interviews. A final stage may utilise the explanatory strategy by attempting to gain greater meaning to the exploratory work through, for example, a case study approach. The important point to bear in mind is that different strategies may work at different stages in the study, depending, of course, on their suitability to answer your research questions and objectives.

## Single, multiple or mixed research methods?

Within your overall strategy, as you can see from the research onion in Figure 5.1, you will face a choice of whether to choose a single method approach to your work or use a multiplicity of methods. For example, a quantitative research design may use a single data collection technique, such as a questionnaire (mono method quantitative study) or combine a questionnaire with structured observation (a multi-method quantitative study). Alternatively, you may choose to base all your data collection on focus groups (mono method qualitative) or combine focus groups with follow- up single interviews (multi-method qualitative). You might also choose to start with semi-structured interviews and use the data collected from these interviews to help design a questionnaire (mixed methods). Mixed methods may be simple (e.g. within a narrow time frame) or complex (over a longer time frame) – see later in this chapter for a discussion of cross-sectional and longitudinal research.

Business and management research lends itself to the use of multiple and mixed methodological choices because these can overcome the drawbacks of using a single method. In addition, they promise deeper and richer data than may result from use of a single method.

Combining approaches and strategies in the pursuit of an answer to your research questions and objectives will usually involve the mixing of research methods. The preceding section on combining research strategies indicates that certain approaches and strategies are better suited to particular stages of the research than others. In the same way, using a variety of data collection methods may present advantages for the following four reasons.

### Reason 1: Some data collection methods are more suited to particular tasks than others

If you wish to establish the extent to which children use Snapchat, this can be done by a questionnaire survey to a sample of children; if you want to understand why some teams work better than others, it is better to use qualitative discussions and interviews. Those two examples are, of course, separate projects. But the same argument applies when you are thinking about one project. Your research objectives may be: 'To what extent do Internet-based suppliers use a multiplicity of carriers for shipping goods?' and 'What are the reasons for the use of multiple carriers?' The first question may collect data through an Internet-based scan by you of leading supplier websites, followed by a questionnaire of a sample of suppliers. You may follow this up with some interviews with the distribution managers of suppliers in order to get a grasp of the reasons for multiple-carrier usage. The different methods are then integrated into a single research design.

### Reason 2: Focusing on different aspects of the study

It may well be that different data collection methods may be better at different research tasks within the study. So you may want to gain an overall view about the way in which companies outsource aspects of their business from studying secondary sources, or even from a quantitative survey. This will probably not give you a sufficient grasp of the reasons why some companies are more likely to be more enthusiastic about outsourcing than others. Nor will it tell you why some functions are greater candidates for outsourcing than others. This may need some interviews with key executives.

### Reason 3: Corroborating your research findings within a study using two or more independent sources of data or data collection methods

When you have finished this chapter, we hope you will have a very clear understanding of the importance of establishing the credibility of your research findings. This topic is dealt with in this chapter's final section (5.6). One way you can do this is through the process of triangulation. Triangulation is the use of two or more independent sources of data or data collection methods within one study in order to help ensure that the data are telling you what you think they are telling you. In an ideal world, a questionnaire, say, will yield highly credible data, particularly if the guidelines to effective survey design and implementation are followed. But if you have triangulated your questionnaire findings with some semi-structured interviews and find that these findings have been confirmed, then you will feel more content in the knowledge that you have done all you can to provide credible results. Of course, it may be that both sets of data are questionable, so even triangulation does not provide final confirmation.

As well as using two or more data collection methods to triangulate your findings, it is possible to vary aspects of the data collection while using the same method. These aspects may be the populations from which you are collecting the data, the time at which the data are collected and the location of the data collection. For example, if you are studying the behaviour of consumers in a supermarket, data collected through observation may differ from town to town, or between mornings and afternoons. If data are broadly the same, this suggests that the findings are robust. Differences may point to the need for more research. If, say, consumers spend more time making buying decisions in the afternoons, this may suggest less busy consumers. Alternatively, it may be that there are fewer customers in the afternoon, which in itself prompts more time to be taken by consumers. So triangulation in this case may not only cause concern over initial findings; it may also indicate the need for a revision of initial conclusions.

It may also be fruitful to triangulate the research by using the same data collection methods and sources of data but changing the data gatherer. So if you are the research manager of a large market research company employing many interviewers, and you notice that one set of data is seriously inconsistent with the others, this may tell you more about the interviewer than sources of the data. It is not unheard of for some data to be invented! But, more usually, two individual researchers conducting semi-structured interviews with similar subjects may generate slightly different data, at least in emphasis, because of, say, the stress put on certain questions or the way in which answers have been followed up.

### Reason 4: Using qualitative methods to explain relationships between quantitative variables

Think again about the sort of research findings you hear in the news every day. We often hear that people in Northern Europe are heavier consumers of alcoholic drinks than those in the South of Europe. This statistic may be of interest as far as it goes, but it doesn't go far enough. What is it about living in Northern Europe that leads to greater alcohol consumption? Is it colder? Are alcoholic drinks cheaper? We don't know from the broad statistics. We need to ask some searching questions to find out what is leading to this particular phenomenon.

### ● Differing time horizons: cross-sectional or longitudinal?

If you are like most of our readers, you will be time-constrained in the completion of your research project. For this reason, you will probably opt for a piece of cross-sectional research. This is a 'snapshot' of a particular research setting at a particular time. On the other hand, a research design which tracks events over time is called a 'longitudinal' design. The main difference between the two designs is the ability of the longitudinal design to note change. Which you choose will probably depend on practical considerations. However, we will show that an element of longitudinal design is perfectly possible within the constraints of one academic year.

## Cross-sectional studies

In a **cross-sectional research** design you would collect data from participants at only one period in time in what is often termed a 'snapshot'. The data are typically collected from multiple groups or types of people in cross-sectional research. For example, data in a cross-sectional study might be collected from male and female consumers, from those of different ages, from people in different socio-economic classes or from consumers with different levels of educational achievement. A classic example of the cross-sectional research design is the opinion poll. It is a way of taking the 'snapshot' of current thinking.

In an opinion poll, the cross-sectional study would usually employ the survey strategy and use a questionnaire to collect quantitative data. As well as describing the incidence of a phenomenon, you can explain statistically the relationship between certain variables: for example, the relationship between expenditure on sales promotions and sales revenue. But a cross-sectional study may also use qualitative methods. For example, interviews conducted over a short time period, either as the sole data collection method or as one of a mixture of methods, may be equally useful.

## Longitudinal studies

As we mentioned earlier, the main advantage of a **longitudinal study** or research design is the capacity that it has to study change and development over time. This may conjure up images of annual visits to managers to track their progress as part of a coaching programme. It could also be that the manager keeps a diary of relevant thoughts and actions, much the same as the personal development journal that you may have come across. These may be powerful ways of collecting data to chart change. But they may be impractical for the student researcher, given time (and, possibly, access) constraints. However, what may be useful is to introduce a longitudinal element to your research by using one of the secondary data sources produced by longitudinal surveys that are available on the Internet, such as the Family Expenditure Survey (see Research in practice 5.3).

---

**Definitions**

**cross-sectional research:** study of a particular topic at a particular time, i.e. a 'snapshot'.
**longitudinal study:** study of a particular topic over an extended period of time.

---

### Research in practice 5.3

#### The UK Labour Force Survey

The Labour Force Survey (LFS) is a survey of households living at private addresses in the United Kingdom. Its purpose is to provide information on the UK labour market which can then be used to develop, manage, evaluate and report on labour market policies. The survey is managed by the Office for National Statistics in Great Britain and by the Central Survey Unit of the Department of Finance and Personnel in Northern Ireland on behalf of the Department of Enterprise, Trade and Investment (DETINI).

Since 1992, the LFS in Great Britain has run as a quarterly survey (1994–95 for Northern Ireland). The quarterly surveys have until spring 2006 operated on a seasonal quarterly basis. However, mostly due to a European Union requirement, in May 2006 the LFS moved to calendar quarters. The 2006–7 data is the first set of HSE data based on the LFS to be affected by this change.

The LFS is intended to be representative of the whole population of the United Kingdom, and the sample design currently consists of around 41,000 responding households in every quarter. The quarterly survey has a panel design whereby households stay in the sample for five consecutive quarters (or waves), with a fifth of the sample replaced each quarter. Thus there is an 80% overlap in the samples for each successive survey.

An extract of the summary of the data for the United Kingdom presented in the October 2016 LFS report is given below:

- Between March to May 2016 and June to August 2016 the number of people in work and the number of unemployed people increased. The number of people not working and not seeking or available to work (economically inactive) fell.

- There were 31.81 million people in work, 106,000 more than for March to May 2016 and 560,000 more than for a year earlier.

- There were 23.23 million people working full-time, 362,000 more than for a year earlier. There were 8.58 million people working part-time, 198,000 more than for a year earlier.

- The employment rate (the proportion of people aged from 16 to 64 who were in work) was 74.5%, the joint highest since comparable records began in 1971.

- The unemployment rate was 4.9%, unchanged compared with March to May 2016 but down from 5.4% for a year earlier. The unemployment rate is the proportion of the labour force (those in work plus those unemployed) that were unemployed.

- The inactivity rate (the proportion of people aged from 16 to 64 who were economically inactive) was 21.5%, the joint lowest since comparable records began in 1971.

- Average weekly earnings for employees in Great Britain in nominal terms (that is, not adjusted for price inflation) increased by 2.3% both including and excluding bonuses compared with a year earlier.

*Source, and more details from:* https://www.ons.gov.uk/employmentandlabourmarket/peopleinwork/employmentandemployeetypes/bulletins/uklabourmarket/october2016

## 5.6    Making sure your research conclusions are believable

When your supervisor or examiner sits back and fixes you with an inscrutable gaze and asks you, 'Why should I believe your theory and/or conclusions?' you should know that all the careful thought you have put into designing your research strategy is going to pay off! All the research design sophistication in the world is of no significance unless you can say with calm authority, 'I have done all I can to ensure that my conclusions are valid'. Well, you cannot guarantee that your conclusions will be valid, but you can do all you can to limit their invalidity.

One way we have used to help people to think about the validity of their research conclusions is to perform the 'reverse test' in examining their validity. This starts with questioning the validity of the theory developed and/or conclusions in relation to the findings that gave rise to them and working backwards from there. So, the key questions are the following:

● Does the theory developed, or do the conclusions, flow logically from the findings?

● Are the summarised findings consistent with the data collected and presented?

● Is it plausible to assume that the data are such that they would have been collected by the methods stated?

● Are the methods employed those that you would expect to find in the research strategy that has been articulated?

● Is there coherence between the research strategy and the research questions and objectives?

Let's examine each of these questions in turn.

### Does the theory developed, or do the conclusions, flow logically from the findings?

You may not end your research with an overall theory. This may not be required. Even if it is not, it may be implicit in what you have written. Let's say that your overall conclusion is that the quality of service in fast food restaurants is the result of effective staff supervision. This sounds reasonable enough. But one of your key conclusions may be that restaurants with high levels of consumer satisfaction reported in consumer surveys are those that have the most experienced supervisory staff, as measured by length of service. Does it necessarily follow that service quality is the result of effective staff supervision? Here you are equating 'length of supervisor service' with 'effective staff supervision'. It may be a valid assumption if those ineffective supervisors have been weeded out and only effective supervisors remain. But you cannot assume it.

### Are the summarised findings consistent with the data collected and presented?

Your presentation of data may lean heavily towards lots of tables and graphs depicting the quantitative data, which you have collected. If this is so, the findings about data representing consumer satisfaction and length of supervisor service must be correlated by the restaurant to support the findings that suggest a link between the two. This implies the need for appropriate statistical techniques, which are covered in section 7.3. In the case of qualitative data, the need for a clear relationship between data and findings suggests the need for skilful and convincing argument. This will ensure that the findings are supported by a narrative which persuades the reader that you have the data to substantiate the findings.

### *Is it plausible to assume that the data is such that they would have been collected by the methods stated?*

Overstatement is a sin punishable by failure! This is particularly an issue with regard to qualitative data collection. For example, it is easy to fall into the trap of making extravagant claims about the data collected when it is based on a very small number of interviews. Let's go back to the example of effective supervision in fast food restaurants. If you have made claims for this as one of your findings, it does raise questions such as 'What is effective supervision in this context?' 'What methods were used to assess the extent to which it is practised?' It is difficult to see how a small number of interviews would enable you to collect data on effective supervision. Some first-hand observation may be required. But even if interviewees are used, it raises questions such as 'Who was interviewed?' 'What were the interviewees asked?' and 'Did the interviewees have sufficient knowledge to be able to answer the questions credibly?'

### *Are the methods employed those that you would expect to find in the research strategy that has been articulated?*

So, you have said in the early part of your research methodology chapter that you are going to pursue a piece of qualitative research using the inductive approach. When your readers look at what you have done, or what you propose to do, they see quantitative questionnaire data or results based on tightly structured observation. This does not mean that what you have done in employing these methods is wrong. But it does suggest presentational incoherence and, worse, muddled thinking.

### *Is there coherence between the research strategy and the research questions and objectives?*

This is the fundamental question and underpins all of this chapter's content. It is a question of 'fit for purpose'. In this case, the purpose is 'credible research findings and conclusions'. If the consumers of your research cannot have faith in what you have said, then what you have done will be of poor quality and questionable utility. So, the question becomes 'Which research strategy will enable me to answer my research questions and meet my research objectives in a way which will yield results that can be depended upon?'

### *Validity and reliability: what is the difference between the two?*

Above, we use the term 'validity' in relation to the credibility of research findings and conclusions. It is an important concept in designing a research strategy. So is reliability. We now explain what we mean by these terms and what practical dangers exist in research strategy design which may threaten the credibility of your research.

## Validity

Put at its simplest, **validity** is concerned with whether the findings are really about what they appear to be about. Obviously, it is a crucial factor in research strategy design. This is because any research can be affected by different kinds of factors which can render your findings invalid. The practical message here is that you must eliminate all factors that threaten the validity of the research. The principal factors are listed in Table 5.1.

**Table 5.1** Principal factors which threaten the validity of research findings and conclusions

| Factor | Refers to |
| --- | --- |
| Subject selection | The biases that may result in selection of particular research subjects which may be unrepresentative of the research population. |
| History | Specific events which occur in the history of the project (for example, between first and second phases of the research) which have an important effect on findings. |
| Testing | Any effects that the data collection process itself may have on the subjects (e.g. participants keen to impress the interviewer). |
| Mortality | The loss of subjects during the research: this is a particularly important issue for the conduct of longitudinal research. |
| Ambiguity about causal direction | Confusion over the direction in which the flow of cause and effect runs: for example, are poor call centre operator performance ratings caused by a negative attitude towards the way their performance was rated, or were the poor ratings causing the negative attitude? |

Table 5.1 refers to 'internal' validity. Another type of validity is 'external' validity. This refers to the extent to which your conclusions are generalisable to other research settings. So, for example, if your research is set in one organisation, there is obviously a question about the degree to which your conclusions are generalisable to other organisations. The simple response to this possible problem is to increase the number of organisations in which you are conducting your research. However, your concern may not be to produce a theory that is generalisable to all populations but to try and explain what is going on in your particular research setting. This is fine, providing that you do not claim that your results, conclusions or theory can be generalised.

> **Definition**
>
> **validity:** extent to which (a) data collection method or methods accurately measure what they were intended to measure and (b) the research findings are really about what they profess to be about.

## Reliability

If your research is to be reliable, it must employ data collection methods and analysis procedures which produce consistent findings. Such consistency refers to the degree to which:

- the measures you use will produce the same results if used on other occasions;
- other researchers, when using the same methods and procedures in the same way, will produce similar results;
- those interpreting your research can see clearly how you came to your conclusions from the data you collected.

As with validity, there are factors which threaten the **reliability** of your research findings and conclusions. These are listed in Table 5.2.

**Table 5.2** Principal factors which threaten the reliability of research findings and conclusions

| Factor | Refers to |
| --- | --- |
| Subject error | Measurement which may take place at different times: for example, a questionnaire administered to night-shift workers may produce significantly different results to day-shift workers. |
| Subject bias | Research subjects giving you unreliable information because they think that telling the truth may, for example, show them in a bad light. |
| Observer error | The way in which different researchers may, for example, ask the same questions in different ways, thus biasing the results. |
| Observer bias | The way in which different researchers may interpret the same data in different ways, thus biasing the findings and conclusions. |

### Definition

**reliability:** extent to which data collection methods and analysis procedures will produce consistent findings.

## Summary

- Considering your research philosophy helps you to 'think about thinking'.
- The main research philosophies are positivism, critical realism, interpretivism, post-modernism and pragmatism.
- The principal approaches to theory development are deduction, induction and abduction.
- Three main purposes of research are exploratory, descriptive and explanatory.
- The main types of research strategy are experiment, survey, case study, action research, grounded theory, ethnography, archival and narrative inquiry.

- There can be significant advantages in combining methods in research design.
- Research studies may be cross-sectional or longitudinal, or combine an element of both.
- Applying the 'reverse test' to the main theory and/or conclusions of the research report is a way of thinking about the research's credibility.
- There are a variety of threats to research validity and reliability which need to be controlled.

## Thinking about your research design

→ Look again at the material on deduction induction and abduction in this chapter. Which of these approaches do you feel (a) appeals to you most, and (b) fits your research question(s) and objectives?

→ Go back to your research question(s) and objectives and think about which of the research strategies is most appropriate. Look again at any studies which are similar to yours and see which strategies they have used and the reasons the authors have given for their choice.

→ Think of your methodological choices. In what way may you combine different research methods in your study? What advantages may there be in using multiple or mixed methods?

→ How might longitudinal and/or cross-sectional time dimensions be used in your design?

→ Make a note of all the threats to reliability and validity contained in your research design.

## References

Barclaycard (2016). The emergence of 'serial returners' – online shoppers who habitually over order and take advantage of free returns – hinders growth of UK businesses. Available at: https://www.home.barclaycard/media-centre/press-releases/emergence-of-serial-returners-hinders-growth-of-UK-businesses.html [Accessed 20 October 2016].

Beynon, H. (1973). *Working for Ford*. London: Allen Lane.

Corbin, J. and Strauss, A. (2008). *Basics of Qualitative Research: Techniques and Procedures for Developing Grounded Theory*, (3rd ed.). London: Sage.

Office for National Statistics (2016). *Labour Force Survey*. Available at: https://www.ons.gov.uk/employmentandlabourmarket/peopleinwork/employmentandemployeetypes/bulletins/uklabourmarket/october2016 [Accessed 20 October 2016].

Saunders, M., Lewis, P. and Thornhill, A. (2016) *Research Methods for Business Students* (7th ed.). Harlow: Pearson Education.

Van Maanen, J., Sørensen, J.B. and Mitchell, T.R. (2007). The interplay between theory and method. *Academy of Management Review*, 32(4), 1145–54.

# Chapter 6

# Collecting data

## 6.1  Why you should read this chapter

You may be thinking, 'I don't need to read this chapter' or 'I can read this chapter later when I need to collect my data'. It might be, as we mentioned in Chapter 4, that your university expects you to use only secondary data for your project and so you feel there is little point in reading this chapter. Alternatively, your university may only require you to write an extended essay or literature review, and so you believe reading a chapter on collecting data will be of limited, if any, use. Or, you might be thinking that, as you have only just started reviewing the literature for your project, it is too early to start learning about collecting data. However, if you are thinking that you don't need to read this chapter on collecting data now, this is not the case.

To assess the suitability of secondary data for your own research project, you need to understand the methods that were used to collect it (section 4.5). Even if your project is an extended essay or literature review, you still need to read this chapter and learn about different methods of collecting data as early as possible. Without this knowledge, you will not be able to evaluate fully the journal articles, reports and book chapters you review (section 2.6). This will reduce your ability to assess the quality of the data used. It will also lessen your ability to evaluate the quality of the findings and conclusions. Even if you are not collecting your own data, you need to know about methods for collecting data. This will help you to infer the quality of potential secondary data for your project, the quality of research reported in the literature you read and the value of both to your own project.

The overall purpose of this chapter is to enable you to answer the question 'Do these data enable the research question to be answered?' By being able to answer this question, you will be able to do the following:

- Assess the value of secondary data to meeting your own research question and objectives.

- Assess the suitability of data used in research you read about in the literature and form judgements about the quality of that research.
- Ensure that you use appropriate data collection methods to collect data to meet your own research question and objectives.

In this chapter, we start by talking about different ways of selecting samples from which data will be collected. We then discuss how particular methods are suited to collecting different sorts of data, considering three frequently used methods of collecting primary data in more detail. In this we look at how to design and distribute questionnaires, including the use of Internet questionnaires; how to design and conduct face-to-face, telephone and Internet-mediated interviews; and how to undertake structured and unstructured observations.

## 6.2 Selecting samples

Throughout your life, you have been selecting samples. Before you download a whole album of songs from iTunes or purchase an MP3 download from Amazon, you will probably listen to one or two tracks from that album to see if you like them. When you were applying to your university for your course, you probably listened to opinions from some current students and lecturers about that course before making your application. You were basing your decision to purchase on feelings after listening to a few rather than all of the tracks on the album, and your decision to apply on the opinions of some rather than all students and lecturers for that course. Each of your decisions was based on a **sample** (sub-group) of the **population** (complete set) that was likely to be available to you. Yet it is unlikely that you spent much time considering your reasons for using these samples rather than different samples, or even the whole population. You also probably did not spend much time thinking about whether the sample you selected was the most appropriate to help you make your decision. These aspects are crucial for all research projects. You need to consider the appropriateness of the sample used in each research article or report you read in relation to the research question being answered. You also need to do this whether you are assessing the usefulness of secondary data, or planning how to collect your own data to answer your own research question. In this section, we look briefly at reasons for selecting a sample rather than collecting data from the whole population, before talking about different ways of selecting samples and their use.

---

**Definitions**

**sample:** a sub-group of all group members or the whole population. The sub-group need not necessarily be a subset of people or employees: it can, for example, be a subset of organisations, places or some of the tracks listed for a music CD.

**population:** the complete set of group members. The population need not necessarily be people or employees: it can, for example, be organisations, places or the complete track listing for a music CD.

# Reasons for selecting samples

Researchers usually collect data from a sample rather than the whole population simply because it is not practicable to collect data from the whole population. This may be because you do not know what the whole population is, because it is difficult to make contact with the whole population or because time or financial constraints prevent you from collecting data from the whole population. However, you should not assume that collecting data from the whole population is always better than just collecting data from a sample.

You have a fixed amount of time to complete your research project because of the submission deadline and your need to complete other work for your course. Within the time you give to your research project, you may have to collect your own data. This means that, like other researchers, if you spend a long time collecting data from a large population, you will have less time to work on the other parts of your project report. Collecting data from a sample of this population will give you more time for the other parts of your project. Some of this time can even be used to test that the methods you use to collect the data will work, providing you collect precisely the data you need to answer your research question and meet your objectives.

# Ways of selecting samples

The way a sample is selected depends, at least in part, on the research question being answered and whether or not you know what the total population is and can get a full list of all its members. This complete list of the population's members is called the **sampling frame**. Let's say an organisation you work for has asked you to use data collected from a sample of all their employees to answer questions that relate to their employees. Your organisation is able to give you a list of all these employees, using their payroll system. Not surprisingly, this list is up to date and complete as employees are keen to ensure they are paid. Using data you collect from the sample selected from this list, you will, providing your sample is selected at random, be able to statistically estimate answers to questions for all employees. This is called using the sample to make statistical inferences about the population. In contrast, it is unlikely that you will get a full list of a supermarket's customers. While the supermarket will record names and contact details of those who have a loyalty card, this includes only some of their customers. In addition, even if you work for the supermarket, it is unlikely that you, as a student, will be given access to the list of loyalty card customers for both commercial and data protection reasons. Consequently, you will, as we discuss later, have to select the sample in a different way.

---

**Definition**

**sampling frame:** complete list of all members of the population. You select the sample from this list when using probability sampling.

For populations where you are able to obtain a complete list, such as an organisation's employees, you can select your sample using one or more sampling techniques that use '**probability sampling**' (Table 6.1). Because you have a complete list, you can select employees at random from your list. You can therefore state the statistical chance or probability that each of these employees has of being selected for your sample from this list. If your complete list contains 200 employees and you select a sample of 100 employees using a probability sampling technique, then, as the sample is selected at random, each employee has a 50% chance of being selected. If you select 50 employees from your complete list of 200 employees using a probability sampling technique, then each employee has a 25% chance of being selected. Providing you have selected your sample using a probability sampling technique, your sample will represent your population statistically, and so you will be able to make statistical inferences about the population. The level of certainty – also known as confidence – with which you can say your sample represents your population and the accuracy of any estimates you make are dependent upon the size of your sample and of your population. Researchers normally work to a 95% level of certainty with a margin of error of plus or minus 5%, or of plus or minus 2%. For a population of 200 employees, you would need to collect data from a sample of 132 employees to be 95% certain that your sample represented that population statistically with a margin of error of 5% (Table 6.2). As you can see in this table, the larger the sample, the more certain you can be that it represents the population precisely. You therefore need to collect data from as large a sample as possible. Like all researchers, you will need to select a probability sample if you want to statistically estimate the characteristics of the population. When you read section 7.3, you will discover that statistical tests also require a sample of at least a certain size to minimise spurious results. In general, this means your data needs to be collected from a probability sample of at least thirty respondents.

Table 6.1  Probability and non-probability sampling techniques

| Probability | Non-probability |
| --- | --- |
| Simple random sampling | Quota sampling |
| Systematic random sampling | Purposive sampling |
| Stratified random sampling | Volunteer sampling |
| | Convenience sampling |

Definition

**probability sampling:** variety of sampling techniques for selecting a sample at random from a complete list of the population. Because you have a complete list and select at random, you know the chance or probability of each member of your population being selected.

Table 6.2 Probability sample sizes required for a 95% confidence level with a 5% margin of error

| Population size | Sample size | Population size | Sample size |
| --- | --- | --- | --- |
| 50 | 44 | 500 | 217 |
| 100 | 79 | 1,000 | 278 |
| 150 | 108 | 5,000 | 357 |
| 200 | 132 | 10,000 | 370 |
| 250 | 151 | 100,000 | 383 |

*Source:* Saunders et al. (2016).

Often the data we and other researchers require cannot be collected using a probability sample. Let's look at your supermarket customers again. As you cannot get a complete list of customers, you do not know how many there are and so will not be able to work out the chance of each customer being selected for your sample. You will therefore have to use one or more of a different group of sampling techniques that do not require a complete list of the population. These are called '**non-probability sampling**' techniques (Table 6.1) and, if you select your sample using these, you cannot say it represents your population statistically. Consequently, you will not be able to make statistical inferences from your data. Rather, you will be normally be using your judgement to select a sample that best enables your research question to be answered. Non-probability samples are often used in conjunction with qualitative data collection techniques such as semi-structured interviews and unstructured observation.

As you read section 6.4, you will discover that, other than for quota samples (normally used with quantitative data collection techniques such as questionnaires), these techniques usually require smaller samples. The actual sample size when collecting qualitative data will also depend in part on your research question. While for some research questions such as those asking whether something exists or requiring a single illustrative exemplar, a sample of one may be sufficient. However, for most research projects, a larger sample will be needed. Following an analysis of the number of interviews used in research published in top organisation and workplace journals, Mark and a colleague noted that while between 15 and 60 interviews are likely to be considered sufficient, the actual number of interviews is dependent on the research purpose and the nature of data collected (Saunders and Townsend, 2016). However, this range refers to research that has been published in top journals, not student projects, and it is unlikely you will have time to undertake so many interviews. Building on advice of others, we therefore

| Definition |
| --- |

**non-probability sampling:** a variety of sampling techniques for selecting a sample when you do not have a complete list of the population. Because you do not have a complete list of the population, you cannot select your sample from this population at random. This also means you do not know the chance or probability of each member of your population being selected.

suggest for questions requiring a sample selected from a population that is homogeneous (similar), such as male UK-born business studies students aged 21 at your university, a non-probability sample size of between 4 and 12 participants is likely to be
sufficient. In contrast, where questions need a sample selected from a heterogeneous
(more varied) populations, such as male and female students of all ages studying any
programme at your university, the sample size is likely to be larger, say between 12 and 30
(Saunders 2011).

## Probability sampling techniques

Having given you a general overview of the difference between probability and non-
probability sampling techniques, let's look first at the probability sampling techniques
listed in Table 6.1 in more detail.

### Simple random sampling

If you have ever bought a lottery ticket, you will have experienced the results of **simple
random sampling**. Simple random sampling uses a series of random numbers, such as
those generated by the =RAND function in Microsoft Excel, to select a sample of members from a population. Like the lottery balls, each member of the population in your
list (sampling frame) is given a unique number. Random numbers are then used to
select the numbers of those members of your population from the sampling frame who
will be in your sample.

Five sets of numbers drawn at random recently for the United Kingdom's National
Lottery Lotto game (selected from the numbers 1 through 59) are:

| | | | | | |
|---|---|---|---|---|---|
| 14 | 16 | 23 | 24 | 25 | 57 |
| 4 | 15 | 19 | 44 | 45 | 49 |
| 20 | 21 | 22 | 24 | 27 | 50 |
| 4 | 10 | 18 | 41 | 42 | 47 |
| 11 | 30 | 38 | 45 | 46 | 49 |

Although each draw of six numbers has been selected at random, you can see that these
numbers are not spread evenly between 1 and 59. Rather, some numbers (such as 23, 24
and 25 in the first draw) are close together and then there are large gaps (for example, 25
and 57 in the first draw). This is a property of random numbers that often occurs when
you use them to select a sample of less than a few hundred members. It means that
researchers, including you, should not use simple random sampling to select a sample
of less than a few hundred if your sampling frame has been sorted in some way. For
example, if your sampling frame is sorted in order of employees' seniority, although

> **Definition**
>
> **simple random sampling:** type of probability sampling in which each member of the population has
> an equal chance of being selected at random and included in the sample. Each member is usually
> selected using random numbers.

your sample of employees will have been selected at random, the occurrence of random patterns such as those illustrated by the five lottery draws may mean that certain levels of seniority in your population are underrepresented and others are overrepresented.

## Systematic sampling

For a **systematic sample**, members of the sample are selected from the sampling frame at regular intervals. To ensure your sample is entirely random, your first sample member is selected using a random number before subsequent members of your sample are selected systematically. If we return to the example of an organisation's employees and the sampling frame that you got from payroll, we can see how this sampling technique works. The list you have been given by payroll is in descending order of salary, the organisation's chief executive being listed first, followed by the most senior managers. The last employee on your list is a newly appointed school leaver who earns the lowest salary. To select a sample of one-fifth of employees (20%), you need to perform the following steps:

1  Select your first employee from the sampling frame at random using a random number, between one and five for a 20% sample, in this example employee number two.

2  As your sample is a fifth (20%) of employees, you then select the 7th, 12th, 17th, 22nd and 27th employee in your sampling frame, continuing to select every fifth employee until you reach the end of the list.

By selecting the first sample employee using a random number, the rest of your sample will also have been selected at random. This technique works well, providing there are no regular patterns in the sampling frame. Let's say your sampling frame consists of UK Premier League football club first-team players who started the match for their team last Saturday. These players are listed in your sampling frame by team starting with the captain of each team, and ending with the goalkeeper. If you were to select a sample of 1 in 11 players (approximately 9%) and the first player you selected at random was the 11th player, then you would subsequently select the 22nd, 33rd, 44th and 55th player until you reached the end of your list. However, your sample would consist entirely of goalkeepers! Providing there are no regular patterns in your sampling frame, this technique usually works well and also has the advantage of being relatively easy to explain.

## Stratified random sampling

Not surprisingly, given its name, **stratified random sampling** is a modified version of random sampling. When using this sampling technique, the sampling frame is divided

---

### Definitions

**systematic sampling:** type of probability sampling in which the first sample member is selected from the sampling frame at random, using a random number. Remaining sample members are selected subsequently at regular intervals from the sampling frame.

**stratified random sampling:** type of probability sampling, in which the sampling frame is first divided into relevant strata. Sample members are then selected at random from within each stratum, using either simple random or systematic random sampling.

into strata or layers that are relevant to your research question, your sample being selected separately from each stratum or layer using either simple random sampling or systematic sampling. Let's say you are selecting a sample of web-based customers for a small web-based retailer, using their complete list of customers as your sampling frame. This alphabetical list includes each customer's name and their postal region (United Kingdom, mainland Europe, North America, rest of the world). You therefore perform the following steps:

1  Split your sampling frame into relevant separate strata or groups (using the four separate postal regions as your strata).

2  Select a random sample from within each stratum or group using either:

   (a)  simple random; or

   (b)  systematic sampling.

By doing this, each postal region or stratum will be represented in the same proportion in your sample as they are in your complete population.

### 🔵 Non-probability sampling techniques

As you read at the start of this section, researchers, including you, are often unable to obtain a list of their population. This means that probability sampling cannot be used as there is no sampling frame. Fortunately, there are a variety of non-probability sampling techniques that can be used. We will now look at those we listed in Table 6.1.

#### *Quota sampling*

You have probably been selected for a **quota sample** at some time in your life. Sometimes when you are shopping, a person with a clipboard asks you if you would be willing to answer a few questions. If you answer 'Yes', the next question you are asked is something like, 'Which one of the following age groups are you in?' after which a number of different age groups are read out to you. This is often followed by a question about your occupation or, perhaps, the newspaper you read (which may be used to indicate your social class). The person asking the questions (interviewer) has been given a number or quota of people to interview, such as '3 working class males aged 25–55' and '2 female students aged 24 or under', and so on. If the interviewer has already filled the quota for the group your answers place you in, you will not be asked any further questions. However, if the interviewer continues to ask you questions from the questionnaire, you will become part of the quota.

Quota samples are used as a substitute for a probability sample to select participants when a sampling frame is not available. This means the sample size is similar to those

---

**Definition**

**quota sampling:** type of non-probability sampling that ensures the sample selected represents certain characteristics in the population that the researcher has chosen.

used for probability samples (Table 6.1), and the data are likely to be analysed using statistical techniques (section 7.3). However, while data used to be collected from the sample by a team of interviewers, each of whom has a quota to fill, this is becoming less common. Rather, as you will read in Research in practice 6.1, the quota samples used by large commercial polling organisations are increasingly selected from an online panel of volunteers, who then agree to take part in answering questions online.

## Research in practice 6.1

### Quota sampling

As a major polling organisation, YouGov conducts online polls about politics, brands and consumer trends. The sample for each poll it conducts is selected from a diverse panel of over five million volunteers from across 38 countries, including over 800,000 in the United Kingdom. YouGov has selected their panel of registered volunteers to represent all groups in society, although not in the same proportions as in the population as a whole. For each poll, an active sample is selected, made up of a number of demographic groups. These groups are specified in much the same way as a quota sample group would be, using data such as volunteers' age, gender, social class and region where they live. This method of sampling is closer to quota sampling than random sampling, email invitations to take part being sent to those who are selected for the active sample. Those who actually take part form part of the responses for a particular demographic group, answering the questions online.

*Source*: Developed from YouGov (2016).

### Purposive sampling

**Purposive sampling** is the most frequently used form of non-probability sampling. It is used particularly to select a small sample when collecting qualitative data. When a researcher selects a purposive sample, the researcher is using their judgement to actively choose those who will best be able to help answer the research question and meet the objectives. Some of the population will have a chance of being chosen by the researcher while others will not.

Let's say you have read a journal article where the researcher has selected two major banks to explore the performance of individual banks after the global financial crisis of 2007–8. These two banks have been selected purposively because they represent the extremes of what happened to banks in one country. The bank at one extreme was nationalised by the government; the bank at the other extreme received no support from the government. The author of the article argues that, when contrasting the

### Definition

**purposive sampling:** type of non-probability sampling in which the researcher's judgement is used to select the sample members based on a range of possible reasons and premises.

findings from these extreme cases, differences will be more obvious and that her findings are relevant in understanding or explaining the performance of other banks. On reading the article, you feel this is an appropriate reason for selecting the sample, which allows her research question to be answered fully. You also feel the generalisations she has made about other banks' performance on which the impact has been less extreme are logical.

You use purposive sampling when you need to understand what is happening so you can make logical generalisations. This means that you, like other researchers who select a purposive sample, need to explain clearly the criteria you have used to select your sample, the reasons for this and the underlying premise on which these are based. Your selection can involve a variety of different purposive sampling techniques, which we have summarised in Table 6.3, along with reasons why you might use them and the underlying premises on which your reasons are based.

**Table 6.3** Varieties of purposive sampling

| Purposive sampling variety | Reasons for use | Underlying premise |
| --- | --- | --- |
| **Typical case** | Sample will be illustrative and considered representative, albeit not statistically. | Sample is typical of the population. |
| **Critical case** | Sample will either make a point dramatically or be crucial to addressing the research aim and objectives. | Topic of interest is most likely to occur in the sample selected, or sample selected is essential to the operation of the process. |
| **Extreme case** | Sample consisting of unusual or special participants will enable you to find out the most. | Findings from extreme cases will be relevant in understanding or explaining more typical cases. |
| **Heterogeneous** | Sample will have sufficiently diverse characteristics to provide the maximum variation possible in the data collected. | Any patterns that emerge are likely to be of particular interest and value, representing key themes. |
| **Homogeneous** | Sample consisting of one particular sub-group will provide minimum variation in possible data collected. | Will allow characteristics to be explored in greater depth and minor differences to be more apparent. |

## Volunteer sampling

**Volunteer sampling** is when potential sample members are either volunteered by someone else or volunteer themselves to take part in the research. It is used particularly when potential sample members are either difficult to identify of difficult to reach.

**Definition**

volunteer sampling: type of non-probability sampling in which the potential sample member either volunteers or is volunteered to be a sample member.

**Snowball sampling** is used when it is difficult to identify members of your population. Let's say that you wish to research people who are working in the informal economy while claiming welfare and unemployment benefits. As these people are difficult to reach, snowball sampling may provide the only possibility for finding potential participants. Alternatively, your population may be like chief executives of Fortune 500 companies, easy to identify but difficult to access. Once again, by using snowball sampling, you may be able to reach such people. To obtain your snowball sample of chief executives of Fortune 500 companies, you would need to do the following:

1 Make contact and collect data from an initial chief executive of a Fortune 500 company.

2 Use the initial chief executive to identify and volunteer a number of other chief executives of Fortune 500 companies and to support your gaining access.

3 Use these chief executives to identify and volunteer further chief executives of Fortune 500 companies and to support your gaining access, so the sample increases in size like a snowball that is rolled.

Remember, those who are volunteered for a snowball sample are most likely to identify and volunteer others who are similar to themselves, resulting in a homogeneous sample.

In contrast, if you ask your sample members to identify and volunteer themselves, say, by putting an advertisement in appropriate media inviting them to take part in your research, you are using **self-selection sampling**. Increasingly, researchers are inviting potential participants using a variety of electronic media such as intranets, blogs and bulletin boards alongside invitations through general letters or all user emails (Saunders, 2011). However, when using self-selection sampling, you need to be careful. Those who self-select and volunteer to be members of your sample often do so because they have strong feelings or opinions about your research topic and consider it sufficiently important or interesting to give it some of their time. This means they are likely to be different from people who do not offer to be involved in some way and so are not representative of the population.

---

**Definitions**

**snowball sampling:** type of non-probability sampling in which, after the first sample member, subsequent members are identified and volunteered by earlier sample members.

**self-selection sampling:** type of non-probability sampling in which possible sample members are asked to identify themselves and volunteer to take part in the research.

**convenience sampling:** type of non-probability sampling in which the sample the researcher uses is those who are easy to obtain rather than because of their appropriateness.

---

## Convenience sampling

The last variety of non-probability sampling which we talk about, **convenience sampling**, is rarely used by researchers and is one, we hope, you will not use for your own research! It simply involves 'using' ('selecting' is too positive a word!) those who are easiest to get hold of for your sample. Say you have to find out managers' views about something. We know you won't do this, but let's pretend that you decide to collect your data from part-time students in your class. These people are only in your sample because of the ease of getting hold of them and have little, if any, relevance to your research. Like most convenience samples, they are likely to be of limited use in answering your research question and meeting your objectives.

## 6.3    Collecting data using questionnaires

**Questionnaires** are used widely to collect data, and we have no doubt that you have completed questionnaires and used data that were collected by questionnaires. Your lecturers will have asked you to complete module evaluation questionnaires so they can find out your, and your classmates', opinions about their modules. You will also have used the results of questionnaires in your assignments, discussing journal articles in which research findings were based on data collected by questionnaires.

The term 'questionnaire' refers to all methods of data collection in which each potential **respondent** is asked to answer the same set of questions in the same order. It therefore includes questionnaires that are used to collect data:

- by the Internet, each respondent reading the questions and recording their own answers;
- by post, each respondent reading the questions and recording their own answers;
- by hand, each respondent reading the questions and recording their own answers;
- by telephone, where an interviewer also records each respondent's answers;
- face to face, where an interviewer also records each respondent's answers.

When a questionnaire is used by an interviewer to collect data, it is often called a **structured interview**.

Questionnaires are a good method for collecting data about the same things from large numbers of respondents. Questionnaires allow you to ask the same set of standardised questions to a large number of respondents. Because the questions are standardised, the data collected by questionnaires are often used either for descriptive research, such as students' opinions of a module they have just taken, or for explanatory research

### Definitions

**questionnaire:** general term that includes all methods of data collection in which each person is asked to answer the same set of questions in the same order. Questionnaires can be distributed face to face by an interviewer, by telephone, by hand, by post and using the Internet.

**respondent:** person who answers the questions in a questionnaire.

**structured interview:** method of data collection using a questionnaire in which each person is asked the same set of questions in the same order by an interviewer who also records the responses.

to test a theory. These data are usually analysed statistically (section 7.3). Let's say you have a theory that the more time students spend working on their projects, the more they will enjoy the work. In explanatory research, you use the data you collect to examine and explain such relationships statistically: in our example, to see whether or not students' enjoyment of their work is statistically related to the amount of time they spend working on their projects.

In this section, we will look at how to:

1  design individual questions;

2  design the questionnaire;

3  write the covering letter or email;

4  conduct pilot testing;

5  distribute the questionnaire to a sample of potential respondents using each of the distribution methods listed above.

## How to design questions

A questionnaire is useful only if:

- it collects data that are needed to answer the research question and meet the objectives;

- it collects data from a large enough number of respondents to answer the research question and meet the objectives;

- the questions asked are understood and interpreted by respondents in the way the researcher wanted them to be understood and interpreted.

This means you need to be very clear about the data you need to collect and to design your questions to collect these data, minimising the chances of questions being misinterpreted. In making sure that your questions (and so your questionnaire) will provide you with enough data to answer your research question and meet all your objectives, you are ensuring what researchers call 'content validity'. By designing your questions carefully and ensuring that they actually collect data about what you intend them to measure rather than something different, you are ensuring what researchers call 'construct validity'. When you are reading about other researchers' research that has used questionnaires, you will need to look at the actual questions that were asked to see if they are valid. This will allow you to better understand and assess the conclusions these researchers reached, based on the answers their respondents gave to these questions.

---

### Definitions

**content validity:** the extent to which a data collection tool, such as a questionnaire, provides enough data to answer the research question and meet all the objectives.

**construct validity:** the extent to which the questions asked actually collect data about what they are intended to measure.

When you design your questionnaire, your first stage will be to design individual questions to collect the data you need to answer your research question and meet your objectives (Ekinci, 2015). When you do this, you can:

- use questions from other researchers' questionnaires (providing you reference the source and obtain permission where necessary);
- adapt questions from other researchers' questionnaires (providing you explain how you adapted them, reference the source and obtain permission where necessary);
- design your own questions.

However, before you decide to use someone else's questions, beware. There are a lot of poor questions and badly designed questionnaires available! You also need to be certain of the wording of each question will be suitable for your intended respondents and the context in which they will complete the questionnaire. If your questions are going to be answered only by accountants, you will be able to use far more specialist language than if they are going to be answered by people in general.

Saunders et al. (2016) highlight seven types of question that can be used in questionnaires. These are listed in Table 6.4, along with a brief description of when to use them and examples.

Table 6.4 Types of question for use in questionnaires

| Type | Use when . . . | Examples |
|------|----------------|----------|
| **Open** | . . . unsure of the response, require a detailed answer, or want to find out what is uppermost in respondent's mind. | If there are any other areas or issues that concern you, please feel free to comment below*<br><br>What do you like most about visiting this theme park? |
| **List** | . . . you need to be sure the respondent has considered all possible answers. | Which of the following fruit juices have you purchased in the past week?<br>[please tick ✓ all appropriate boxes]<br>Apple ☐<br>Orange ☐<br>Cranberry ☐<br>Pineapple ☐<br>Tomato ☐<br>Other (please say) ......................... |
| **Category** | . . . you need to ensure the respondent's answer will only fit into one category. | Are you in receipt of a state pension?<br>(*Interviewer, listen to the respondent's answer and tick the correct box*).<br>Yes (receives state pension) ☐$_1$<br>No (does not receive state pension) ☐$_2$ |

**Table 6.4** Continued

| Type | Use when . . . | Examples |
|---|---|---|
| **Ranking** | . . . you want the respondent to place a list in rank order. | Number each of the holiday destinations listed below in order of their attractiveness to you for your next holiday. Number the most attractive holiday destination 1, the next 2 and so on. If a destination is not attractive, leave blank. <br><br> *Destinationn*    *Attractiveness* <br> England    [ ] <br> Scotland    [ ] <br> Wales    [ ] <br> Ireland    [ ] <br> France    [ ] <br> Germany    [ ] <br> Spain    [ ] <br> Holland    [ ] |
| **Rating** | . . . you want a respondent's opinion or belief. | For the following statement please tick ✓ the box that matches your opinion most closely. <br><br> *Agree*  *Tend to agree*  *Tend to disagree*  *Disagree* <br> I generally believe what my manager tells me  ☐  ☐  ☐  ☐ <br><br> How likely do you believe it is that you will pay off your overdraft within a year of graduation? <br> *Very likely*  *Quite likely*  *Not sure*  *Quite unlikely*  *Very unlikely* <br> ☐  ☐  ☐  ☐  ☐ |
| **Quantity** | . . . you want the respondent to tell you a number or amount. | How many dependent children do you have living with you? <br> [ ] [ ] <br> (*For example, for 2 write:* [ ] [ 2 ] ) |
| **Matrix** | . . . the responses to two or more questions are selected from the same set of possible answers. | The following statements ask about your feelings regarding the future of the Happy Toy Manufacturing Company. <br><br> *Strongly agree*  *Agree*  *Disagree*  *Strongly disagree* <br> I feel the future for the company is getting brighter  ☐  ☐  ☐  ☐ <br> I would be happy to spend the rest of my career at the company  ☐  ☐  ☐  ☐ |

*Some researchers would term this a 'request' rather than a 'question'.

The example questions in Table 6.4 show how the answer you get depends on the way your question is worded. Looking at the first open question, this could result in some respondents writing hundreds of words commenting about the issues that concern them, and others writing only a few words or even nothing! In contrast, the second open question asks the respondent to only answer what they like most. For all your questions, you will need to decide the data you need to answer your research question and meet your objectives and, therefore, in how much detail you want your respondents to answer. However, beware of including too many open questions; they are extremely time consuming to analyse.

Next, compare the list question and the ranking question in Table 6.4. You can see that, although the list question asks about fruit juices and the ranking question asks about holiday destinations, only the list question allows the respondent to include another response of their choice. The list question gives the respondent the option 'other (please say) . . .' while the ranking question names eight holiday destinations, giving no space for the respondent to add her or his own destination. Including the 'other (please say)' option alters the data collected, something you need to beware of both when reading about others' research and designing your own questions. This is because it allows respondents to have a free choice in how they answer rather than be constrained by the options you have given them.

Now look at the two examples of rating questions. The first of these questions has an even number of possible answers (four) while the second has an odd number of possible answers (five). By giving an even number of possible answers, you are forcing your respondents to make a choice between, in the first rating question, agreeing and disagreeing. You are not allowing them to neither agree nor disagree. In contrast, in the second example, the respondent is allowed to be 'not sure' being neither 'quite likely' nor 'quite unlikely'. Once again, this emphasises that you need to be clear about the precise questions asked, both when reading reports of others' research and when designing your own questionnaire.

Finally, look at the category question. A number in a smaller font size has been added next to each possible response: '1' next to 'yes (receives state pension)' and '2' next to 'no (does not receive state pension)'. These numbers are the codes that will be used to represent each respondent's answer on a paper questionnaire when the data are entered on a spreadsheet, such as Excel or statistical software such as IBM SPSS Statistics, for statistical analysis. Wherever possible, we suggest you add code numbers to possible question responses on paper questionnaires at the design stage. This will save you having to code the answers later! However, if you use an online survey tool, such as SurveyMonkey™ or Qualtrics™, to design your Internet questionnaire and collect your data, codes are added automatically. Once you have collected your data via the Internet, it will only take a few clicks of the mouse to download and save it as a spreadsheet file. This is far quicker than entering the data yourself; it also means your data set is less likely to contain errors!

### How to design the questionnaire

Your questionnaire should be pleasing to look at and, of equal importance, easy for respondents to read and fill in their answers. This means you need to ensure your questionnaire is easy to read and for Internet questionnaires optimised for viewing on laptops, tablets and mobile phones. You also need to tell the respondents what the questionnaire is about and why you want them to answer the questions. The order of questions needs to be logical to those answering rather than to you. Your questionnaire should be as short as possible, although you obviously need to ask enough questions to collect all the data you need to answer your own research question and meet your objectives! These design points, along with others, are listed in Table 6.5.

**Table 6.5** Points to remember when designing a questionnaire

| *Layout* | *Question order* |
| --- | --- |
| • Title should be clear and a larger font size. | • At the start, ask more straightforward questions. |
| • Introduction should be brief and explain why the topic is important and what the respondent should do. | • At the start, ask questions that are related clearly to the stated topic of the questionnaire. |
| • Questions should be displayed clearly on the page or screen. | • Ask more complex questions in the middle of the questionnaire. |
| • The typeface (font) should be easy to read. | • Group questions into sections that will be obvious to the respondent. |
| • Questions' typeface (font), font size, spacing and formatting should be consistent throughout. | • Use filter questions to stop the respondent answering questions that are not relevant. |
| • When printed, it should be on good-quality paper/card. | • Make sure the wording of questions is consistent throughout the questionnaire. |
| • Details of how to return the completed questionnaire should be given at the end. | • At the end of the questionnaire, ask personal or sensitive questions. |

If you look at Research in practice 6.2, you will see that sometimes you need to ask only a few questions. This short questionnaire is designed only to collect a limited amount of data about diners' experiences at the restaurant. Yet, despite it being short, the design includes many of the points made in Table 6.5. Starting with the layout, the questionnaire has a clear title ('How did we do?') in a larger font, which also describes the topic. The brief introduction is friendly in style and explains why ('to know what you think'), and what the respondent should do ('tell us what you think') in a little more detail. The questions do not appear squashed and are printed using the same typeface throughout. Despite this, you probably think that there is not enough space for an answer to the open question at the end. We agree with you! We are told that the questionnaire is printed on card, hopefully good quality, and that the return postal address is printed on the other side. It would also have been helpful if respondents were told there was a box for completed questionnaires to be put in, perhaps by the exit.

If you now look at the actual questions, you will see that these are both straightforward to answer and, other than the 'Date of visit', relate clearly to the stated topic. It may be that the waiter or waitress fills this in before the questionnaire is given to the customer. The first three questions are grouped as a matrix into one section and are phrased consistently: 'what was the . . . like?' However, the last open question has an error: it should say 'us' rather than 'use'. Unlike the designer of this questionnaire, you need to proofread your questionnaire very carefully, remembering that a spell check will not pick up mistypes that result in the wrong word being included.

Research in practice 6.2 does not include any sensitive questions or filter questions. Whether or not a question is sensitive will depend on what is being asked and the person who is answering it. It will therefore be a matter of judgement. Fortunately, as you

## Research in practice 6.2

### Questionnaire design

Often when you visit a restaurant, you are given a 'comment card' with your bill similar to the one below. This is usually printed on card rather than paper. After a short introduction asking you to respond, there are a few questions about your experiences in the restaurant and some space for you to add your own comments and feedback. You are then expected to either place the card in a box as you leave or, alternatively, post the card to the restaurant. The postal address is printed on the other side of the card, and usually the postage has been prepaid to encourage you to send it back.

---

#### *How did we do?*

At Mark 'n Phil's restaurant we're always keen to know what you think . . . so if you've got any comments about your visit we'd like you to tell us.

Date of visit? dd............. mmm.......... yy......

| | Excellent | Good | Average | Poor | Awful |
|---|---|---|---|---|---|
| What was the quality of your food like? | ☐ | ☐ | ☐ | ☐ | ☐ |
| What was the service you received like? | ☐ | ☐ | ☐ | ☐ | ☐ |
| What was your overall experience like? | ☐ | ☐ | ☐ | ☐ | ☐ |

If you have anything else you would like to tell us, please do so below . . .

---

will see later, this can be checked as part of pilot testing. Filter questions are used to route your respondents through your questionnaire so they miss out questions that are not relevant. Let's say you have a questionnaire that includes some questions that are only relevant to respondents who are members of a professional body. Your filter question is:

| | | | |
|---|---|---|---|
| 22. | Are you a member of a professional body? | Yes | ☐ |
| | *(If no, go to question 30)* | No | ☐ |

The following (open) question is then only answered if the respondent has answered 'yes'. It asks:

23. Please name your professional body: ........................................................

Questions 24 to 29 are also about the respondent's membership of a professional body.

If you are using an online survey tool, answering the filter question will, as far as the respondent is concerned, just take them to the next relevant question; in our example, to question 23 if they answered 'yes' and to question 30 if they answered 'no'. However, if you are using a paper questionnaire in which the respondent fills in answers, the respondent will have to find the next relevant question. Unfortunately, some respondents will not follow your filter question's instructions and will try to answer the following questions whether they are relevant or not! You therefore need to use filter questions sparingly in paper questionnaires.

## What to write in the covering letter or email

In Research in practice 6.2, the purpose of the questionnaire was only explained briefly to potential respondents. When you distribute a questionnaire by post or the web, you will need a more detailed covering letter or email to explain the purpose of your questionnaire. The structure and contents of your covering letter are summarised in Table 6.6. You will often be expected to put a copy of your covering letter and a blank questionnaire as appendices in your project report.

**Table 6.6** Structure of a covering letter or email

| Section | Contents |
| --- | --- |
| Letter/email head | Official, with a logo, address, telephone number and email address. On good-quality white paper if for a paper questionnaire. |
| Name and address of potential respondent | Use name and full postal address for personal approach if for paper, otherwise just name. |
| Date | In full, e.g. 8th July 2017. |
| Greeting | Use title and name if possible, e.g. Dear Mrs Penny. |
| Heading or email subject | Brief descriptive title of questionnaire |
| 1st paragraph | What research is about, why it is useful, how respondent's time is needed and their answers are of value. |
| 2nd paragraph | Whether responses will be confidential and/or anonymous. |
| 3rd paragraph | How results will be used. Whom to contact if there are any questions, with telephone number and/or email contact details. Explanation of how to return the questionnaire, to whom and by when. |
| Closing remarks | Thank recipient in advance for help. |
| Signature and name | Sign by hand if letter. Also put sender's title, forename and surname. |

## Why pilot testing is important

Before distributing your questionnaire to potential respondents, you need to check that it will work; that your respondents will have no problems in answering the questions and that their responses will be recorded correctly. This is important for both Internet and paper questionnaires. Even if you are really short of time, you still need to try out your questionnaire and covering letter with a small number of people who are like those who will answer it in your research. This is known as **pilot testing** and will also help to confirm that your actual respondents will understand the meaning of your questions and will be able to follow the instructions on the questionnaire. Remember, it is far easier to correct mistakes in your questionnaire at the pilot stage than to have to recollect your data because mistakes had been overlooked.

---

**Definition**

**pilot test:** trying out of a questionnaire, interview schedule or other method of data collection with a small group of respondents who are similar to those who will be used in the actual research to see if it works. Any problems that arise in the pilot test can then be sorted out before the actual research is undertaken.

---

## How to distribute the questionnaire

At the start of this section (6.3), we listed five ways in which you might distribute your questionnaire to potential respondents and so collect data from your sample. Whichever way you are using, you are trying to get as many completed questionnaires returned to you as possible. Although response rates from questionnaires vary considerably, research by Baruch and Holtom (2008) based on looking at 490 academic studies using questionnaires provides a clear indication of the rate you might expect. The average response for studies where data were collected from individuals was 52.7%, while that for questionnaires to organisations was lower, being an average of 35.7%. Studies using Internet or telephone distribution reported higher response rates than traditional paper-based questionnaire distribution.

### Distributing Internet questionnaires

Internet questionnaires are normally distributed using an email with a hyperlink to the actual questionnaire or using a link to a website that has a hyperlink to the question-naire. For the first, this means you need to have a complete and up-to-date list of your sample's email addresses. For the second, you will need to invite people to contribute and direct them to your website and your questionnaire. If you choose to do this, you must follow the general guidelines for using the Internet. This is called netiquette and means you should do the following:

- Only send emails and posting to relevant user groups.
- Remember that postings to more than 20 user groups at once are unacceptable to many web users.

- Avoid sending junk emails or spam.
- Avoid emailing multiple mail lists as this will mean some people will get more than one copy.
- Avoid using email attachments as these may be thought to contain viruses.

To distribute an Internet questionnaire, you need to observe the following:

1  Ensure the Internet questionnaire is set up in the online survey tool and works as you wish, the data set is generated automatically and that you have noted the direct hyperlink to include in your accompanying email or on your website.

2  If you are emailing potential respondents, let them know in advance that you will be emailing a hyperlink to a questionnaire or to a website that has a hyperlink to the questionnaire.

3  Email potential respondents with your covering email and the hyperlink to the questionnaire or advertise your website widely, highlighting the closing date.

4  If you are emailing potential respondents with the hyperlink, email them again a week after the questionnaire has been distributed, thanking those who have returned the questionnaire and encouraging others to respond.

### *Distributing postal, or delivery and collection questionnaires*

The distribution of postal questionnaires and delivery and collection questionnaires is very similar. As you will have worked out from their names, the only real difference is that the former is delivered and returned by post, while the latter is delivered and collected in person. To distribute a questionnaire using either of these ways, you need to observe the following steps:

1  Ensure that the questionnaires and accompanying letters are printed and the envelopes addressed.

2  Contact potential respondents to let them know in advance that you will be posting/delivering by hand a questionnaire to them.

3  Post or deliver by hand the questionnaire.

4  Contact potential respondents a week after the questionnaire is posted/delivered by hand, collecting the questionnaire (delivery and collection) or thanking those who have returned the questionnaire (postal) and encouraging others to respond.

### *Conducting telephone or face-to-face structured interviews*

The quality of your structured interviews, whether conducted using a telephone or face to face will depend on your interviewing ability. For telephone-structured interviews, the clarity and tone of voice with which you read the questionnaire questions will be crucial, while for face-to-face structured interviews, your appearance will also be important. To conduct a telephone or face-to-face structured interview using a questionnaire, you need to pay attention to the following points:

1  Ensure that the questionnaires are printed or set up in an online survey tool so that you can record responses easily.

2 Where possible and resources allow, contact potential respondents to let them know in advance that you will be telephoning/visiting them within the next week to conduct a structured interview.

3 Try to contact each potential respondent in person, noting down the date and time of contact and whether or not the structured interview took place. If you arrange an alternative appointment, note it down and visit then!

4 Try to contact each potential respondent at least twice more, each at a different time and on a different day, noting down the same information.

## 6.4 Collecting data using semi-structured or unstructured interviews

Every day of your life you read about, listen to and watch interviews. Journalists interview politicians and business leaders, chat show hosts interview celebrities of all kinds and business investors known as 'dragons' interview entrepreneurs with new business ideas. All these interviews have one thing in common: they are purposeful discussions between two or more people. Although you might argue that the purpose of some of these interviews is to entertain rather than gather data for research, they still give you a real insight into the process of asking questions and the preparation and skills you need to interview people.

In the previous section (6.3), we talked about the structured interview: when each respondent is asked the same standard questions from a questionnaire by an interviewer, either by telephone or face to face. In this section, we will look at two other forms of interview: semi-structured and unstructured interviews. These are sometimes also referred to as qualitative research interviews, the person answering your semi-structured or unstructured interview questions being called the **participant**. Like other researchers, you will find these types of interview particularly useful where you:

- wish to gather data about a particular topic;
- generate data to enable theory development;
- encourage participants to tell stories from their own perspectives;
- gain insights into indivduals' experiences or lifeworlds (Cassell, 2015).

In a **semi-structured interview**, you (or the researcher) will have a list of topics to be covered and questions to be asked, although the order in which you ask them will vary

---

**Definitions**

**participant:** the person who answers the questions in a semi-structured or unstructured interview.

**semi-structured interview:** a method of data collection in which the interviewer asks about a set of themes using some predetermined questions but varies the order in which the themes are covered and questions asked. The interviewer may choose to omit some topics and questions and ask additional questions as appropriate.

from interview to interview depending on the responses from the participant. For some semi-structured interviews, you may decide not to ask some of your questions or not to cover one or two topics if they are not relevant to that participant. You may also decide to ask additional questions to find out further details and explore your objectives in more depth or, alternatively, to check that your understanding of what the participant is telling you is correct. **Unstructured interviews** are more informal and are used to explore a general topic in which you (or the researcher) are interested in more depth. Unlike semi-structured interviews, you do not have a list of questions to ask, although you still need to be clear about the topics you wish to talk about. In unstructured interviews, you want your participants to talk openly and widely about the topic with as little direction from you as interviewer as possible. For this reason, they are sometimes called non-directive interviews.

As you have read academic journal articles, you will have found out about research that has used semi- and unstructured interviews. In many of these articles, such interviews will have been used to collect data that were analysed qualitatively (section 7.4). These data will have been used to either explore what is happening and gain new insights or describe what is happening and identify general patterns. Semi- and unstructured interviews may also have been used along with other data collection techniques. For topics where little is known, the researcher may start by using unstructured interviews to explore what is happening. Alternatively, researchers start by collecting data using a questionnaire, analyse these data statistically and then use semi-structured interviews subsequently to understand the statistical relationships their analysis has revealed.

Some years ago, we along with another colleague used a questionnaire to collect data from a manufacturing company about employees' use of and feelings about different communication methods. Our statistical analysis showed that office employees looked at the company's noticeboards to find out what was happening, while production employees rarely looked at these noticeboards. The reasons for this difference were unclear from our questionnaire data. In our subsequent semi-structured interviews with both office and production employees, we probed for reasons why this happened. The office employees did not know why. However, the production employees we interviewed all provided a compelling reason. The noticeboards were in the main entrance hall where office employees entered each day. In contrast, the production employees used a different entrance where there were no noticeboards. Not surprisingly, we recommended the company put up noticeboards at the entrance used by the production employees.

If you are going to use semi- or unstructured interviews, you need to prepare for the actual interview. As part of your preparation, you will need to be clear about the topics

| Definition |

> **unstructured interview:** a method of data collection in which the participant talks openly and widely about the topic with as little direction from the interviewer as possible. Although there is no predetermined list of questions, the interviewer will have a clear idea of the topics to explore.

you are going to cover to collect the data you need to answer your research question and meet your objectives, as well as the location of the interview and your appearance. Next, you will need to think carefully about how you might ask questions about these topics. Following a pilot interview, you will have to conduct the interviews, making sure that you test your understanding when necessary and show that you are listening at the same time as taking notes or audio-recording the conversations. We will now look at each of these.

## How to prepare for semi- and unstructured interviews

Imagine you have a meeting with an important client of the public relations company for whom you work. Before going to this meeting, you would prepare carefully. You would make sure you knew about the client you were meeting and their organisation so that you were credible. You would also think carefully about the likely conversation you would have, the questions you would ask and the likely questions you would be asked and how you would answer them. Preparing for a semi-structured or unstructured interview involves thinking about similar things. In particular, you need to pay attention to the following:

- Make sure you have found out as much as possible about the person you are going to interview and, where appropriate, the organisation where they work.
- Develop an interview guide, listing the topics you want to discuss and initial questions you will ask for each topic.
- Choose a location that is convenient for your participant, where that person will feel comfortable and you will not be disturbed.
- Make sure your clothing and appearance is appropriate for the interview.
- Work out how you will use your body language to show your interest and that you are listening attentively.

These are illustrated in Research in practice 6.3. However, as well as these, to prepare for an interview you will also need to:

- develop a consent form;
- think how you are going to record the data: if you are going to audio-record the interview, make sure that your audio recorder works, it has sufficient memory to store a day's interviews and you have spare batteries.

### Research in practice 6.3

#### Preparing for the interview

Neve was preparing to interview small business owner-managers about the impact of the new workplace pensions that had recently been introduced by the government. She had obtained permission from an organisation that represented small businesses in her university town to use of a small 'interview room' in their offices. The administrative assistant had assured her that this room would be quiet and contained a low table and two comfortable chairs. Neve prepared a notice for the room's door which said 'Interview in progress. Please do not disturb.'

Neve was pleased the room had a low table as this meant there would not be a physical barrier between her and the owner managers she was interviewing. She was more worried about the comfortable chairs as she knew that, if she sat back and relaxed, her body language might suggest she was not interested. Neve therefore decided she would lean forward attentively and ensure she maintained eye contact with each interviewee. She also thought it was important she dressed formally for the interviews as many of her participants would probably be wearing suits.

As her first interview was in a few days' time, she began to develop her interview guide:

---

**Impact of workplace pensions research**

**Introduction**

- Thank person for attending.
- Explain purpose of research and interview, emphasising that it is participant's own opinions that are important.
- Ask if willing to be interviewed and stress this is their decision.
- If willing, ask them to read and sign the consent form; if not, thank them for their time and close the interview.

**Interview**

1  To what extent have the introduction of workplace pensions impacted on your business?

   (a) *Probe*: In what ways? (ask for examples)

   (b) *Probe*: Can you give me an example (if possible) of how you think workplace pensions will benefit your business?

   (c) *Probe*: Can you give me an example (if possible) of how you think workplace pensions will cause problems for your business?

2  Do you think the government have provided sufficient guidance for small businesses regarding workplace pensions?

   (a) *Probe*: How has this guidance been provided?

   (b) *Probe* (*if insufficient guidance*): What extra guidance is needed?

---

In section 3.8 we talked about the importance of getting participants' consent for your research. Many universities expect you to ask each interview participant if they are willing to take part in the research and, if they are, to sign a consent form like that in Figure 6.1. This is important, as participants have the right to refuse to take part in your research or withdraw from the interview whenever they wish.

**Consent form**

***Title of the research project***

Researcher's name, Final year student at University of Anycity

*Please initial box*

1. I confirm that I understand what the research is about and have had the opportunity to ask questions.

2. I understand that my participation is voluntary and that I can withdraw at any time without giving a reason.

3. I agree to take part in the research.

*Please initial box*

Yes     No

4. I agree to my interview being audio recorded.

5. I agree to the use of anonymised quotations in publications.

Name of participant: ................................. Signature: .................................

Researcher's name: ................................. Signature: .................................

Date: .................................

**Figure 6.1** Participant consent form here
*Source:* Developed from Saunders et al. (2016).

As you can see from the consent form (Figure 6.1), the choice of whether or not to audio-record the interview is the participant's, not yours! Although audio recordings provide an accurate and unbiased record and allow you to listen again to the interview, if the participant does not wish you to record the interview, then you will have to rely entirely on the notes you take. This is not easy to do at the same time as interviewing, so we suggest you practise beforehand. As well as noting what the participant says, you will need to note where and when the interview was held and relevant background information about the participant. After each interview, we suggest you word-process your notes immediately. Leaving your notes for a few days means you are less likely to be able to read what you wrote!

## ◉ How to ask questions in semi- and unstructured interviews

In both semi-structured and unstructured interviews, you will have to ask questions carefully and listen attentively to answers given. As in designing a questionnaire, you will need to make sure the questions you ask are worded clearly using appropriate and unbiased language. However, unlike when using a questionnaire, you will be able to test your interpretation by summarising the response and, where necessary, asking further questions. Brinkmann and Kvale (2014) identify a number of types of questions to use in interviews. We have listed those our students have found most useful in Table 6.7, along with a brief description of when to use them, and examples.

**Table 6.7** Types of question for use in interviews

| Type | Use when . . . | Examples |
| --- | --- | --- |
| **Introductory** | . . . you are starting a new topic. | Could you tell me about . . .? |
| **Probing** | . . . you want to find out more detail, but without saying what. | Can you say a bit more about that? Could you let me have a bit more detail? |
| **Specifying** | . . . you want to find out more detail about a specific aspect already discussed. | Can you say a bit more about why you purchased a hybrid car rather than an electric car? How did you feel when your 91-year-old mother was sent home from the hospital to an empty cold house? |
| **Direct** | . . . you want answers about a topic introduced by the interviewer to apply to the participant. | Have you ever received a bonus for good performance? Have you used a consultant in the past? |
| **Indirect questions** | . . . you want answers about a topic introduced by the interviewer to apply to others. | How do other patients feel about their treatment at this hospital? |
| **Structuring** | . . . you want to show questions on a theme have been completed. | I would now like to ask you about another topic. Is that all right? |
| **Interpreting** | . . . you want to check interpretation of the participant's response is correct. | You mean that . . .? Is it correct that . . .? So what you are saying is . . .? |

If you look at Research in practice 6.4, you will see that the types of question you use and the order in which you use them depends on the responses you receive from the participant during the interview. This means that, unlike with a structured interview, it is not possible to work out all the questions you will ask or the order in which you will ask them. This makes semi-structured and unstructured interviews difficult to conduct. In the short extract in Research in practice 6.4, the interviewer (Deborah Meadon) opens the interview

## Research in practice 6.4

### Interviewing

In the BBC reality business television show *Dragons' Den,* entrepreneurs present their business ideas to a group of investors (Dragons) in the hope of getting investment capital in return for a stake in their business. After their presentations, the Dragons interview entrepreneurs about their business ideas.

In 2014 Scott Cupit asked the Dragons for an investment of £65,000 in his Swing Dance Business 'Swing Patrol'. After a swing dance-inspired presentation, he was interviewed by the five Dragons, which included the entrepreneur and investor Deborah Meadon and businessman and investor Piers Linney. An extract from a transcript of the televised interview shows some of the questions asked by Meadon and Linney and the responses from Scott Cupit.

*Meadon:* Scott, let's look at the business. I think you called yourself the biggest swing and dance school in the world. How does that turn into cash?

*Cupit:* The revenue has had a steady growth over the last five years. It started at, perhaps, 36,000 and it gone up to 84, 120, 180, 210 and the last financial period is 280 thousand. Gross profit has reached 190 thousand.

*Meadon:* And net profit?

*Cupit:* This year was 67 thousand. It's had a solid growth and all the projections are it should continue to grow.

*Linney:* So how does it work? It's like a Sumba really isn't it in terms of the model?

*Cupit:* We wouldn't pretend to be as big as Sumba because it's so massive . . .

At the end of the televised interview one of the Dragons, Meadon, agreed to an investment of £65,000 in Swing Patrol London in return for a 20% stake in the company. The entertainment brand now boasts a community of over 12,000 dance troop members and the Guinness World Record for the world's largest Charleston dance with 975 people.

Sources: *Dragons' Den* (2014), Dunsby (2016).

with the introductory question 'I think you called yourself the biggest swing and dance school in the world.' Without giving participants time to answer, this is followed with the specifying question, 'How does that turn into cash?' The participant's response, although detailed, does not provide sufficient detail about profit. A further specifying question is therefore asked: 'And net profit?' Another 'interviewer' (dragon), Peter Linney, introduces a new topic asking: 'So how does it work? It's like Sumba really isn't it in terms of the model?' Although two questions have been asked, only the second is answered. This illustrates clearly how participants often fail to answer all questions if more than one is asked at the same time. It is therefore better to only ask one question at a time.

### Why a pilot test is important

Before conducting your interview with selected participants, you need to pilot-test your interview and technique and check that your questions are likely to be understood, are not leading and will provide you with the data you need. This will give you an idea of possible problems with questions as well as how long each interview is likely to take. You also need to be sure that your audio recorder works properly, or you can take sufficient notes while interviewing. This is important for both semi-structured and unstructured interviews. Even if you are really short of time, you still need to pilot-test your interview with a small number of people who are like those who will be participating in your research. It is worth remembering that, unlike with questionnaires, it may be possible to partially overcome mistakes made in early interviews, such as missing out a topic that later appears to be important, by amending later interviews.

### How to conduct semi- and unstructured interviews

Semi-structured and unstructured interviews can be conducted face to face, by telephone or Internet-mediated using email, messaging software such as Messenger™, web conferencing or video chat apps such as Skype™ and Facetime™. For such interviews, the crucial issue is the number of participants you will need to interview to answer your research question. This depends on the nature of your research question and your population. Many texts recommend you establish the number of interviews you need inductively, simply continuing to conduct interviews until **data saturation** is reached, that is, until each additional interview provides no new insights. While this is good advice, it is not particularly helpful when you are assessing research undertaken by others using semi-structured and unstructured interviews, particularly as, for the former, this is not always stated in journal articles. When planning your own interviews, use the suggestion in section 6.2 that for homogeneous populations the sample size is likely to need to be between 4 and 12, while for heterogeneous populations the sample size will need to be larger, say between 12 and 30. Although this does not remove the need for you to ensure you have enough data to answer your research question or establish data saturation has been reached, it provides an idea of the likely number of interviews needed.

> **Definition**
>
> **data saturation:** where additional data collection provides few if any new insights into the research question and objectives.

### Conducting semi-structured and unstructured interviews face to face

Conducting semi-structured and unstructured interviews face to face makes full use of your interviewing skills. The clarity and tone with which you ask questions will be crucial, as will your appearance and body language. To conduct these interviews face to face, you need to take the following steps:

1  Ensure that your interview checklists and consent forms are printed.

2  Contact potential participants, explain the purpose of your research and invite them to take part, providing a clear indication of the likely amount of time the interview will take.

3 If they agree to take part, arrange a mutually convenient appointment and place to conduct the interview.

4 Arrive for your interview early and make sure the room is set as you wish.

5 Conduct the interview, making sure you also:

    (a) thank the participant for attending;

    (b) explain the purpose of the research, offering assurances of anonymity and confidentiality as appropriate and explain that they can withdraw at any time;

    (c) if using an audio recorder, ask for permission to record the interview;

    (d) ask participant to sign the consent form;

    (e) remember to also take notes.

6 At the end, thank the participant for their time.

7 Word-process your notes as soon as possible.

At the end of the interview, some researchers suggest it is a good idea to offer participants a summary of the findings or a copy of your notes of their interview. This is up to you. We would, however, stress that, if you do make an offer, it is essential that you actually do provide your participants with the summary of the findings or a copy of the interview notes. If you do not, they will be less willing to participate in research in the future.

### Conducting semi-structured and unstructured interviews by telephone

The process of conducting semi-structured and unstructured interviews by telephone appears very similar to conducting them face to face, although without the visual contact! This lack of visual contact means conducting such interviews by telephone is not easy. Remember, the purpose of semi- and unstructured interviews is to explore your participants' responses in detail. You will be unlikely to be able to do this unless you have gained their trust, something that is often difficult to do if you have only talked on the telephone. You will also not be able to see your participants' body language, meaning you may interpret some of their answers incorrectly. We therefore recommend that you only use a telephone for these forms of interview either where you already have met the participant face to face and gained that person's trust, or you have already established a trusting relationship.

To conduct a semi-structured or unstructured interview by telephone, you need to pay attention to the following:

1 Ensure that your interview checklists are printed.

2 Contact potential participants by telephone, explain the purpose of your research and invite them to take part, providing a clear indication of the likely amount of time the interview will take.

3 If they agree to take part, arrange a mutually convenient time to telephone and conduct the interview.

4 Telephone and conduct the interview, making sure you also:

    (a) thank the participant for their time;

(b) explain the purpose of the research, offering assurances of anonymity and confidentiality as appropriate and explain that they can withdraw at any time;

(c) ask for their consent and permission to record the interview (if using an audio recorder);

(d) remember to take notes.

5 At the end, thank the participant for their time.

6 Word-process your notes as soon as possible.

### *Conducting semi-structured and unstructured interviews using the Internet*

Internet-mediated interviews can be divided into three groups:

- those that are conducted in real time (synchronous) using instant messaging software such as WhatsApp™ or Messenger™;

- those that are conducted in real time (synchronous) using Voice over Internet Protocol (VoIP) or web conferencing services such as Skype™;

- those that are, in effect, conducted offline (asynchronous), such as through emails, forums or discussion groups.

Providing your participants are IT-literate and have good access to the Internet, all three groups have a significant advantage, enabling you to interview participants who are geographically dispersed. In addition, your participants' responses can often be recorded automatically for both typed and audiovisual conversations, although you should obtain consent to save these recordings.

You will already be familiar with synchronous interviewing software through your use of Messenger™ and WhatsApp™. These and other instant messaging software can be used to undertake real-time semi-structured interviews, providing netiquette (section 6.3) is observed. Similarly, you will also be familiar with asynchronous interviewing software through your use of Internet forums, blogs and email. Internet forums or discussion groups and blogs usually deal with one topic and need to remain open for at least a few weeks if they are to generate sufficient posts (data). Participants can read and comment on each other's posts, but cannot edit them. Posts are normally made by a variety of participants, and so they are really group interviews. In contrast, email interviews consist of a series of email exchanges between the interviewer and a participant, each consisting of a small number of questions and the associated answers. Although it is possible to email one long list of questions, this is really just a questionnaire and means you will not be able to adapt later questions depending on participants' responses to earlier ones. Because of the delay between questions being asked and their being answered, such interviews can often take more than a week.

To conduct semi-structured and unstructured Internet-mediated interviews, you need to remember the following:

1 Ensure that your synchronous or asynchronous means of asking questions is set up and works as you wish.

2  If you are using:

   (a)  Email, instant messaging, or VoIP services to conduct your interview – contact potential participants by email, explain the purpose of your research and invite them to take part, providing a clear indication of the likely amount of time the interview will take.

   (b)  Internet forums or blogs – invite people to join your discussion.

3  If you are using:

   (a)  Email to conduct your interview and those invited agree to take part – ask a few questions at a time rather than all together.

   (b)  Instant messaging or VoIP services to conduct your interview and those invited agree to take part – arrange a mutually convenient time to conduct the interview.

4  Conduct the interview, making sure you:

   (a)  thank the participant for their time;

   (b)  explain the purpose of the research, offering assurances of anonymity and confidentiality as appropriate and explain that they can withdraw at any time;

   (c)  ask for their consent and permission to record the interview or use the transcript for research purposes;

   (d)  (where permission has been given) remember to save the interview recording or transcript.

5  At the end, thank the participant for their time.

## 6.5  Collecting data using observation

We spend our lives observing. When we sit in a coffee bar or café 'people watching', we are observing. When we look at the length of the different check-out queues in our local supermarket, we are collecting data by observing, although, compared with people watching, our observation has a more clearly defined focus and purpose – to establish which queue is the shortest so that we have to wait the least possible time.

In the earlier sections of this chapter, we have focused on collecting data by asking people questions. Yet an obvious way of finding out what people do is, rather than ask them questions, watch and listen to them do it; in other words, to systematically observe and record their behaviours. We call a person whom we are observing an **informant**. In this section, we will look at two forms of collecting data that already exist: structured observation and unstructured observation. **Structured observation** is

### Definitions

**informant:** a person who is being observed using structured or unstructured observation.

**structured observation:** a method of observing with a high degree of predetermined structure in the seeing, hearing and subsequent recording of data to answer questions concerned with how much or what happens.

concerned with questions such as 'What happened?' 'How much?' 'How many?' 'How often?' or 'How long?' Given its name, it is not surprising that what is going to be observed is both predetermined and highly structured. What is seen and heard by the researcher is recorded systematically to provide quantitative data on the frequency of actions, or how long specified actions will take, such as the length of time it takes a crew member in a burger restaurant to undertake each of the tasks needed to serve a customer. In contrast, **unstructured observation** is concerned with answering 'why' questions. It is far less structured, focusing on the physical setting, those being observed and their activities, and the processes and emotions involved. It uses what the researcher sees and hears as she or he observes the activities of the research subjects fully to provide more qualitative data about actions such as their meanings or explanations. This might include how customers respond to different particular crew members, or the reasons why people consider the service received from a particular waiter or waitress in a restaurant to be exceptional or awful.

In undertaking a structured observation, you make the assumption that what is being observed, such as a meeting or the serving of a customer in a burger restaurant, can be broken down into a series of discrete aspects or elements. You define these, using the literature you have reviewed, use a recording sheet to provide focus when collecting the data and passively observe rather than take part. For unstructured observation in its most extreme form, you immerse yourself fully within the situation you are observing, taking part fully in what you are observing and developing a narrative account of what is going on. You might, for example, be employed by the organisation in which you are undertaking the observation. Alternatively, it might involve you taking part in a particular experience such as a summer working holiday in North America. Because you participate fully, you come to understand the world you are observing, allowing a deep and nuanced understanding of the interactions and the associated meanings. Whilst both structured and unstructured observation can offer the advantages of collecting in-depth data in real time and within context, they are extremely time consuming. In addition, particularly for overt observation, those you are observing (the informants) may act differently because they are being observed; this is known as the Hawthorne effect.

---

### Definition

**unstructured observation:** a method of observing in which the researcher observes the activities fully and there is limited structure in the seeing, hearing and subsequent recording of data to answer questions concerned with why.

---

## How to prepare for observation

Like semi-structured and unstructured interviews, undertaking observation involves careful preparation, including ensuring you have both ethical approval and consent to undertake the research (Figure 6.1). Having decided whether structured or unstructured observation will be most appropriate to answering your research question, you need to make sure you know about the people you are observing and the context in which you will be observing them. You also need to think carefully about what you want to observe, the degree of focus of your observations and how you will record them to ensure you have the data you need to answer your research question. For structured observation, it is likely you will use some form of observation sheet to record your observations (Research in practice 6.5). In contrast, for unstructured observation, it is more likely that you will record, usually in note form, as detailed a descriptive account as possible of what you saw.

### Research in practice 6.5

#### Preparing for the interview

Colin was preparing to observe how team members and the team leader interacted in team meetings using structured observation. Drawing on the academic literature, he devised six categories of interaction he was interested in observing. These were:

- Providing facts or information
- Seeking facts or information
- Checking others' understandings

**MEETING OBSERVATION SHEET**

**Date of Meeting:**

**Location of meeting:**

**Purpose of meeting:**

|  | Providing facts or information | Seeking facts or information | Checking others' understandings | Providing clarifications | Expressing opinions | Summarising what has been said |
|---|---|---|---|---|---|---|
| Team Leader |  |  |  |  |  |  |
| Team member 1 |  |  |  |  |  |  |
| Team member 2 |  |  |  |  |  |  |
| Team member 3 |  |  |  |  |  |  |

- Providing clarifications
- Expressing opinions
- Summarising what has been said

He then devised an observation sheet so he could record each time a team member or the team leader undertook one of these types of interaction using a tally mark. This provided a quick way of recording interactions in groups of five. He made one vertical line for each of the first four interactions, the fifth interaction being recorded by a diagonal line across these four.

Colin obtained written permission from the company's owner to observe the meeting. He had stated that he would observe the meeting overtly and knew he would have to explain to those he was observing how he would preserve their anonymity. For this reason, he did not record names on his observation sheet. Although he was concerned that his presence in the meeting and his obvious note taking would have an impact on the interactions he was observing, he believed the impact would lessen over time as they became used to his sitting in the corner of the meeting room.

How you plan to record your data will also depend a great deal on the nature of your observation. In particular, it relates to whether or not you intend to reveal your identity as a researcher to those you are observing and whether or not you will take part in the activity you are observing. This gives four possible scenarios (Figure 6.2).

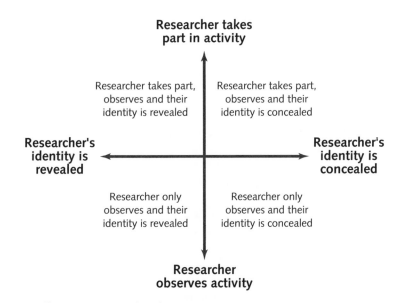

**Figure 6.2** Different scenarios for observation

If those you will be observing will know you are observing them, then it is likely to be possible for you to make notes as things happen, providing you are not taking part. However, if you plan to undertake covert observation, then making notes immediately, even if you are not taking part in the activity, may be difficult. You therefore need to think carefully about where and when it will be possible to make notes. One of Mark's students who observed customer behaviour in a café frequented by tourists wrote most of her notes on postcards, as she felt this would be a normal activity in a tourist café. Obviously, if you plan to take part in the activity you are observing, it will be more difficult to record your observations, particularly if you are observing covertly. We have both heard of researchers undertaking covert observations who wrote most of their notes while taking a comfort break on the toilet! Whether your observations are overt or covert, or whether you are taking part or just observing, we strongly recommend that you plan to record your observations as soon as possible and always on the same day as they occur. If you do not manage to do this you will, unfortunately, lose valuable data.

In preparing for observation in particular, you therefore need to:

- Be clear about the purpose of the observation and how the data you intend to collect will help you answer your research question.

- Make sure you have found out as much as possible about the person or people you are going to observe, the situation you intend to observe them in and, where appropriate, the organisation where they work.

- Be clear about whether you will be taking part in the situation you intend to observe or just observing.

- Be clear about whether you will identify yourself to those you are observing or, alternatively, your observations will be covert and the likely implications for how those you are observing will act.

- For structured observation, develop an observation sheet (Research in practice 6.5) listing those aspects you want to observe and the detail you wish to record for each. This will be informed by the literature you have already reviewed.

- For unstructured observation, think carefully about the aspects you want to observe and how you will record your observations when you immerse yourself in the research setting.

- Make sure your clothing and appearance is appropriate for how you intend to conduct your observation, be it face to face, Internet-mediated, or using videography.

## How to conduct observation

Observations can be conducted in-person (face to face), mediated by the Internet and by using videography. **Internet-mediated observation** involves collecting data by

> **Definition**
>
> **Internet-mediated observation:** an adaptation of in-person observation from oral and visual observation to textual and digital observation in a virtual environment of an online community or communities.

observing online communities replacing the oral aspects of observation with the text, and the visual aspects with the digital images. As with in-person observation, you can either take part in the activity you are observing or just observe. Depending on the accessibility of an online community, it may also be possible for you to enter a discussion group or online forum as a guest without revealing your identity and without participating other than reading or viewing the available material. This is known as lurking and as your purpose as a researcher is not revealed, it may be considered unethical by your university. This can lead to your being asked to leave if you reveal yourself as a researcher and ask to undertake research overtly. Observation using **videography** involves recording moving images electronically as observational data. It can therefore be used to record research informants in a research setting such as through a body-worn camera. You can also ask informants to record their own video diaries, something that is very useful where it is difficult to gain personal access as an observer.

---

**Definition**

**videography:** the recording of moving images and associated sound as observational data.

---

The way in which you conduct your observation will, as highlighted earlier, depend on whether or not you reveal your identity, whether or not you are taking part in what you are observing and whether your observation is structured or unstructured.

### Conducting observation in person

Conducting observations in person share a number of similarities to conducting interviews. To conduct both structured and unstructured observation, you need to:

1 Ensure you are as clear as possible about the purpose of your observation.

2 Be clear about what it is you want to observe, ensure you have sufficient copies of the means of recording your observations, such as an observation sheet (structured observation) or notebook (unstructured observation) and sufficient consent forms (if your identity as researcher will be revealed) printed.

3 Ensure you are clear how you will manage observing and recording data, particularly where you are taking part in what you are observing.

4 Arrive for your observation early and, if you are not taking part, make yourself as unobtrusive as possible.

5 Conduct your observation maintaining a positive but non-threatening self-image and trying to ensure that those you are observing do not depart from their usual ways of doing things. Where your identity is revealed:

   (a) thank those being observed for allowing you to observe them;

   (b) explain the purpose of the research, offering assurances of anonymity and confidentiality as appropriate and explain that they can withdraw at any time;

(c)  ask for permission to record electronically what is observed using the text or video files;

(d)  ask the participant to sign the consent form.

Remember, many universities will not give ethical approval where the researcher's identity is not revealed.

6  Record your observations as precisely as possible and as close to the time they occur:

(a)  for structured observation, use your observation sheet;

(b)  for unstructured observation, include descriptions of people, events and conversations as well as your own actions and feelings in relation to what you are observing.

7  At the end, if you have revealed your identity, thank those you have been observing for their time.

8  Word-process your observation notes as soon as possible.

### Conducting Internet-mediated observation

The process of conducting Internet-mediated observations appears very similar to conducting them in person, although without the personal contact. However, you will also need to determine whether what you are observing online represents all of the interactions, or whether those in the community also interact offline. You also need to be aware that members can adopt different personas online to both protect the identities and so they can offer views that they would never talk about face to face.

When conducting Internet-mediated observation you need to pay attention to the following:

1  Ensure you are as clear as possible about the purpose of your observation.

2  Be clear about what it is you want to observe, that you are able to record your observations either electronically or by paper and that your consent form is available electronically.

3  Conduct your observation maintaining a positive but non-threatening self-image and trying to ensure that those you are observing do not depart from their usual ways of doing things. Where you reveal your identity:

(a)  thank those being observed for allowing you to observe them;

(b)  explain the purpose of the research, offering assurances of anonymity and confidentiality as appropriate and explain that they can withdraw at any time;

(c)  ask for permission to observe;

(d)  ask participants to sign the consent form electronically.

Remember, many universities will not give ethical approval where the researcher's identity is not revealed.

4  Record what you are observing electronically as precisely as possible and as close as possible to the time they occur. For unstructured observation, remember also to record descriptions of people, events and conversations as well as your own actions and feelings in relation to what you are observing.

5  At the end, if you have revealed your identity, thank those you have been observing for their time.

6  Word-process your observation notes as soon as possible.

### Conducting observations using videography

You can collect your own observational data by, for example, videoing what you are observing or asking your informants to provide you with their own videos. These are relatively easy from a technical perspective, due to the relatively high-quality video recording available on mobile phones. They can be undertaken both overtly and covertly, the latter using a hidden camera. However, beware, recording an observational video is not as easy as it seems and we strongly recommend that you practice with the equipment before observing for your research. Despite this, we have already noted, it is easy to miss important data when undertaking observation, and video-recording can go some way towards overcoming this problem. Although the place from which the video is shot gives a particular viewpoint, recording allows the video to be replayed to gain a deeper understanding as you reflect on what is being observed.

When conducting observation using videography, you need to pay attention to the following:

1  Ensure you are as clear as possible about the purpose of your observation.

2  Be clear about what it is you want to observe and, even if you are using your mobile phone to record the video, ensure that you are able to use the video equipment to record your observations, alongside printing sufficient consent forms (if your identity as researcher will be revealed).

3  Conduct your observation, maintaining a positive but non-threatening self-image and trying to ensure that those you are observing do not depart from their usual ways of doing things. Where you reveal your identity:

   (a)  thank those being observed for allowing you to observe them;

   (b)  explain the purpose of the research, offering assurances of anonymity and confidentiality as appropriate and explain that they can withdraw at any time;

   (c)  ask for permission to observe;

   (d)  ask informants to sign the consent form.

Remember, many universities will not give ethical approval for covert video-recording.

4  Video-record what you are observing. For unstructured observation, remember to also note descriptions of people, events and conversations as well as your own actions and feelings in relation to what you are observing.

5  At the end, if you have revealed your identity, thank those you have been observing for their time.

6  Word-process your observation notes as soon as possible.

## Summary

- Your choice of sampling technique depends on whether or not you can obtain a complete list of the population (sampling frame), your research question and your objectives.

- If you can obtain a sampling frame, you can use probability sampling techniques such as simple random, systematic random and stratified random sampling. You use probability samples if you want to estimate statistically the characteristics of the population.

- If you cannot obtain a sampling frame, you must use non-probability sampling techniques such as quota, purposive, snowball and self-selection sampling. We recommend you do not use convenience sampling. You use non-probability samples when you want to make logical generalisations.

- Questionnaires are used when you want to collect data by asking each person to answer the same set of questions in the same order.

- Before designing your questionnaire, you need to know what data you need to collect to answer your research question and meet your objectives. Individual questions should then be designed before putting the questionnaire together. In designing your questionnaire, use as few open questions as possible. Remember to design the questionnaire so it is easy to read and respond to questions.

- Questionnaires can be distributed face to face by an interviewer, by telephone, by hand, by post and by using the web.

- Semi-structured and unstructured interviews are used when you are unsure of the answers respondents will give, your questions are complicated or you need to vary the order of questions or the actual questions asked.

- In semi-structured interviews, you ask about a set of themes, only some questions being predetermined. The order in which the themes are covered and questions asked can be varied. You can choose to omit some topics and questions and ask additional questions as appropriate.

- In unstructured interviews, the participant talks openly and widely about the topic with as little direction from you as possible. Although there is no predetermined list of questions, you will have a clear idea of the topics to explore.

- To prepare for semi-structured and unstructured interviews, you need to be clear about the topics you are going to discuss, the questions you are going to ask, the location of the interview and your appearance. When you conduct the interviews, you need to test your understanding as necessary, show that you are listening and make a record of the conversation.

- Semi-structured and unstructured interviews can be conducted face to face, by telephone and using the web.

- Observation is used when you want to find out what people do by watching them rather than asking questions.

- Structured observation is concerned with systematically recording what has happened, often using a recording sheet, to provide data that is often quantified.

- Unstructured observation is concerned with recording what is happening more broadly. It is concerned with the physical setting, those being observed, the activities, the processes and your associated emotions and observations.

- In preparing for both structured and unstructured observation, you need to be clear about whether or not you will take part in the activity you will be observing, and whether or not you will reveal your identity as a researcher to those you are observing. These decisions will impact on how you record your observations.

- Observation can be conducted in person, mediated by the Internet or using videography.

## Thinking about collecting data

→ As you continue to read and note the literature, use your knowledge about samples, questionnaires and interviews to help you assess the appropriateness of the methods used by other researchers and the value of their research findings (section 2.7).

→ Think about the data you will need to answer your research question and meet your objectives.

→ If you are going to use secondary data, use your knowledge about samples, questionnaires, interviews and observation to help you assess the suitability of the secondary data for your own research (section 4.5). Make notes about this, as you will need this level of detail to write the method section of your project report.

→ If you are going to collect your own (primary) data, use your knowledge about samples, questionnaires, interviews and observation to help you choose the most appropriate data collection method or methods (Chapter 6).

→ If you are going to collect your own (primary) data, make notes about the reasons for your choices about selecting your sample and the method or methods you will use to collect your data. Also, make notes explaining why you need to collect the data you wish to collect, linking these data explicitly to your objectives. You will need this level of detail to write the method section of your project report.

## References

Baruch, Y. and Holtom, B.C. (2008). Survey response rate levels and trends in organizational research. *Human Relations*, 61(8), 1139–60.

Brinkmann, S. and Kvale, S. (2014). *InterViews: Learning the Craft of Qualitative Research Interviewing*, (3rd ed.), Los Angeles, CA: Sage.

Cassell, C. (2015). *Conducting Research Interviews for Business and Management Students*, London: Sage.

*Dragons' Den* (2014). 'Scott Cupit and Swing Patrol on BBC's Dragon's Den' YouTube. Available at: https://www.youtube.com/watch?v=lHYnxtR1u0I [Accessed 8 November 2016].

Dunsby, M (2016). *Dragons' Den Success Stories: Swing Patrol*. Available at: http://startups.co.uk/dragons-den-success-stories-swing-patrol/ [Accessed 8 November 2016].

Ekinci, Y. (2015). *Designing Research Questionnaires for Business and Management Students*, London: Sage.

Saunders, M., Lewis, P. and Thornhill, A. (2016). *Research Methods for Business Students* (7th ed.). Harlow: Pearson

Saunders, M.N.K. (2011). Choosing research participants. *in* C. Cassell and G. Symons (eds), *The Practice of Qualitative Organizational Research: Core Methods and Current Challenges*. London: Sage.

Saunders, M.N.K. and Townsend, K. (2016). Reporting and justifying the number of interviews participants in organisation and workplace research. *British Journal of Management*, 27(4), 836–52.

YouGov (2016). *Panel Methodology* Available at: https://yougov.co.uk/about/panel-methodology/ [Accessed 7 November 2016].

# Chapter 7

# Analysing data

## 7.1　Why you should read this chapter

In Chapter 6, we noted how it was important to know about and understand different methods of collecting data, even if you were not collecting data yourself for your research project. We now make similar comments about analysing data. Obviously, if you collect your own data, you will need to analyse these data to answer your research question and meet your objectives. Similarly, if you're using secondary data (Chapter 4) for your own research project, you will still have to analyse these data. However, even if your project is an extended essay or literature review, you will still need to know about different techniques for analysing data. Without this knowledge, you will not be able to understand or evaluate fully the journal articles, reports and book chapters you review. If you only understand partially how the data were analysed and are unclear about the reasons why particular techniques were used, your ability to assess the quality of analysis, understand the research findings or follow the discussion of these findings will be reduced. In addition, a reasonable understanding of techniques for analysing data will help you to be clear about the value of research reported in the literature to your own project.

So what do you need to know about analysing data to help you do your project and write the project report? Well, whether you're collecting your own data, using secondary data or basing your project entirely on the literature, you still need to know the same things. You need to know how to get data ready for analysis, when to use different analysis techniques and how to interpret the results of these different analysis techniques. In addition, you need to know a bit about different types of data and the analysis techniques you should use depending on the type of data you have.

The first section of this chapter is about the different types of data you might be analysing or reading about. As you would expect from reading about collecting data (Chapter 6), this section looks at both quantitative and qualitative data. Following a similar structure to Chapter 6, the next section looks at how to analyse data quantitatively. Within this, we look at how to prepare your data for quantitative analysis using a spreadsheet such as

Microsoft Excel or statistical analysis software such as IBM SPSS Statistics. We also look at when you should use different tables, graphs and some of the more straightforward statistics as well as what the results of your analysis mean. Our final section looks at how to analyse data qualitatively. Once again we will look at how to prepare your data for analysis, this time looking mainly at manual analysis. Within this, we talk about ways of coding and analysing your data as well as what the results of your analysis mean.

## 7.2　Different types of data

Data can be split into two main types: quantitative data that are numerical or whose values have been measured in some way, and qualitative data that are not numerical and have not been measured in some way (Figure 7.1). As we saw in section 6.3, quantitative data are collected in a standardised way, such as by using questionnaires. These data are collected about different variables (we defined this term in section 1.7), which are the building blocks of quantitative analysis. Your variables are usually described using numbers and analysed using diagrams and statistics, including testing hypotheses.

In contrast, qualitative data are collected usually in a non-standardised way, such as interviews (section 6.4). These data are analysed by developing and testing propositions, using justified argument. To be able to analyse both quantitative and qualitative data, you need to know more about each of these types, as they will dictate the analyses you can do.

### ⬤ Quantitative data

As you can see in Figure 7.1, quantitative data are split into two main types: categorical and numerical data. Categorical data, as the name suggests, are data that have been grouped into a descriptive set or put in rank order. Let's say you have collected data

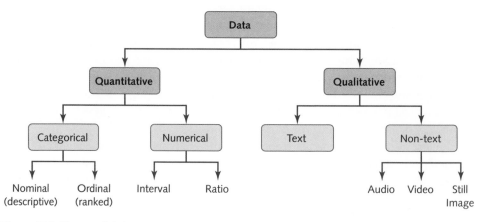

**Figure 7.1** Types of data

from a sample of students at your university using, among others, the category question:

| | | |
|---|---|---|
| In which faculty are you studying? | Arts and Humanities | $\square_1$ |
| | Business and Law | $\square_2$ |
| | Physical Sciences | $\square_3$ |
| | Social Sciences | $\square_4$ |

The data you get from this category question will be descriptive, your variable 'faculty in which studying' being made up of a descriptive set of categories that are the four faculties in your university. Although these data are coded using numbers, the numbers do not mean that the Arts and Humanities faculty is first, Business and Law second and so on; they are just codes, and there is no relevance to the number order. In contrast, **ordinal data** are categorical data that have been put into rank or definite order. These are often called **ranked data**. In your questionnaire, the next question is one that also appeared in Table 6.3:

| | | |
|---|---|---|
| How likely do you believe it is that you will pay off your overdraft within a year of graduation? | Very likely | $\square_1$ |
| | Quite likely | $\square_2$ |
| | Unsure | $\square_3$ |
| | Quite unlikely | $\square_4$ |
| | Very unlikely | $\square_5$ |

This rating question collects data on the variable 'likelihood of paying off overdraft within a year of graduation'. The responses are in ranked order, 'very likely' being ranked first, 'quite likely' second and so on.

Numerical data are where the data are measured using numbers and can be measured using either intervals or ratios. For **interval data**, you can state the difference between any two data values: such as, the difference between 3° Celsius and 9° Celsius is 6° Celsius. However, you can't say that 9° Celsius is three times as hot as 3° Celsius! For **ratio data**, you can say what the actual difference and what the relative difference are between two values. For example, if one student's overdraft is £15,000 and another student's overdraft is £30,000, you can say that the difference between them is £15,000, the second student having twice as large an overdraft.

---

**Definitions**

**ordinal or ranked data:** categorical data that are put into a definite order.

**interval data:** numerical data whose values are measured numerically so that the numerical difference between two values can be stated, but not the relative difference.

**ratio data:** numerical data whose values are measured numerically so that both the numerical and the relative difference between two values can be stated.

Numerical data can take either discrete values (**discrete data**) or any value (**continuous data**). If we return to your student questionnaire, we can again use questions to illustrate these two types of numerical data. In your questionnaire, the next question is:

> On how many days did you visit the library last week?                              [   ]
> (For example, for 2 write: [ 2 ] )

This quantity question collects discrete numerical data on the variable 'number of days visited the library last week'. The values for this variable can only be 0, 1, 2, 3, 4, 5, 6 or 7, depending on the number of days a respondent visited the library last week. In contrast, your next quantity question collects continuous data for the variable 'time spent studying last week'. Although this variable is measured to the nearest hour, these data could theoretically take any value, depending on the level of accuracy used:

> How much time did you spend studying last week to the nearest hour?        [   ] [   ] hours
> (*For example, for 2 hours, 15 minutes write*: [   ] [ 2 ] hours)

You will notice from the definitions above that **nominal data** are sometimes called **descriptive data**, and ordinal data are sometimes called ranked data. Where these terms are used, you will often find that numerical data has been divided into continuous and discrete data rather than interval and ratio data. Don't worry; it's just a different way of grouping data variables!

---

**Definitions**

**discrete data:** numerical data whose values are measured numerically as quantities in discrete units and can therefore only take a finite number of values.

**continuous data:** numerical data whose values are measured numerically as quantities and can theoretically take any value, depending on the level of accuracy with which they are measured.

**nominal or descriptive data:** categorical data that are grouped into sets (categories) that have no obvious rank order.

---

## Qualitative data

Looking again at Figure 7.1, you can see that qualitative data are also split into two main types: text and non-text. Text data, as the name suggests, are data in the form of words that have been recorded as text and are usually word-processed. They therefore include written answers to requests such as, 'If there are any other areas or issues that concern you please feel free to comment below', in Table 6.3. The majority of audio recordings, and the audio parts of video recordings, are transcribed and word-processed and then analysed as text data. As we discovered in Research in practice 6.4, these are known as interview transcripts and contain both the questions asked by the interviewer and the participant's answers. These transcripts often also record details about the research setting as well as the interviewer's and the participant's non-verbal behaviour. In contrast, although methods of analysing visual data such as video and other images are developing, they are not yet in widespread use and consequently are outside the scope of this text.

## 7.3 Analysing data quantitatively

### How to prepare your data

If you're analysing your sample data quantitatively, you will almost certainly be using either a spreadsheet or statistical analysis software. These software require your data to be in the format of a **data matrix**. Look at Figure 7.2. This extract from a spreadsheet data matrix has one column for each variable, representing questions in your student questionnaire (section 7.2). The first row in the spreadsheet contains a short description of each data variable. Each of the remaining rows contains the data for all these variables for one student, each cell containing the code representing a student's response for a particular variable.

The codes for each variable mean different things. If you look at the first row of data (row 2 in the spreadsheet), you can translate the codes. The first cell in the row contains the student identifier. This is not to identify the student by name! Rather, by writing this number on the questionnaire containing these data, you can link the questionnaire to your data matrix. This makes it much easier for you to check your data for possible typing errors. Student 1 is studying in the 'Faculty of Business and Law' (code 2).

|   | A | B | C | D | E |
|---|---|---|---|---|---|
| | | | Likelihood of paying off overdraft within | | Hours spent |
| 1 | Student identifier | Faculty in which studying | year of graduation | Days visted library last week | studying last week |
| 2 | 1 | 2 | 2 | 3 | 28 |
| 3 | 2 | 2 | 5 | 4 | 34 |
| 4 | 3 | 2 | 5 | 3 | 57 |
| 5 | 4 | 3 | 5 | 2 | 34 |
| 6 | 5 | 1 | 5 | 0 | 8 |

**Figure 7.2** Data matrix in Excel

---

**Definition**

**data matrix:** the table format in which data are typed into spreadsheets or statistical analysis software. Each column represents a separate data variable, and in each row a separate member about whom data have been obtained.

The likelihood of this student's overdraft being paid off within one year of graduation is 'quite likely' (code 2). This student visited the library three times last week and spent 28 hours studying. Numeric codes have been used because they make subsequent analysis more straightforward. In addition, numbers are quicker to type in and you're less likely to make errors.

If you have collected your own data, but not used an Internet questionnaire, you will need to code it and type it into your analysis software as a data matrix. To do this, you will need to do the following:

1　Work out the number of variables and give them clear names.

2　For each variable, work out a coding scheme (if you collected your data using a questionnaire, you should have already done this for most variables; see section 6.4).

3　Code each variable, leaving variables with no data blank.

4　Set up your data matrix as in Figure 7.2.

5　Type in your data, saving your file regularly and also making a backup copy.

6　Check your data for typing errors.

No matter how carefully you type in your data, you're almost certain to make a few errors. You should always check your data for errors before starting your analysis. This will save time as it prevents you having to redo analyses because your data were wrong. Two common errors you should look for are:

- *Illegitimate codes* – these are code numbers which appear in a data variable that you have not used for that data variable.

- *Illogical relationships* – these are relationships that are very unlikely to occur in your data, such as a person aged 91 who is still in full-time work.

As we pointed out in section 4.2, online secondary data are in formats that can be read directly into your data analysis software as a data matrix. These data have already been checked for errors and, as you will not have to type the data in yourself, you will save time. However, don't forget to download the codebook and list of definitions so you know exactly what everything means and can interpret the data correctly.

## How to present data

Your first stage of any quantitative data analysis is to explore and understand your data. The easiest way to do this, and we believe a most helpful way, is by presenting your data as tables and graphs. Those that are most useful in helping you answer your research question and meet your objectives will also appear in your project report. However, before you start designing tables and graphs, you need to be aware of the following:

- Particular tables or graphs are better than others for highlighting certain aspects of your data (Saunders et al., 2016).

- Categorical and numerical data often require different tables and graphs.

- All tables and graphs must be labelled clearly and designed so as not to distort the data.

In this section, we look at how to highlight different aspects of your quantitative data using tables and graphs. Within this, we talk about those tables and graphs which are used to present categorical data and those which are used to present numerical data, also looking at the importance of clear design and labelling. These are summarised in Table 7.1.

**Table 7.1** Presenting data using tables and graphs

| For . . . | use a . . . | to present . . . | which allows the . . . |
|---|---|---|---|
| categorical data | table | a summary | individual values to be read |
| categorical data | bar graph | values for each category | highest and lowest values for a variable to be seen[2] |
| numerical continuous data[1] | histogram | values for data grouped in categories | highest and lowest values for a variable to be seen |
| categorical data[1] | pie chart | proportions in each category | relative proportions in each of a variable's categories to be seen |
| numerical data | line graph | values for a variable over time | trend over time to be seen[2] |
| numerical and categorical ranked data | scatter graph | a relationship | relationship between two variables to be seen |

[1] Numerical data will need to be grouped into categories.
[2] To also compare variables, use a multiple bar chart or a multiple line graph.

## How to summarise data so specific values can be read

Tables are used when you want to summarise data so that specific values can be read easily. When your table summarises the data for one variable, such as the number in each category for a question such as 'In which faculty are you studying?' it is sometimes called a frequency table or frequency distribution.

Now read Research in practice 7.1. The table Harry pasted into his project report summarises the number of hectares used for organic farming in each member of the European Union's 27 member states. Each EU member state is represented by a separate row. The table contains data for more than one variable. The total number of hectares used for organic farming in 2010 and 2015 for each member state is represented by the second and third columns. A further variable, represented by the fourth column, has been included. This has been calculated using the second and third columns of data.

While the individual values in this table are easy to read, their meaning is less easy to understand. This is because Harry has simply cut and pasted this table into his project report rather than thinking! He needs, as pointed out by his supervisor, to make sure the table has a clear title, states the source of the data and that the various abbreviations and notes are explained more fully.

## Research in practice 7.1

### Designing and labelling tables

As part of his research project on the market for organic food, Harry decided to present some of the secondary data on the growth of organic farming, using a table he had found on the European Commission's website. This showed the organic crop area in EU member states. He cut the table from the web page and pasted it into his chapter, which he later emailed to his project supervisor for comments. The extract below includes his supervisor's comments.

*Do you mean "member state" or "country". Use clear labels for all column and row headings*

*I presume this is the total for the EU. It is more usual to put the total at the bottom*

*I am pleased you have used country names rather than abbreviations. However it would help to present them in alphabetical order or, perhaps, order of area if you wish to emphasise those member states that have the highest and lowest area under organic cultivation.*

*What does this mean? Ensure notes are clear and easy to understand*

| In hectares | 2010 | 2015 | Change (%) |
|---|---|---|---|
| EU | 9 195 813 | 11 139 595 | 21.1% |
| Belgium | 49 005 | 68 818 | 40.4% |
| Bulgaria* | 25 648 | 118 552 | 362.2% |
| Czech Republic | 435 610 | 478 033 | 9.7% |
| Denmark | 162 903 | 166 788 | 2.4% |
| Germany | 990 702 | 1 060 291 | 7.0% |
| Estonia | 121 569 | 155 806 | 28.2% |
| Ireland | 47 864 | 73 037 | 52.6% |
| Greece | 309 823 | 407 069 | 31.4% |
| Spain | 1 615 047 | 1 968 570 | 21.9% |
| France | 845 442 | 1 361 512 | 61.0% |
| Croatia | 15 913 | 75 883 | 376.9% |
| Italy | 1 113 742 | 1 492 579 | 34.0% |
| Cyprus | 3 184 | 4 699 | 47.6% |
| Latvia | 166 320 | 231 608 | 39.3% |
| Lithuania | 143 644 | 213 579 | 48.7% |
| Luxembourg | 3 614 | 4 216 | 16.7% |
| Hungary | 127 605 | 129 735 | 1.7% |
| Malta | 24 | 30 | 25.0% |
| Netherlands | 46 233 | 44 402 | -4.0% |
| Austria | 538 210 | 552 141 | 2.6% |
| Poland | 521 970 | 580 731 | 11.3% |
| Portugal | 210 981 | 241 375 | 14.4% |
| Romania | 182 706 | 245 924 | 34.6% |
| Slovenia | 30 689 | 42 188 | 37.5% |
| Slovakia | 174 471 | 181 882 | 4.2% |
| Finland | 169 168 | 225 235 | 33.1% |
| Sweden | 438 693 | 518 983 | 18.3% |
| United Kingdom | 699 638 | 495 929 | -29.1% |

* 2015 data are provisional.
The source dataset can be found here.

*There is no table number or title! Make sure the title is clear and describes contents of table. I had no idea what this table was showing.*

*Units of measurement are clear -good*

*You MUST state the source of the data clearly. I presume it is the European Commission.. Don't forget to put the full reference in your list of references.*

*Potentially a useful table that seems to support your arguments. Please see my other comments to improve it.*

*Source of table*: © Eurostat Press Office (2016).

### How to present data so the highest and lowest values can be seen

As you can see from Research in practice 7.1, tables do not emphasise any particular values. If you wish to do this, you need to use a bar graph (sometimes called a bar chart) for categorical data or a histogram for numerical data. The bar graph in Figure 7.3 shows visually the organic farming area for each European Union member state: Spain has the largest area of organic farming, while Cyprus, Luxembourg and Malta have the smallest areas of organic farming. Because of the scale at which the graph is drawn, it is not possible to be sure which of these three countries has the smallest area. However, if you look at the specific values in the table in Research in practice 7.1, you will find out that the lowest member state is Malta, with only 30 hectares of organic farming.

More complicated forms of bar graphs can be used to compare the highest and lowest values for two or more variables. These are known as multiple bar graphs. When you draw these, you need to make sure the data you want to compare are represented by bars that are next to each other. So, if Harry wished to compare the total organic farming area in each EU member state between 2010 and 2015, he would draw the two bars for each member state next to each other. For each member state, the first bar would represent the total organic farming area for 2010 and the second the total area for 2015.

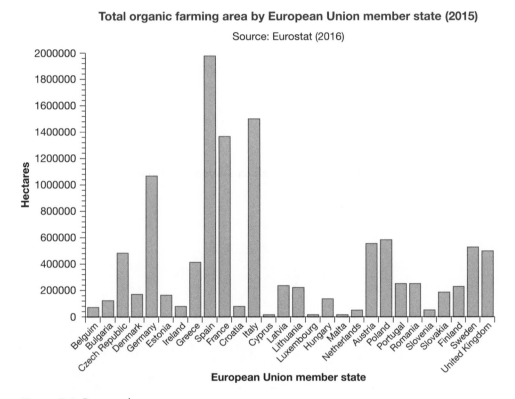

**Figure 7.3** Bar graph
*Source:* Eurostat (2016).

Histograms are used if you have numerical continuous data, the continuous nature of the data on the horizontal access being shown by there being no gaps between the bars. Let's look at numerical data you collected from students using the question:

How much time did you spend studying last week to the nearest hour?        [   ] [   ] hours
*(For example, for 2 hours, 15 minutes write:* [   ] [ 2 ] hours)

These data would consist of a series of numbers, such as 23, 34, 8, 14, 46 . . ., each number being the number of hours a student had spent studying last week. To draw a histogram, you could place these data into a series of equal width categories such as:

| | |
|---|---|
| less than 5 hours | 25 to less than 30 hours |
| 5 to less than 10 hours | 30 to less than 35 hours |
| 10 to less than 15 hours | 35 to less than 40 hours |
| 15 to less than 20 hours | 40 to less than 45 hours |
| 20 to less than 25 hours | 45 hours or more |

As one of these categories ends, the next starts, the lack of a gap between the categories reflecting that your data are continuous. Your histogram would consist of 10 bars, the area of each bar representing the total number of students whose time was spent study-ing last week for a five-hour time period (Figure 7.4). Because there is no gap between each of your categories, there is no gap between each of the bars in your histogram (Figure 7.4). Once again, the highest and lowest values are easy to see: the most frequent amount of time spent studying last week by students was 20 to less than 25 hours, the least frequent being 45 hours or more.

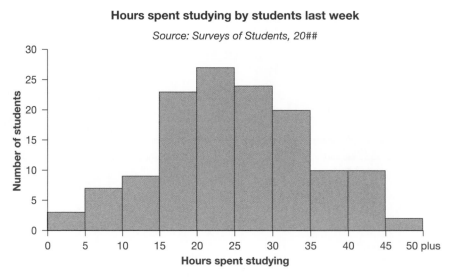

**Figure 7.4** Histogram

## How to present data so that proportions can be seen

As we are sure you already know, pie charts are useful if you want to show the propor-tions in different categories for a variable. As with histograms, if you're using numerical data, you need to put these data into categories. The pie chart in Figure 7.5 has been drawn using categorical data collected from your student questionnaire which used responses to the question, 'In which faculty are you studying?' The largest segment, Business and Law, represents the faculty that had the greatest proportion of students responding. We've added the annotations to remind you how to design and label graphs, whatever type you're using. You will notice that one annotation states '(Two-dimensional graph used so as not to distort or misrepresent the data)'. While it is fun to draw three-dimensional graphs using multiple colours viewed from weird angles, a quick look at some of graphs in newspapers shows how easy it is to use them to misrepresent data. You should not do this in your project report.

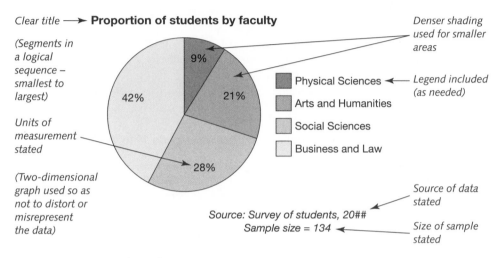

**Figure 7.5** Annotated pie chart

### *How to present data so that a trend can be seen*

You should use line graphs to highlight changes in numerical data over time (Table 7.1). For most research projects, your line graphs will be drawn using secondary data such as that available from government websites (Research in practice 7.2) or online market and financial databases. If you want to compare trends over time for two or more variables, you simply draw an additional line for each variable, adding a legend so you know what each line represents.

### *How to present data so interdependence between two variables can be seen*

Interdependence or the relationship between two numerical variables is best shown using a scatter graph, sometimes called a scatter plot (Table 7.1). Let's say an organisation has asked you to find out if there is any relationship between how well its 30 sales employees performed in an aptitude test and their sales performance. The first of your variables is each employee's aptitude test score out of 100. The second is the value of each employee's total sales for the past month recorded in pounds sterling. As you feel that sales performance is likely to be affected by aptitude, you decide that sales performance is your dependent variable and so should be plotted against the vertical axis of your scatter graph. Aptitude is the independent variable, and so you plot this on the horizontal axis (Figure 7.6). Each point (cross) on your scatter graph represents an

## Research in practice 7.2

### Presenting a trend

Ahmed's research project was looking at long-term economic trends. In particular, he was interested in changes in countries' balance of payments since the end of the Second World War and the relative importance of different goods and services over the years. Using the UK Government's website (www.statistics.gov.uk) as one of his sources of secondary data, he downloaded the Balance of Payments time series data set free of charge. This contained a summary of the UK's total trade in goods recording the value of imports, exports and the balance of trade for the years 1946–2015. To show the trend in the balance of payments for trade in goods, he used a line graph. This showed a clear decline over time, this decline being most rapid between 2011 and 2013.

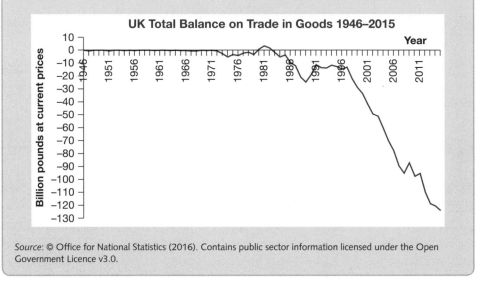

*Source*: © Office for National Statistics (2016). Contains public sector information licensed under the Open Government Licence v3.0.

employee. The closer these points on your scatter graph are to an imaginary straight line (not shown on Figure 7.6 as it is imaginary!), the stronger the relationship between the two variables. Looking at your graph, you decide that there appears to be a strong relationship between an employee's aptitude test result and their sales performance. As we will see later, you decide to explain this cause-and-effect relationship statistically.

### How to describe data using statistics

We're sure that you've already studied statistics at some time in the past. However, we wouldn't be surprised if you had forgotten at least some things. We don't intend to give you a lecture on how to calculate lots of different statistics in this section. After all, there is no real need to do this, as you will be using either a spreadsheet or

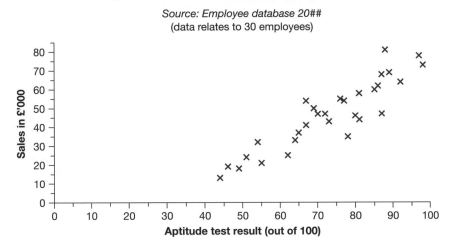

**Figure 7.6**  Scatter graph

some other statistics software to calculate the statistics for you. Rather, we will talk about the statistics you should use to describe different types of data and, when you have calculated the statistics using a spreadsheet or statistical analysis software, what each one actually means. The statistics we will look at are summarised in Table 7.2.

Let's start by looking at the statistics you can use to describe a data variable. When you do this, you're describing one of three things:

- The **central tendency**, which is the common, middle or average value.

- The **dispersion**, which is how the data values are spread, or dispersed, around the central tendency.

- The **trend**, which is how the data values change or move in one direction over time.

### How to describe the central tendency and dispersion

As you can see from Table 7.2, if you have categorical data variables, such as the answer to your student questionnaire question 'In which faculty are you studying?' the only

**Definitions**

**central tendency:** the value for a variable that represents the common, middle or average. Statistics that describe data in this way are called 'central tendency measures'.

**dispersion:** the value for a variable that represents how the data are spread or dispersed around the central tendency. Statistics that describe data in this way are called 'dispersion measures'.

**trend:** the movement or change in one direction of the values for a variable over a period of time.

**Table 7.2** Describing a variable using statistics

| For . . . | use the . . . | to describe the . . . | which represents the . . . |
|---|---|---|---|
| categorical data | mode | central tendency | category that occurs most often |
| numerical data | mode *or the* | | value that occurs most often |
| | median *or the* | | middle value when all the data values are put in rank order |
| | mean | | average value |
| numerical data | range *or the* | dispersion | difference between the highest and lowest data values when they are put in rank order |
| | inter-quartile range *or the* | | difference within the middle 50% of data values when they are put in rank order |
| | standard deviation[1] | | extent the data values differ from the mean (for normally distributed data, 95% of values will lie within plus or minus 1.96 standard deviations of the mean) |
| numerical data | index number[2] | trend | relative change in a series of data values over time |

[1] only use if the data are normally distributed.
[2] only use if the data have been collected over time.

statistic you can use to describe the central tendency is the mode. This describes the category that occurs most often, for this question the Faculty of Business and Law. You can't describe the dispersion or the trend for categorical data.

For numerical data, you can describe the central tendency, the dispersion and, where the data have been collected over time, the trend. The mean and the median are used normally to describe the central tendency for quantitative data. However, you might use the mode to describe the most common value. Let's use statistics to describe the variable 'employee sales last month' which we used for the scatter graph in Figure 7.6. Table 7.2 tells you that you can calculate the mode, median, mean, range, inter-quartile range and standard deviation for this numerical data variable. You decide to do this using IBM SPSS Statistics and get the output shown in Figure 7.7. Although your output does not give you the inter-quartile range, you could easily work it out by subtracting the 25th percentile from the 75th percentile. You use the output to describe employee sales in your project report:

Mean sales last month for the organisation's 30 employees were £46,600. As the mean, median and mode are virtually the same, this suggests these data are normally distributed. Consequently the standard deviation of 18.46 indicates that 95 per cent of sales fell within the range £10,318 to £82,682, the complete range being £68,000.

**Definition**

**normal distribution:** the symmetrical distribution of data values around the mean for a quantitative variable forming a bell-shaped curve. In a normal distribution the values of the mean, median and mode are the same.

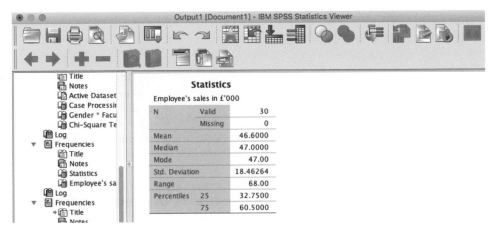

**Figure 7.7** Descriptive statistics output in IBM SPSS Statistics

*Source:* SPSS © 2016 International Business Machines Corporation. Reproduce courtesy of IBM.

### How to describe the trend

You will have seen in Figure 7.7 that we did not calculate index numbers for the variable 'Employee's sales in £'000'. This is because these data were not collected over time and so can't be used to show a trend. However, we can do this for the data used to draw the line graph in Research in practice 7.2. Let's say Ahmed is now focusing his research on the trend for the 'Balance of payments – trade in goods' since 1981. Ahmed represents the value of his data for this starting date, known as the base year, on his spreadsheet using the number 100 (Figure 7.8). Increases in subsequent years would be represented by positive index numbers greater than 100 and decreases by positive index numbers less than 100, providing the balance of payments was in surplus. As you can see in Figure 7.8, this was not the case for the years 2006 onwards. For these years, the deficit in the balance of payments is represented by a negative index number. As the deficit is greater than the initial surplus in

| | A | B | C |
|---|---|---|---|
| | Year | Balance of Payments - total trade in goods | Index number (1981=100) |
| 1 | | | |
| 2 | 1981 | 2986 | 100.00 |
| 27 | 2006 | -78963 | -2644.44 |
| 28 | 2007 | -90540 | -3032.15 |
| 29 | 2008 | -95026 | -3182.38 |
| 30 | 2009 | -86624 | -2901.00 |
| 31 | 2010 | -97384 | -3261.35 |
| 32 | 2011 | -94955 | -3180.01 |
| 33 | 2012 | -110907 | -3714.23 |
| 34 | 2013 | -120664 | -4040.99 |
| 35 | 2014 | -122575 | -4104.99 |
| 36 | 2015 | -126437 | -4234.33 |
| 37 | | | |

**Figure 7.8** Describing the trend using index numbers

the base year (1981), the negative index numbers are greater than 100. Concentrating mainly on the last 10 years, Ahmed interprets the index numbers in his project report:

> Using 1981 as the base year it can be seen that the balance of payments for trade in goods went into deficit increasing rapidly up to 2008, the index number of –3182.38 in 2008 indicating the deficit for this year was over 31 times the surplus in 1981. The index number of –2901.00 in 2009 indicates a decline in the deficit from the previous year (index number –3182.38). However, subsequent to 2011 the trade gap in goods has grown year on year, particularly between 2011 and 2012.

## How to examine and assess the significance of interdependences (relationships) using statistics

We will now look at the statistics you can use to examine and assess 'relationships' between two or more data variables when you have selected your data from a larger population using probability sampling (Chapter 6.2). When examining a 'relationship' using statistics, you're calculating a test statistic to look at one of five things:

- The independence between two variables.
- The relationship between two variables.
- The difference between two or more variables.
- The explanation of one (dependent) variable by one or more other (independent) variables.
- The prediction of one (dependent) variable by one or more other (independent) variables.

You're also assessing how likely the outcome you see in your sample data (the 'relationship' represented by your test statistic) is to have occurred by chance to establish whether you can use this to infer the characteristics of the population from which it was selected. This means as well as a test statistic, you have to work out both a statistic and the probability (likelihood) of this test statistic or one more extreme occurring by chance alone. The process of assessing the significance of findings is known as **significance testing**, the classical approach to assessing statistical significance being **hypothesis testing**. If this probability is small (usually 0.05 or lower), then you

---

**Definitions**

**significance testing:** the process of assessing statistically how likely it is that the characteristics observed in a sample have occurred by chance.

**hypothesis testing:** the classical approach to assessing the statistical significance of findings from a sample.

**hypothesis:** a tentative (usually testable) statement about the 'relationship' between two or more variables; often referred to as $H_1$.

**null hypothesis:** a statement about the 'relationship' between two or more variables that the researcher hopes to reject, thereby accepting the opposite; often referred to as $H_0$ or $H_a$, the *alternative* hypothesis.

have a relationship that is statistically significant. Statisticians refer to this as 'rejecting the null hypothesis and accepting the hypothesis'. When you reject a null hypothesis, you're rejecting a testable statement such as 'There is no relationship between . . .' and accepting a hypothesis such as 'There is a significant relationship between . . .'

As you can see in Table 7.3, different statistics are used to test each of the five things we listed above. You will also see that the statistic you use depends on the data you have, and that there are far more statistics to choose from for numerical data than for categorical data. This means you need to think carefully about which statistic you use and why. Table 7.3 should help you in this!

**Table 7.3** Examining and assessing the significance of interdependencies (relationships) between variables using statistics

| For . . . | use . . . (symbol in brackets) | to examine and assess the significance of . . . | which, if the null hypothesis is accepted, represents the . . . |
|---|---|---|---|
| categorical data | chi-square test ($\chi^2$) | independence | association between two variables and the probability of this or one more extreme occurring by chance |
| categorical ordinal (ranked) data | Spearman's rank correlation coefficient ($\rho$) or | correlation | strength of the relationship between two variables and the probability of this or one more extreme occurring by chance |
| | Kendal's rank correlation coefficient ($\tau$) | correlation (when data contains tied ranks) | strength of the relationship between two variables and the probability of this or one more extreme occurring by chance |
| numerical data split into two groups using a categorical variable | independent groups $t$-test ($t$) | difference | size of the differences between two groups relative to the variation in the sample and the probability of this or one more extreme occurring by chance |
| numerical data split into three-plus groups using a categorical variable | Analysis of variance (ANOVA) ($F$) | difference | size of the variation in the sample means relative to the variation in the sample and the probability of this or one more extreme occurring by chance |
| pairs of numerical data for two variables measuring the same feature under different conditions | paired $t$-test ($t$) | difference | size of the differences between the two variables relative to the variation in the sample and the probability of this or one more extreme occurring by chance |

*(Continued)*

**Table 7.3** Continued

| For . . . | use . . . (symbol in brackets) | to examine and assess the significance of . . . | which, if the null hypothesis is accepted, represents the . . . |
|---|---|---|---|
| numerical data | Pearson's product moment correlation coefficient ($r$) | correlation | strength of the relationship between two variables and the probability of this or one more extreme occurring by chance |
| | Coefficient of determination ($r^2$) | explanation | strength of a cause-and-effect relationship between a dependent and one or more independent variables and the probability of this or one more extreme occurring by chance |
| | Regression equation ($y = a + b\,x$) | prediction | formula to predict the values of a dependent variable, given the values of one or more independent variables |

### How to examine and assess the significance of independence (association)

Let's say you, in your questionnaire to a sample of students, collected data on each student's gender (male or female) as well as the faculty in which she or he was studying. These are both categorical data variables. You look at Table 7.3 and see that, as these data are not ranked, the only statistic you can use to examine and assess the association between gender and faculty is the chi-square test. You use this statistic to test the null hypothesis 'The faculty in which students are studying and their gender are independent' using IBM SPSS Statistics. Your output is shown in Figure 7.9.

Your output gives you both a crosstabulation of the data and another table headed 'Chi-Square Tests'. The first row of the 'Chi-Square Tests' table contains the (Pearson) chi-square statistic (11.716) and the probability (Asymptotic Significance) of this or one more extreme occurring by chance (.008). Next to the chi-square statistic is a reference to a footnote which states '0 cells (0.0%) have expected counts of less than 5 . . .' This is important, as for the statistic to give usable results, no more than 25% of cells can have expected values of less than five. Fortunately, this is not the case and, since the probability of this chi-square statistic or one more extreme occurring by chance is less than 0.05, you can reject your null hypothesis, 'The faculty in which students are studying and their gender are independent', and accept the hypothesis 'There is a significant association between the faculty in which students are studying and their gender'. You use the table and the chi-square statistic to interpret the relationship between gender and faculty in your project report:

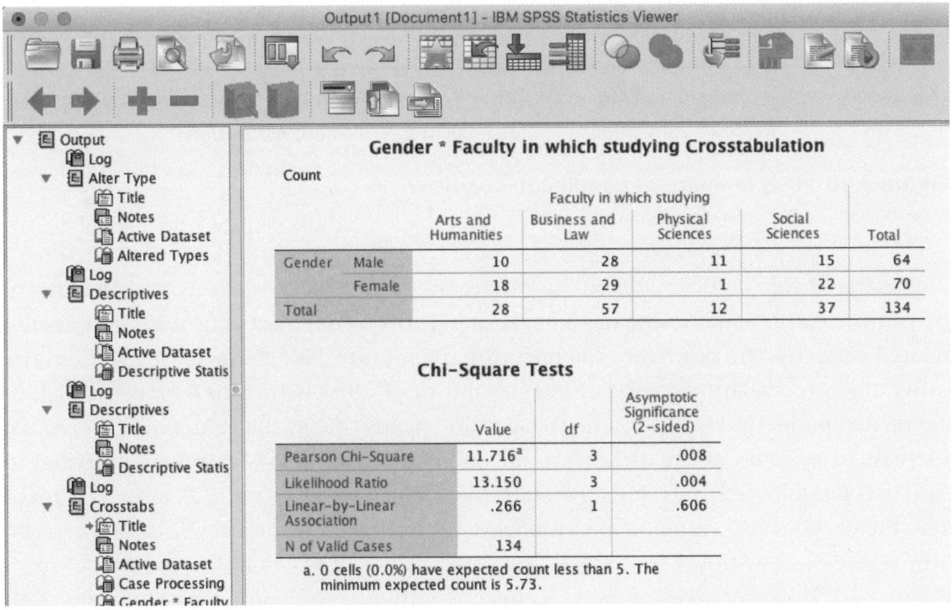


**Gender * Faculty in which studying Crosstabulation**

Count

| | | Faculty in which studying | | | | |
|---|---|---|---|---|---|---|
| | | Arts and Humanities | Business and Law | Physical Sciences | Social Sciences | Total |
| Gender | Male | 10 | 28 | 11 | 15 | 64 |
| | Female | 18 | 29 | 1 | 22 | 70 |
| Total | | 28 | 57 | 12 | 37 | 134 |

**Chi-Square Tests**

| | Value | df | Asymptotic Significance (2-sided) |
|---|---|---|---|
| Pearson Chi-Square | 11.716[a] | 3 | .008 |
| Likelihood Ratio | 13.150 | 3 | .004 |
| Linear-by-Linear Association | .266 | 1 | .606 |
| N of Valid Cases | 134 | | |

a. 0 cells (0.0%) have expected count less than 5. The minimum expected count is 5.73.

**Figure 7.9** Examining and assessing the significance of association between variables using a chi-square test

*Source:* SPSS © 2016 International Business Machines Corporation. Reproduce courtesy of IBM.

There is a significant association between the faculty in which students are studying and their gender (chi-square = 11.716, *df* = 3, *p* = 0.008). Students in both the Arts and Humanities and Social Sciences faculties are more likely to be female, while those in the Physical Sciences faculty are more likely to be male. Students in the Business and Law faculty are more evenly divided between genders.

### *How to examine and assess the significance of interdependencies (relationships)*

The only other categorical data statistics we highlight in Table 7.3 are for ranked (ordinal) data. You will see in this table that there are two possible statistics that can be used to measure the strength of the relationship between two ranked variables:

- Kendall's rank correlation coefficient;
- Spearman's rank correlation coefficient.

Both these statistics assume your sample has been selected at random, but they do not need your data to be normally distributed. If your data for a variable contains tied ranks, let's say two or more students came equal second in an examination, it is better to use Kendall's rank correlation coefficient. Otherwise, you should use Spearman's rank correlation coefficient.

Like all correlation coefficients, the value of both Spearman's and Kendall's rank correlation coefficients will always be somewhere between –1 and +1 (Figure 7.10). This

**Figure 7.10** How to interpret correlation coefficients
*Source:* Developed from Hair et al. (2009).

means that if your value is outside this range, an error has been made in the calculation! If your correlation coefficient has a value of +1, this means that your two variables are related perfectly, the positive value meaning that as one variable increases, so does the other. If your correlation coefficient has a value of −1, this also means your two variables are related perfectly. However, a negative value means that as the values of one variable increase, the values of the other variable decrease. Beware: it is extremely unusual to find two variables that are related perfectly. As you can see in Figure 7.10, a correlation of zero means your two variables are independent, not being related at all. You have probably worked out by now how to interpret other values of a correlation coefficient from Figure 7.10. However, to allow you to check whether or not you have got it right, let's look at two different values: a correlation coefficient of −0.23 represents a weak negative correlation; a correlation of coefficient of 0.7 represents a strong positive correlation.

When you interpret a correlation coefficient, you also need to see how likely the relationship between these variables in your sample is to have occurred by chance. As with the chi-square test, this is called significance testing and represents the probability (likelihood) of your statistic or one more extreme occurring by chance. Once again, if this probability is small (usually 0.05 or less), then you can say your relationship is statistically significant. Again, this is referred to as 'rejecting the null hypothesis and accepting the hypothesis'. When you reject a null hypothesis for a correlation coefficient, you're rejecting a statement such as 'There is no correlation between . . .' and accepting a hypothesis such as 'There is a significant correlation between . . .'

If you haven't done so already, now read Research in practice 7.3. This looks at the use of statistics in a journal article a student is reading for her extended essay. Towards the end of this Research in practice, the student, Samantha, looks at how the author of the article has used Pearson's product moment correlation coefficient. As the data used to calculate Pearson's product moment correlation coefficient are numerical, she feels rightly that the correct statistic has been used. For each potential relationship between brand consciousness and the six socialization factors, the article's author has given both the statistic ($r$) and the probability ($p$) of that relationship or one more extreme occurring by chance. Where this probability is less than or equal to 0.05, the author has implicitly rejected the null hypothesis 'There is no relationship between . . .' and accepted the hypothesis 'There is a significant relationship between . . .' This practice of not stating either the null hypothesis or hypothesis often happens in academic journal articles, so don't worry too much if they are not actually stated in an article you're reading. Although the article's author has not provided an indication of how to interpret the strength of the significant correlations, Samantha recognises that they are not particularly strong. If you look again at Research in practice 7.3, you will see that the

## Using *t*-tests, analysis of variance and correlation

Samantha was writing an extended essay on brand consciousness. Within her essay, she was particularly interested in the factors that influenced people's awareness of different brands and how this differed according to their demographic characteristics. During her search of the literature, she had found a 2011 article by Zaharah Ghazali in the *International Journal of Management and Marketing Research*. This article used a sample of 230 students at a Malaysian university to investigate how socialisation factors such as the media, parents and peers all influenced students' brand consciousness for clothing. Within the article, Ghazali also looked at how brand consciousness differed according to the students' demographic characteristics.

Ghazali's article outlined how the data for each of the variables had been collected using a questionnaire, which Samantha considered had an excellent (88%) response rate. The article also stated that the questions used to collect the data were all derived from previous questionnaires, although Samantha noted the source for some of the questions was not always referenced clearly. Variables used in the analysis included the following:

- Gender – categorised as male or female.
- Ethnicity – categorised as Malay, Chinese, Indian or other.
- Socialisation factors:
  - exposure to television media – measured on a numerical scale;
  - exposure to radio media – measured on a numerical scale;
  - exposure to online media – measured on a numerical scale;
  - exposure to movie media – measured on a numerical scale;
  - exposure to parents' influences – measured on a numerical scale;
  - exposure to peers' influences – measured on a numerical scale;
- Brand consciousness – measured on a numerical scale.

Ghazali had undertaken a variety of statistical analyses using these variables, such as:

- Independent sample *t*-tests for gender differences in brand consciousness.
- One-way analysis of variance for ethnicity differences in brand consciousness.
- Pearson's correlations between exposure and each of the six socialisation factors with brand consciousness.

Based on the first of these, Ghazali (2011) commented in her article that there was a significant difference in brand consciousness between genders stating the *t*-test value and its significance ($t = -2.495$, $p = 0.013$). This Ghazali interpreted as indicating that females were more likely to be highly brand-conscious than males.

Samantha felt that the *t*-test was the correct statistic to use. She looked at the table in the article that showed the results of the *t*-test and noted the mean brand consciousness score for males (2.98) and females (3.24). This provided further support for Ghazali's statement that females were more likely to be highly brand-conscious than males.

Interpreting the one-way analysis of variance statistic ($F = 8.732$, $p \leq 0.001$), Ghazali (2011) commented there was a significant difference in brand consciousness between ethnic groups. This she interpreted as students from her category of 'other ethnic groups' (including those of Siamese, Singaporean and Indonesian origin) being more likely to be highly brand-conscious than students of Malay, Chinese and Indian origin.

Samantha felt that analysis of variance was the correct statistic to use. She looked at the table in the article showing the results of the analysis of variance. This gave the mean brand consciousness score for 'other' (3.95), as well as the Malay (3.09), Chinese (3.10) and Indian (3.13) ethnic groups. This supported Ghazali's interpretation that students in the other ethnic groups were more likely to be highly brand-conscious than Malay, Chinese and Indian students.

Finally, using Pearson's product moment correlation coefficient, Ghazali (2011) discussed the relationship between brand consciousness and socialisation factors such as media socialisation, parents and peers. She noted the various factors differed in their relationships: movie-viewing having a negative relationship with brand consciousness ($r = -0.369$, $p < 0.01$), while parental influence ($r = 0.134$, $p < 0.05$) and peer influence ($r = 0.486$, $p < 0.01$) both showed positive relationships.

Samantha considered Ghazali's discussion of the findings in relation to the correlation statistics presented in the associated table in the article. She felt that the use of Pearson's correlation was appropriate for numerical data. Although these statistics had been interpreted correctly, she felt that none of the correlations were particularly strong. She noted that, while there were correlations between brand consciousness and exposure to each of movie media, parents' influences and peers' influences were statistically significant, the correlations with exposure to television, radio and online media were not. Although this point was made by Ghazali in her article's discussion section, Samantha decided to note down the remaining correlation statistics with brand consciousness and their significance levels for use in her extended essay. These were exposure to television media ($r = -0.081$, $p > 0.05$), exposure to radio media ($r = -0.020$, $p > 0.05$), and exposure to online media ($r = 0.067$, $p > 0.05$).

negative correlation between exposure to movies and brand consciousness ($r = -0.369$, $p < 0.01$) and the positive correlation between exposure to peer influence and brand consciousness ($r = 0.486$, $p < 0.01$), although both significant, might only be interpreted as a moderate relationship. In contrast, the relationship represented by the positive correlation between exposure to parental influence and brand consciousness ($r = 0.134$, $p < 0.05$), although significant, might be interpreted as 'none', owing to the very low value of the correlation coefficient. None of the remaining correlations with brand consciousness are assessed as significant, the value of $p$ for each being greater than 0.05.

## How to examine and assess the significance of differences

Research in practice 7.3 also shows how two statistics, the independent groups' $t$-test and the analysis of variance, can be used to analyse differences when a numerical variable is split into two or more groups. In the article Samantha is reading, the author split the numerical variable 'brand consciousness' into two groups using the categorical variable 'gender', and then uses the independent groups' $t$-test statistic and associated $p$ value to assess whether the difference between males and females in her sample is significant. The independent groups' *t*-test was used because the author was examining differences between two groups. It is worth noting here that a paired *t*-test was not used because the data in the two variables were not collected in pairs, one from each group. Although a paired *t*-test is calculated in a slightly different way, its interpretation is exactly the same. As the *p* value of 0.013 was less than 0.05, the probability of this test statistic or one more extreme occurring by chance alone in the population was considered significant. A null hypothesis such as 'There is no difference in brand values between males and females' could be rejected, and a hypothesis such as 'There is a significant difference in brand values between males and females' could be accepted. Once again, neither the null hypothesis nor the hypothesis was stated in the article.

The author of the article also split the numeric variable 'brand consciousness' into four groups, using the categorical variable 'ethnicity', and then used the analysis of variance statistic to see if the difference in brand consciousness between Malay, Chinese, Indian and other ethnic groups was significant. Looking at Table 7.3, you can see that analysis of variance was used because brand consciousness was now split into more than two groups. The probability of the recorded *F* ratio ($F = 8.732$) or one more extreme occurring by chance in the population was less than 0.001 ($p \leq 0.001$). This means a null hypothesis such as 'There is no difference in brand values between ethnic groups' could be rejected, and a hypothesis such as 'There is a significant difference in brand values between ethnic groups' could be accepted. As previously, the null hypothesis and hypothesis were not stated in the article.

## How to explain and predict cause-and-effect relationships

You've already looked at a cause-and-effect relationship using a scatter graph to display the relationship between all sales employees' aptitude test results and their sales performance for the past month (Figure 7.6). When you plotted these data on your scatter graph, you plotted aptitude test result as the independent variable and sales performance in £'000 as the dependent variable. This scatter graph suggested there was a cause-and-effect relationship between employees' aptitude (the cause) and their sales performance (the effect). As we stated you would, you now test this statistically by calculating the coefficient of determination (Figure 7.11). As your data relate to all sales employees, the population, there is no need to calculate the likelihood (probability) that this coefficient of determination has occurred by chance.

| | A | B | C | D | E | F | G | H | I | J |
|---|---|---|---|---|---|---|---|---|---|---|
| 1 | Aptitude te | Sales in £ '000 | | | | | | | | |
| 2 | 44 | 13 | | Coefficient of determination: | | | 0.83 | | | |
| 3 | 46 | 19 | | | | | | | | |
| 4 | 49 | 18 | | Gradient (b): | | | 1.11 | | | |
| 5 | 51 | 24 | | | | | | | | |
| 6 | 54 | 32 | | Intercept (a): | | | -34.58 | | | |
| 7 | 55 | 21 | | | | | | | | |
| 8 | 62 | 25 | | | | | | | | |
| 9 | 64 | 33 | | Regression equation: | | | Sales in £'000 = -34.58 + 1.11 Aptitude test result | | | |
| 10 | 65 | 37 | | | | | (y | = a | + b | x) | |
| 11 | 67 | 41 | | | | | | | | |

**Figure 7.11** Coefficient of determination and regression equation

Your coefficient of determination of 0.83 means that 83% of the variation in your dependent variable, sales in the past month, can be explained by the independent variable, aptitude test result. This means that the aptitude test is a very good predictor of sales performance for the past month as it's rare to obtain a coefficient of determination larger than 0.8. Note: the value of a coefficient of determination must always be between zero and one. If it is outside this range, then there has been an error in the calculation!

The regression equation you've calculated in Figure 7.11 can be used to predict the value of your dependent variable, sales for the past month, if you know the value of the independent variable, aptitude test. This means, for example, if a potential employee scores 70 in an aptitude test taken as part of the selection process, you can use the regression equation to predict what their sales in £'000 would have been for the past month:

$$\text{Sales in £'000} = -34.58 + (1.11 \times 70)$$
$$= -34.58 + 77.7$$
$$= 43.12$$

You could therefore predict that this potential employee would have made sales of £43,120 for the past month.

## 7.4  Analysing data qualitatively

At the start of this chapter, we said that we would focus on analysing text data qualitatively, only talking about the analysis of non-text data such as audio recordings and the audio parts of video recordings where these have been transcribed and so could also be analysed as text data. If you're collecting your own data, perhaps by interviewing, you will probably have already begun to think about what these interviews are telling you. This is quite normal. We would expect you to begin to analyse your qualitative data before you've collected them all. Doing this will allow you to follow up initial insights suggested by early interviews in later interviews, as well as to recognise when you have reached data saturation (we talked about this in section 6.3). In this section, we will start by looking at how you prepare text data so that they are suitable for qualitative analysis. As you do this, you will begin to immerse yourself in your data and so begin to understand it better. Next, we will talk about how you develop propositions and then how you use these propositions to build or test theory by looking for patterns in your data. Finally, we will look at how you assess the credibility and dependability of qualitative research findings reported by others.

### How to prepare your data

If you're analysing your data qualitatively, you may or may not be using specialist qualitative data analysis software. Although in some universities computer-aided qualitative data analysis software (**CAQDAS**), such as QSR International's NVivo, is

> **Definition**
>
> **CAQDAS:** a general term for all computer-aided qualitative data analysis software such as NVivo, ATLAS.ti and MAXqda.

## Research in practice 7.4

### Annotated interview transcript

As part of her research project on employees' reactions to change, Xue had conducted and audio-recorded semi-structured interviews with 12 participants, each of whom signed a consent form. She found the transcription of the interviews very time consuming as, although each only lasted on average half an hour, word-processing each audio recording took between three and four hours. She emailed her first transcript to her supervisor and asked him to see if there were any ways it could be improved. The extract below from the start of the interview includes her supervisor's comments relating to preparing the transcript for analysis. It does not include any of the supervisor's comments about Xue's interviewing skills.

I presume names have been changed to preserve anonymity

**[organisation name] Interview 2**

Include more details such as date, time and place of interview

XUE: *Thank you for agreeing to be interviewed. Now, just to give a little bit of context, we're going to be talking about you in relation to your work and the changes at [organisation name] in the interview. But first, can you give me an idea of which bit of [organisation name] you work in and what sort of job you do? (...) Can you give me a quick overview?*

Use of italics makes questions easy to see

Use of capitals makes names easy to see

PHIL: I work in Financial Services in the payroll section and I work within the control section of the payroll section running payrolls and thatsort of thing (...)

I presume dots inside the single brackets mean a pause

XUE: *So what is your job title Phil?*

PHIL: Well (...) at the moment it is Project Officer (...) or something like that, I mean (...).

I know there are no typographical errors here, but check there are none in all your transcripts

XUE: *Basically what you are doing is running the payrolls?*

I presume the double bracket means this is your description inside the brackets

PHIL: Well we've gone on to a new payroll system in the last twelve months and are also involved in setting up (......) I WAS involved in the project in setting it up (...) and NOW I have just sort of moved back into the payroll section, and running payrolls, dealing with queries, dealing changes to the system, that sort of thing at the moment ((appears to be unhappy about this)). There is a restructuring going on in the section, so the job title and what I do could, again, be changed into something else.

I presume more dots inside the single brackets means a longer pause

DON'T FORGET TO SAVE EACH INTERVIEW AS A SEPARATE FILE

I presume capitals means this word was spoken more loudly than the others

---

used by students for undergraduate and master's research projects, this is not always the case. In addition, some researchers prefer to analyse qualitative data manually. As a consequence, although you will be expected to use a spreadsheet or statistical analysis software to analyse quantitative data, you're less likely to be expected to use CAQDAS to analyse qualitative data. However, the things you need to do to prepare your text data for qualitative analysis are similar whether or not you intend to use CAQDAS.

Research in practice 7.4 examines an annotated extract from a student's interview transcripts, showing you how to prepare an audio recording as text for qualitative analysis.

As you can see from how Xue has prepared her transcript, when preparing data as text for qualitative analysis, you need to do the following:

- Include details of the date, time and place where the data were collected.

- Anonymise both the organisation's and the respondents' names, using the alternatives consistently.

- Consistently use *italics* to signify questions asked.

- Consistently use capitals to highlight the names of the interviewer and the respondents.

- Consistently use (. . .) to show a pause in speech, the number of dots showing the relative length of the pause.

- Consistently use CAPITALS within the transcript to show those words that were spoken more loudly than others.

- Consistently use (( )) to enclose your description of what is happening such as the participant's tone of voice, facial expressions or other visual cues.

- Make sure there are no typographical errors and that words are spelt consistently throughout.

- Save each interview transcript as a separate file.

Having just read this list, you will see that being consistent when preparing qualitative text data such as transcripts for analysis is crucial. If you're going to analyse web-based interview data where questions and responses were automatically captured as they were typed in, it is unlikely that these data will have been recorded consistently or in precisely the right format for CAQDAS. If you're going to analyse other forms of text data, including secondary data such as online business news reports, these data are also unlikely to be in quite the right format for CAQDAS. Although you will not need to anonymise secondary text data that are available publicly such as news reports, you will still need to add full details of when it was collected and the source where you found it. It is also likely that such data will contain some typographical errors and inconsistencies that you will need to correct. You will therefore need to spend time preparing your text data for qualitative analysis by following the points outlined above, whatever its source.

You only need to read this paragraph if you're going to analyse your data using CAQDAS! If you are, you need to find out if the software you are thinking of using will enable you to do the analysis you are thinking of doing. Fortunately, most CAQDAS software websites, for example QSR International's NVivo 11, provides considerable detail on what the software can do. Many also offer you the option to download a free trial version. Do take this opportunity, especially if the software is not available to download from your university as part of their site license.

### How to develop propositions to build or test theory

We are sure that sometime in your life you have at least had a go at completing a jigsaw puzzle. When you started to make the puzzle, you probably looked first at the picture on the box lid. Let's say it was a photograph of the Sydney Opera House in Australia, although unlike Figure 7.12, it would be in colour. You then tipped all the pieces out of the box onto a table and turned them picture side up before sorting them into different groups or

**Figure 7.12** Sydney Opera House
*Source:* © Mark Saunders, 2015.

categories that had similar characteristics. To help you with your sorting, you looked at the picture to get some ideas for categories. These would have included categories such as part of the 'Opera House', the 'sky', the 'sea', 'vegetation' as well as the 'edge of the puzzle'. Inevitably, you could have put some of the puzzle pieces into more than one category, such as being at the 'edge of the puzzle' and also part of the 'sky', or being part of the 'sea' and part of the 'Opera House'. You then fitted pieces in each category together, completing different parts of the puzzle such as the sky, the river or the Opera House. You then used those pieces that were in more than one of your categories such as the 'sky' and 'Opera House' to join together the different parts of the puzzle you had already completed, before fitting the remaining pieces. Finally, you compared the puzzle picture with that on the box lid.

You're no doubt wondering why we've spent so much time talking about completing a jigsaw puzzle. The answer is simple! Analysing qualitative data and, in particular, looking for patterns by categorising data is similar to completing a jigsaw puzzle. Let's start with the lid of the puzzle box. In addition to the picture of the completed puzzle, it normally says how many pieces there are in the puzzle and how difficult it is to complete. This is similar to your critical review of the literature (section 2.2), as the lid provides an overview of significant information about the puzzle and a clear idea of how the pieces should fit together. The information on the box lid therefore represents the existing knowledge about how the puzzle pieces relate to each other. From this existing knowledge you develop **testable propositions**. For example, looking at the picture on the box lid

(Figure 7.12), a testable proposition would be that the pieces of sky are at the top of the picture. Another would be that the sea is at the bottom of the picture. Pieces that can be put in two or more categories show the interrelationships within the theory, such as the relationship between the Opera House and the sky. You test these propositions (and others) by categorising the pieces and making the puzzle. If the picture on the box is the same as the puzzle picture you have made, then the propositions you have developed are supported!

What you have done in using the picture and other information on the puzzle box lid is analyse your data (the puzzle pieces) deductively (we talked about both deductive and inductive approaches in more detail in section 5.3). This is because you started with what was already known about the puzzle (the picture and other information on the box) and used this as a guide to develop your series of testable propositions. You then designed your analysis (categorised your pieces and made the puzzle) to test these propositions. If you're analysing qualitative data deductively for your project report, you're looking for things in the data to answer research questions and test the propositions that you have developed using your understanding of the academic literature. Like the picture on the puzzle box lid, the literature on which your research questions and propositions are based give a clear direction of the categories that are important and, where a piece falls into two or more categories, how they should fit together. By systematically categorising your data and seeing if particular patterns occur, you're testing your propositions. Remember, as we pointed out in section 6.4, as you collect and analyse your data, you may get new insights into your testable propositions that you did not initially expect and so may need to revise them.

If your puzzle had no picture on the box lid or any other information, then you would have had to analyse your data inductively. You would have started without a clear theory from which to develop testable propositions of what the puzzle looked like, the number of pieces and how they were related. You would have done this by sorting the pieces into different categories that had similar characteristics. However, as there was no information on the box, you would have had to use ideas you generated by looking at (analysing) the puzzle pieces to decide on your categories. You would have found that some of the categories you first thought of were less useful than others and may well have decided later not to use them. If you're analysing qualitative data inductively for your project report, you do not have (or need) a clearly defined theoretical framework. Rather, you're identifying possible propositions (theories) from your data and then developing questions to test them. Like a puzzle about which you have no information, your theory about how the pieces fit together will develop as you systematically analyse your data and collect more data, and the most relevant patterns become clearer.

Look at the first two paragraphs of Research in practice 7.5. In his research, Mark developed three testable propositions from the literature. Each proposition was carefully worded, often as a possible explanation, to enable it to be tested. Reread Mark's first proposition:

1. Students adopt particular habits when they write.

## Research in practice 7.5

### Developing testable propositions and categorising data

Mark was working with a group of students who, like many, found writing their project report difficult. During his preparation, he used a number of academic sources on writing, including the book *Writing for Social Scientists* (Becker, 2007). Using this, he developed three testable propositions:

1  Students adopt particular habits when they write.

2  Students adopt these habits because they:

  (a)  find writing difficult,

  (b)  are easily distracted from writing,

  (c)  are afraid that what they write will be wrong.

3  The habits students adopt differ between male and female students.

He decided to test these propositions and asked each of the students to describe in writing how he or she wrote. He explained he was interested not in the students' scholarly preparations, but in the details of what they actually did when they were writing. The students' word-processed descriptions were subsequently anonymised and formed Mark's data. Mark also developed an initial set of categories to attach to this data:

| | |
|---|---|
| Habit | *Unsure what these could be. Develop categories from the data.* |
| Reason | – difficult |
| | – distraction |
| | – afraid wrong |
| Gender | – male |
| | – female |

The following extract of a student's description shows these categories attached to units of data, each of which is one sentence of the description:

| | |
|---|---|
| GENDER MALE | **Male student** |
| HABIT | I always compose directly into a word processor. I usually have |
| HABIT | hand-written notes to work from which give me an overall |
| | structure, but the thoughts are typed directly in. Before starting, |
| HABIT | I make sure that my desk is relatively clear, other than for the |
| | notes and articles I'm going to use. I also make sure I have a |
| HABIT | fresh cup of tea. The computer is in a room which I always use |
| REASON—COMFORT/DIFFICULT | for writing and I feel comfortable there. To be honest, I find it |
| HABIT | difficult to write anywhere other than this room. The word |
| HABIT | processor software is set to my preferences: Times New Roman |
| | 12, and no auto spell corrections. I've turned off the underline |
| REASON—DISTRACTION | for misspelled words because it puts me off. I don't have any |
| REASON—DISTRACTION | distractions in the room where I write – no music or television, |
| | although there is a telephone. I nearly always start early in the |
| HABIT | morning (7.30) and work through until about 10.30–11.00 |
| | before I have a break. I like to have full days for writing as it |
| HABIT | helps me organise my thoughts . . . |

Although this proposition does not offer a possible explanation, whether or not the students adopt particular habits when they write, it can be tested by looking for patterns in the data Mark has collected.

Now look at Mark's second proposition:

2. Students adopt these habits because they:
   (a) find writing difficult,
   (b) are easily distracted from writing,
   (c) are afraid that what they write will be wrong.

This suggests three possible explanations for students adopting particular habits when they write: (a) they find writing difficult, (b) they are easily distracted from writing and (c) they are afraid that what they write will be wrong. The data Mark collects in the form of students' descriptions of how they write will enable each possible explanation to be tested. When testing these explanations, it will be important that Mark also looks for alternative explanations, such as other reasons why students might adopt these habits. It may be that some students do not even adopt particular habits when they write! If you do not look for alternative explanations, you will probably only notice evidence that supports your own opinions, resulting in your findings being biased and subjective. By testing your own propositions and looking for alternative explanations through looking for clear patterns, you will be able to develop clearly justified, credible conclusions from your data.

Finally, look at Mark's third proposition:

3. The habits students adopt differ between male and female students.

Like Mark's first proposition, this can be tested using the data Mark has collected. As with his other propositions, he will test this by looking for patterns in the data.

## How to build or test theory by looking for patterns

Our earlier jigsaw puzzle example emphasises that, whether you're using a deductive or an inductive approach to look for patterns to build or test your propositions, you need to take the following steps:

1 Develop meaningful **categories** or codes to describe your data.

2 Decide on the **unit of data** that is appropriate for your analysis and to which you will attach relevant categories.

3 Attach relevant categories to units (pieces) of your data.

---

**Definitions**

**categorising data:** developing meaningful categories and attaching those categories that are relevant to specific units of data.

**unit of data:** a predetermined piece of data such as a line of a transcript, sentence, paragraph or response.

If you're using a deductive approach, your categories will be based on terms used in the literature, often being drawn from existing theory. In contrast, if you're using an inductive approach, your categories will emerge from your data. For both deductive and inductive approaches, it is likely that you will refine your categories to ensure they are meaningful as you look for patterns during your analysis to test your propositions. Your choice of the unit of data to which you will attach a relevant category or categories depends on what works! You need units of data that are large enough to highlight where there are relationships between categories, and yet not so large as to be described by all your categories. Depending on the analysis, we've found units of a line of transcript; a sentence and an individual response can all work well.

Let's now look at the categorising of the student's description in Research in practice 7.5. In this research, Mark created hierarchical categories to test three propositions he developed from the literature. However, other than the source of categories, the process he has used is the same for both deductive and inductive approaches. For his first category, 'habit', Mark was unsure what these might be and so decided to develop more detailed sub-categories from the data. This means that for these detailed sub-categories, he will be working inductively. Although the extract shows only part of one student's description, it implies, as suggested in proposition one, students do have habits associated with how they write. Possible sub-categories of 'habit' that Mark could use to group his data suggested by the extract include 'computer use', 'refreshment' and 'room'. If these sub-categories also proved suitable for categorising other students' descriptions, they would reveal that the habits were common. It is likely that further new sub-categories would be revealed by the other students' descriptions of how they write. For his second category, 'reason', Mark worked deductively using the literature to provide three sub-categories: 'difficult', 'distraction' and 'afraid wrong'. The first two of these have been used when categorising units of data in the extract. In addition Mark has introduced a new sub-category: 'reason – comfort' based on the data. This indicates he is looking for alternative explanations. Mark's use of the category 'gender – male' provides descriptive data about the student and will allow him to test his third proposition by looking for differences in patterns between male and female students.

We'll now look at how categorising these data has already begun to suggest a possible pattern with which to test the second proposition. Proposition two offered three reasons why students adopted these habits associated with writing. If we look at the student's description, we can see that the 'reason' sub-categories 'difficulty' and 'distraction' are both in close proximity to the category 'habit'. This provided Mark with an indication that there may be a pattern. Looking at the actual data, you can see that the 'reason' for the 'habit' of using a particular room is because it is 'difficult' to write anywhere else and, towards the end of the extract, because there are no 'distractions'. Obviously from such a short extract, Mark can't be sure that this is a pattern. Analysis of the other students' descriptions of how they write will enable him to test the proposition further and confirm whether a similar pattern occurs.

### ■ How to assess the value of qualitative research reported by others

You're probably now thinking: this is all very well but, when I read articles reporting qualitative research, how do I know that patterns that are discussed and the insights offered are of value? Your question is a good one! As with you, the researcher's biases, preferences and so on will influence at least to some extent the way the data have been collected, analysed and interpreted. This means that when you read an article you need to carefully assess whether the author's claims are credible and dependable, being justified by methods used and supporting evidence that has been offered. To do this, we suggest you use the following questions:

1  Is the method used to collect the data explained clearly (section 6.4)?

2  Is the method used to analyse the data explained clearly (section 7.4)?

3  Are the findings explained thematically?

4  Are the findings related explicitly to research objectives, questions or propositions?

5  Do the arguments and the evidence presented support the claims made? For example:

    (a)  Are the quotations used placed in context, and do they support points made?

    (b)  Are data included that do not support the claims made and an explanation offered as to why?

---

### Research in practice 7.6

#### Assessing findings from interviews

Simone's research project was an extended literature review about how ethnic minority small businesses (EMSBs) managed their customer relationships. In her search of the Business Source Premier database, she had found an article by Altinay, Saunders and Wang (2014) that explored the influence of culture on trust judgements in the development of customer relationships by EMSBs. Altinay and colleagues had analysed data from 134 face-to-face interviews with Turkish entrepreneurs working in London. Each interview covered a wide range of issues including relationship marketing practices and how relationships with both ethnic and British mainstream customer groups were managed, and the entrepreneur's understanding of trust and its importance in customer relationship development.

Simone felt that the article outlined the data collection and analysis clearly, providing sufficient detail for her to see precisely how both had been undertaken. This gave her confidence in the findings. The authors had organised their findings to address their research objectives on the influence of culture thematically using three dimensions of trust judgement outlined widely in the literature (benevolence, honesty and competence) to provide a clear structure.

As part of the findings about how ethnic minority small businesses saw the link between acting benevolently and managing customer relationships Altinay et al. (2014: 67) had written:

They considered relationship development as a process of social exchange, something they saw as a weakness of their large counterparts. The vast majority of EMSB owners explained how they tried to ensure that customers felt there was a family atmosphere, indicating this was the most important element of Turkish hospitality. A retail shop owner emphasized the importance of being sincere and demonstrating good intention: 'Our biggest strength is that we have a lot to offer from our hospitable culture. When the customers go to the bigger stores, they do not know the employees very well. Employees do not talk to them properly. They sometimes do not even know the products well. Whereas with us, I talk to customers informally, I talk to them about football, traffic, weather, family and develop an informal relationship.' . . .

During our interviews, most participants highlighted the importance of demonstrating friendship in business transactions. They stated that this mindset inspired them in their relationship development with customers.

Starting dialogue with customers was perceived to be an effective way of demonstrating friendship and good intentions. One grocery shop owner explained: 'We are very good at developing customer relationships. We take the initiative and start off conversation with our customers about anything.' An accountant's comments summarized the "mentality" dominating the trust development with customers: 'We treat them as "people" not as customers. We value them with their characters and personalities.

In line with arguments by Carson and Gilmore (2000) and Altinay and Altinay (2008), our findings revealed that the value sets of the business owner determine the marketing orientation of firms. Since relationship development was well embedded in the values of Turkish EMSB owners who saw this as a competitive advantage over large counterparts, they equated relationship marketing to their firms' marketing philosophy . . ."

*Source:* Altinay et al., (2014: 67–68) Copyright © 2014 John Wiley & Sons. Reproduced by permission of the publisher

Simone felt that this extract, along with the rest of the findings section on the link between the three components of trust and customer relationship development, provided credible evidence of the role of trust in the development of customer relationships by ethnic minority small businesses. She also recognised that, although the quotations used in the article provided credible supporting evidence regarding how the ethnic minority small businesses EMSBs interviewed had operationalised trusting behaviours, there was no need to include them in her extended literature review. Her supervisor agreed and suggested she just refer to the key findings, where appropriate, when discussing particular themes in her review.

If you haven't done so already, now read Research in practice 7.6. This looks at a journal article using qualitative research a student is reading for her extended essay. The student, Simone, feels that the methods used to collect the data and to analyse the data have been explained clearly in the article (questions 1 and 2 from the list above), and we'll believe her! We're also told that the findings have been organised thematically, each of the authors' research objectives being considered (questions 3 and 4 from the list above). This suggests the findings are based on a dependable method.

Using the extract from the article, we can now consider whether or not we agree with Simone's assessment that the article 'provides credible evidence' to support the claims made. To do this, we'll use the final question (5) from the list above. Look at the first quotation in the extract. Although this quotation is more than four lines in length, it has not been indented. If you're including quotations in your project report, check your university's regulations. Often quotations of five lines or more are indented rather than just being included within the main text of the paragraph. This first quotation provides credible evidence from a retail shop owner to support the authors' claim that the vast majority of owners tried to ensure their customers felt there was a family atmosphere (question 5a). As you read on, you will see that subsequent quotes from a grocery shop owner and an accountant offer further insights regarding how this atmosphere was developed and the importance of friendship.

You will notice that all of the data in this extract does supports the claims being made. This would suggest that the answer to question 5b, 'Are data included that do not support the claims made . . .?' is 'No'! You will have to take it from us that such data were included in this article, illustrating clear differences in how ethnic minority small businesses developed relationships with different customer groups. In particular, these data highlighted differences in those trust components that were important for relationships with other ethnic minority groups and those that were important for relationships with mainstream British nationals (Altinay et al., 2014). Following this discussion, we can say we agree with Simone's assessment and that the article 'provides credible evidence' to support the claims made.

## Summary

- The data that you and others analyse can be divided into two types: quantitative data that are numerical or whose values had been measured in some way, and qualitative data that are not numerical and have not been measured in some way.

  - Quantitative data can be split into categorical data (nominal and ordinal) and numerical data (interval and ratio).

  - Qualitative data can be divided into text data and non-text data (audio, video and still image).

- When preparing quantitative data for computer analysis, you should enter it as a data matrix. Secondary data can often be downloaded in this format. You should check data for errors before undertaking analyses.

- Tables and diagrams are used to present quantitative data. The tables and diagrams you use depend on the type of data you have and what you want to show.

- Statistical analyses are used to describe data and to examine and assess relationships. The statistics you use depend on the type of data you have, what you want to describe, examine or assess and whether you can meet the assumptions of the test. For data that is a sample from a larger population, you will need to work out the probability of the finding or one more extreme occurring by chance.

- Qualitative data are often analysed in text form. When preparing qualitative data for analysis as text, you should transcribe it as a word-processed document, ensuring you use transcribing conventions consistently. You can either analyse qualitative data manually or use computer-aided qualitative analysis software.

- You can undertake the process of qualitative data analysis both deductively and inductively.

- In both inductive and deductive qualitative analysis, you can use propositions to develop theory. This involves looking for patterns in your data and testing alternative explanations for these patterns using your data. To look for patterns, you need to:

  - develop meaningful categories or codes to describe your data;

  - decide on the unit of data that is appropriate for your analysis and to which you will attach relevant categories;

  - attach relevant categories to units (pieces) of your data.

- It is important that, in analysing data, the arguments you offer and the findings you present support claims you're making clearly and logically.

## Thinking about analysing data

→ As you continue to read and note the literature, use your knowledge about quantitative and qualitative data analysis to help you assess the value of other researchers' findings (section 2.7).

→ Think about the analyses you will need to undertake to answer your research question and meet your objectives.

→ If you're going to use or are using secondary data (Chapter 4), use your knowledge about different types of data and how to prepare data for analysis to help you assess which data analysis techniques will be most suitable. Make notes about the reasons for your choices, as you will need this level of detail to write the method section of your project report.

→ If you're going to collect or have collected your own (primary) data, use your knowledge about different types of data and how to prepare data for analysis to help you assess which data analysis techniques will be most helpful. Make notes about the reasons for your choices, as you will need this level of detail to write the method section of your project report. If possible, make your assessment of techniques before you collect your data. You may find you need to change parts of your collection methods, such as questionnaire questions (Chapter 6).

→ Also, make notes explaining how the analyses you have chosen will mean you can answer your objectives. You will need this level of detail to write the method section of your project report.

## References

Altinay, L., Saunders, M.N.K. and Wang, C. (2014). The influence of culture on trust judgments in customer relationship development by ethnic minority small businesses. *Journal of Small Business Management*, 52(1), 59–78.

Becker, H.S. (2007). *Writing for Social Scientists* (2nd ed.). Chicago: University of Chicago.

Eurostat Press Office (2016). Organic crop farming on the rise in the EU. *Eurostat News Release 208/2016*. Available at: http://ec.europa.eu/eurostat/documents/2995521/7709498/5-25102016-BP-EN.pdf/cee89f9e-023b-4470-ba23-61a9893d34c8 [Accessed 21 November 2016].

Ghazali, S. (2011). The influence of socialization agents and demographic profiles on brand consciousness, *International Journal of Management and Marketing Research*, 4(1), 19–29.

Hair, J., Black, W., Babin, B. and Anderson, R. (2009). *Multivariate Data Analysis* (7th ed.). London: Pearson.

Office for National Statistics (2016). *Balance of Payments Time Series Dataset*. Available at: https://www.ons.gov.uk/economy/nationalaccounts/balanceofpayments/datasets/balanceofpayments [Accessed 20 November 2016].

Saunders, M., Lewis, P. and Thornhill, A. (2016). *Research Methods for Business Students* (7th ed.). Harlow: Pearson.

# Chapter 8

# Writing and presenting the research proposal

## 8.1 Why you should read this chapter

When we sat down to plan this text, we thought long and hard about the order in which the chapters should appear. The most difficult decision was where to place this chapter. It had to appear at the beginning of the text or at the end. We could have put it at the beginning. Setting out the recommended content of the research proposal could have acted as a route map from which you could plot your path through the text. This would have ensured you were familiar with the role of, say, the literature review and the details you should include about your proposed methods. We decided against this. We thought that you should be familiar with the major concepts and techniques that the conduct of research involves before you think about your proposal. In short, we felt that you would be better equipped to write an effective research proposal having read and understood the previous seven chapters.

Writing an effective research proposal is a vital part of the research process. We explain the reasons for this in the first section of this chapter. Perhaps you feel it is unnecessary to elaborate on this. After all, your university may require you to produce a written research proposal as the assessment vehicle for the research methods module, so this reason is sufficient. But the research proposal is a vital document for reasons other than assessment necessity. Indeed, you may be reading this text to help you prepare a research proposal which will be a vital starting point in your research. For example, you may be embarking upon a research project required by your work organisation. Whatever the purpose, writing an effective research proposal is vital.

We then consider at which point in the research process you should be writing your research proposal before considering the most important topic addressed in the chapter: the content of the research proposal. The chapter ends with two discussions which we hope you will find useful. The first is on the writing style you should adopt when compiling your research proposal. This is something many of us have found difficult, and confusing, in our academic careers and is something worth thinking about. Finally, we return to the subject of assessment and ask just what is it that the assessor(s) of your research proposal will be looking for when that all-important judgment is made.

## 8.2   The importance of the research proposal

The overall purpose of the research proposal is to present and justify a research idea you have and to explain the practical way in which you think this research should be conducted. In effect, it is a 'contract' between you and your reader(s) which sets out precisely what it is you aim, or would aim, to do and the way in which you will do it. You can also think about this contract as a personal document which binds you to your stated intentions in the event that you are tempted to break the contract! So think about the research proposal as an essential discipline measure in a process which has the potential to become extremely undisciplined!

Now let's look at some of the more specific reasons the research proposal is so important.

### It clarifies your ideas and helps you organise those ideas

Another reason we decided to place this chapter at the end of the book is that you will realise now that assembling your research ideas is a very difficult process. Moreover, assembling them in a way that they will make sense to an audience which is far less familiar than you with those ideas is even more difficult.

We have already made the point in Chapter 2 that writing can be the best way of clarifying our thoughts. This is a valuable purpose of the research proposal. There is nothing quite so frightening as sitting in front of a screen with just the heading 'Research proposal' to concentrate the mind. The very blankness of the screen forces you to come up with some ideas. If all else fails, we always suggest to our students to do what we do ourselves (and, in fact, what we did in planning this chapter): to turn to Rudyard Kipling! There is a section in one of his 1902 *Just So Stories* where he wrote:

> I KEEP six honest serving-men
> (They taught me all I knew);
> Their names are What and Why and When
> And How and Where and Who.

*Source*: Kipling (1902, reprinted 2007).

To use Kipling to help you in framing your research proposal, you can build the content around the answers to:

- What are the research questions I am seeking to answer?
- What are my research objectives?
- Why is the research I propose significant?
- When are the key dates in the research process?
- How will I go about collecting the necessary data to answer the research questions?
- Where will I be conducting my research (e.g. organisation, sector, country)?
- Who are the key participants in the research process (e.g. gatekeepers, respondents)?

Not only will this technique clarify your thoughts but it will help you to organise your ideas into a clear statement of your research intent. Clarity, in this sense, means organising your ideas in such a way that they are coherent and rigorous. Coherence means that they make sense, are plausible and can be understood easily: by rigorous, we mean that the ideas will stand up to searching analysis and can be defended by you in the face of demands for you to justify their inclusion in your proposal. Your assessor will be looking for this standard of work in your proposal.

### It serves as a route map to guide you through the research process

If you are going on to do the research that you have detailed in your research proposal, the proposal will be a very useful check for you to ensure that you are doing what you said you will do. This may sound an obvious point, but few of us have not had our imaginations fired by a great idea during the research process only to be deflated by a supervisor who says 'yes, that's a super idea, but look again at your research objectives; explain to me how this new idea fits'. Too often the response is 'mmm . . . I see what you mean' when it is apparent that the new idea does not fit.

We have found that some students benefit from putting up on their study wall a copy of their research question(s) and objectives in large, bold type so that they can revisit them frequently to ensure they are on the right track.

---

**Research in practice 8.1**

**Defining research questions**

Freya was a final-year undergraduate who had to prepare a research proposal for her research methodology module assessment. For her topic, she had chosen to explore the extent to which work experience during a undergraduate course impacted upon job performance in the graduate's first job. Her interest in the topic stemmed from her own spell in a large non-profit organisation which she felt prepared her well for her entry into paid employment. So her overall research question was 'To what extent and in what ways does the degree student placement affect the job performance of the newly recruited graduate?'

As a result of a lot of reading of reports, particularly in the educational media, Freya generated the following research objectives:

1 To establish whether there is a link between the experience of a placement by the undergraduate and the performance in the first career job.

2 To discover whether the type of placement (e.g. duration, amount of responsibility) is associated with level of job performance.

3 To identify the variables which may be most strongly associated with job performance (e.g. quality of experience gained, personal confidence, closeness of relationship between placement duties and first-job duties).

Freya's proposal went on to detail her research strategy and methods that she would adopt. Her main data collection method was that of interviews with two samples of UK

→

students, one who had completed a work placement and one who had not done so. She also suggested interviews with managers to whom the first-job graduates were responsible.

Freya was praised for her proposal which raised an interesting question that would be of considerable use to future students. However, her assessor criticised the lack of consistency between her objectives and her data collection methods. In particular, her assessor thought that the language of her objectives was couched in precision (e.g. duration of placement, amount of responsibility and, most importantly, actual job performance) whereas Freya's data collection method was more consistent with subjective impressions. In short, there was a mismatch between her objectives and method. The overall comment of her assessor was 'you may have been wiser to stress in your objectives the quality of experience of the graduate in the first job rather than the performance: the first suggesting subjective impressions, the second, objective measurement'.

## It shows you have a good knowledge of the existing work

Your research proposal is your opportunity to demonstrate your expertise on the subject you have chosen. This will largely result from your close acquaintance with the relevant literature. From this you will gain the insights that will help you to produce an interesting proposal. Later in this chapter we talk more about the place of the literature in the research proposal. At this stage, we must stress that there is a world of difference between the proposal which merely lists some references at the end and that which clearly uses the literature to inform the choice of topic, the question(s) and objectives and the research approach, strategy and methods.

If you have read thoroughly in preparation for your research proposal, this will shine through because it will demonstrate that you are up to date with the current news and debates concerning your topic. This will be at two levels: first, the news level where the latest developments in, say, outsourced marketing are reported; and second, where academic research has been done to reach a deeper level of understanding of the topic. Of course, current knowledge of the second level means that you don't submit a research proposal which merely replicates research done by other researchers, risking quite justifiable criticism from your assessor. But even if your proposal is similar to that already done by another researcher, you can demonstrate novelty and knowledge of current literature by building on existing research and, perhaps, approaching the research from a different perspective, or in a different context.

## It demonstrates to the assessor(s) that the research is viable

If you have to submit a research proposal without having to actually conduct the research, there is a danger that you will not give sufficient thought to the practical issues which would be faced by the researcher. The focus here is on resources.

As a management and business expert, your assessor will be mindful of the cost implications of your proposal. This relates to the direct costs involved, such as travel and possible accommodation expenses, and indirect costs, most particularly your time.

You will have other things to do in your degree programme, so submitting a proposal which implies that it will take up more of your time that you can reasonably afford to devote is not a good idea. It is not only the amount of time that is important, but the length of time of the proposed research from start to finish that you should consider. It is no good suggesting a research project which, say, plots the effect of management coaching on longer-term job performance if the timescale is longer than you have allocated.

But perhaps the most important resource of which you may underestimate the importance is data availability. There may be little point in developing a proposal which examines the importance of the vision that Sir Richard Branson brings to the Virgin Group if you cannot get access to the man himself! In the example shown in Research in practice 8.1, the proposal specifies the role of job performance. This assumes that job performance data will be made available to the researcher. This is problematic, given issues of confidentiality.

Two further points about the viability of the research are relevant for those of you who are not only submitting your proposal for assessment but are going to conduct the research you have included in that proposal. The first relates to the extent to which you indicate that you are capable of doing the research. This may be implied in all that has gone before in terms of evidence of quality of thought. But you also have the opportunity to show that you are creative and innovative, not only in the research objectives you set but in the way in which you set out to achieve them. A genuine interest in the research you propose is something that will be clearly evident in what you have written. The second point about the viability of the research concerns the practical planning for the research from your university's perspective. A clear and timely proposal is often used to decide who would be the most suitable supervisor for you.

## ● It ensures that your research meets the requirements of your university

It is likely that your proposal may have to contain your assurance that you have considered the requirements of your university. An example of these requirements is the university which states in its code of practice that an ethics committee needs to consider all research proposals which actively involve human participants. In another UK university, the research proposal must clarify exactly what is meant by guaranteeing anonymity and confidentiality to research participants when they participate in the research. Here, anonymity refers to concealing the identity of the participants in all documents resulting from the research. Confidentiality is concerned with the right of access to the data provided by individual participants and, in particular, the need to keep these data secret or private. In addition, many ethics committees require researchers to state the steps they will take to ensure protection of respondents' identities and ensure that the information collected is stored securely. We go into the subject of research ethics in more detail in section 3.8.

For those of you who are going to conduct the research you have outlined in your proposal, you are justified in thinking that a proposal which is deemed acceptable implies that the research itself promises to be successful. Obviously, this cannot be guaranteed. But it is reassuring to know that at least you started your research journey with a suitable destination and journey plan.

## 8.3    When you should write your research proposal

In our view, the proposal could be started at day one of your research module. At that stage, it may bear little or no resemblance to the finished article, but there are enormous benefits to be gained from starting early, not the least of which is committing thoughts to writing. Once again, we make the point that writing is a great way of clarifying your thoughts. At the first stage of thinking about your research, you will probably not be able to note any more than outline topics in which you are interested. As your thoughts develop, you may add some initial research questions and then follow these with research objectives. All the time, expect that you will amend what you have written. But do keep a copy of the various main versions of your proposal document. You never know when you may need to resurrect a previous idea. Treat your proposal as work in progress rather than seeing it as a 'one off' – something which you write up and submit after your thinking, discussing and planning stage.

We have always encouraged our students to adopt this approach to the development of their research proposals. This has proved to be beneficial to us too. When we sit and discuss our students' research ideas, it is so helpful to have a shared document to form the basis of that discussion, even if it is in a very early stage of development. Also, we keep copies of earlier drafts which show us how thoughts have developed and become more concrete. We also have the ability to look back at ideas which may have become 'lost' and may be usefully reconsidered.

The earlier the research proposal is discussed with your supervisor, the better. Often the supervisor will suggest that the scope of what you are considering is too ambitious. This will usually be because the work proposed is not viable for one of the reasons we have explained in section 8.2. Whatever amendments you need to make, and for whatever reason, the sooner you begin preparing your research proposal, the better.

## 8.4    What you should include in your research proposal

To a great extent, the content of your research proposal will be governed by the format required by your university and by the proposal content itself. What we offer here is a guide to the sections that you will most likely need to include.

### Research overview

You may think of this first section as an abstract or an executive summary. As such it is a brief statement of what you intend to do for the research. It should be no more than a paragraph or two and should describe the proposal content to busy readers in no more than a few words.

## Title

Try here to reflect as accurately as possible the content of the proposal. The economist Adam Smith may not have written a research proposal for his famous book, but it seems to us that you can't be more precise than the title he chose: *An Inquiry into the Nature and Causes of the Wealth of Nations* (1904).

You may want to leave composing the title until you have finished the body of the proposal. Alternatively, this may be your start point. If this is the case, don't be afraid to amend the title as your work progresses.

## Introduction to the research

This is an important part of the proposal. You should place the proposed study in a context which will assist your assessor in understanding why it is you have chosen this particular topic. You may wish to demonstrate the topical relevance of your proposal if it is concerned with something that is generating current debate. An example here would be the way the retail banks are trying to overcome their negative public image through their marketing strategies. Alternatively, you may wish to concentrate upon a problem being experienced by an organisation with which you are familiar. Here, an example may be the difficulty the organisation has with retaining key employees.

In either of these two cases, your assessor will be keen to see if you are knowledgeable about the topic and can relate it to existing theory. So in the case of the retail bank proposal you may show how this is drawn from, and/or may contribute relevant marketing theory. Similarly, you may use the literature on employee retention strategy theory in the second example.

It will help to persuade your assessor of the quality of your proposal if you can explain why you are interested in the topic. This may be because you have worked in the particular organisation or have studied the retail banks in another module.

If your proposal is the precursor to your going on to conduct the research, it will be helpful if you show that you are enthusiastic about the research topic. This will help convince your assessor you have sufficient commitment to sustain your effort over the life of the research.

In short, the real value of this background section is to convince the assessor that the research is worth pursuing; not just by you as part of your course, but by a competent researcher who will add to an understanding of the particular topic you are studying.

## Research Question(s)

In section 1.7 we explain what is meant by research questions and research objectives and the difference between the two. To recap, the research question may be one overall question, or a number of questions that the research process will address which are often the forerunner of research objectives. Research objectives are clear, specific statements that identify what the research process seeks to achieve as a result of doing the research. So the movement from research questions to research objectives is a developmental one: objectives follow questions to provide precision to that which is more general.

This progression from research questions to research objectives is reflected in the order we suggest for the sections in the research proposal. We propose that the literature review section separates them. The reason for this is that we see the research question as directing and leading you into the relevant literature, whereas the research objectives are developed as a result of careful consideration of the literature. Of course, the process is not that straightforward. Our model implies that reading generally on the topic of your interest may fire your imagination sufficiently to raise workable research questions; and having developed a research question(s), you then embark on more specific reading to develop your question(s) into objectives. The reality is that the three processes of reading, question development and objective development may take place in no coherent order or, more likely, simultaneously without you really sensing that there is a particular order. There are some examples of research questions in section 1.7.

## Literature Review

Chapter 2 explains in detail the role of the critical literature review in doing research and ways in which this may be accomplished. A critical literature review is something that you would normally include in a final written project report. Here we are more concerned with that which you should include in your research proposal. It is important to show in your proposal that you are knowledgeable about the literature that relates to your research topic. More specifically, you should use this opportunity to explain how your proposal relates to the academic debate which is being conducted in the literature. You will be expected to show a clear link between the previous work that has been done in your field of research interest and the content of your proposal. Put simply, you should show in your review of the literature where your research question(s) came from and how your research objectives will move the debate forward by, say, applying a new perspective or setting your research in a new context: the literature is both a point of departure and a signpost pointing to your destination.

This all suggests that it is insufficient in your research proposal just to provide an overview of the key literature sources from which you intend to draw. Clearly you should include references to key articles and texts, but you must also show relevance to your research.

### Research in practice 8.2

#### A research proposal about power

James was a part-time student. His full-time job was in the fire service where he led a team of firefighters. His organisation had recently been through a major change programme which had been only partly successful. James had noticed that in some parts of his organisation, the programme had been implemented more effectively than others. In particular, he felt that this might relate to the leadership style adopted by the manager in charge of the individual departments.

James's initial theory was that a leadership style which was based on the principle of 'leading by example' was more likely to yield positive results than one rooted in autocracy.

James had studied leadership as part of his course and had decided to examine his organisation's change programme as his research project. He was interested in the idea of power and how this related to leadership and particularly attracted by the typology of power used by Raven and French (1959), still a key influence in the power literature although written half a century ago.

The section below is from James's research proposal, where he outlines the way in which he plans to incorporate the idea of power into his study.

This study will draw on the theory of power as noted by Raven and French (1959), and reviewed more recently by Elias (2008). Power is defined here as the ability to influence others to believe and act in such a way that those in power would wish.

Raven and French argue that power manifests itself in five main forms. These are:

- Coercive Power
- Reward Power
- Legitimate Power
- Referent Power
- Expert Power

1. Coercive Power

   This form of power is based upon the idea of coercion. This means that someone is forced to do something, typically against their will. The main objective of coercion is compliance.

   Coercive power can lead to unhealthy behaviour and dissatisfaction at work.

   Leaders who use this leadership style rely on threats in their management styles. Often these threats can relate to dismissal or demotion.

2. Reward Power

   This form of power is based on the idea that as a society we are more inclined to do things well when we are getting something in return for this. The most popular forms of reward are pay rises, promotions or compliments. The problem with this form of power is that when the reward does not have enough perceived value to others, the power is weakened. One of the frustrations when using rewards is that they often need to be bigger than the last time if they are to have the same effect. Even then, when they are given regularly, employees can become accustomed to the rewards and as a result, they will lose their effectiveness.

3. Legitimate Power

   Legitimate power is usually based on a role. People traditionally follow the one person with power which is solely based on their position or title. This form of power can

→

easily be overcome as soon as someone loses their position or title. This form of power can be an ineffective way to persuade and convince other people.

4.  Referent Power

Leaders in this form of power are often seen as a role models. Their power is often treated with admiration. This power emanates from a person that is highly liked and people identify strongly with them in some way. Leaders with referent power often have a good appreciation of their environment and therefore tend to have a lot of influence. But individual responsibility flowing from referent power is heavy.

5.  Expert Power

This form of power is based on in-depth information, knowledge or expertise. The leader who has a particular expertise within an organisation can often persuade employees, who trust and respect them, to do things for them. This expertise is greatly appreciated and forms the basis of this type of leadership.

James's plan was to construct an initial theoretical model which related the variables of organisational change effectiveness and power in leadership. He proposed to define indicators of each and collect data noting the extent to which these indicators were present in the change programme.

**References**

Raven, B. H. & French, J. (1959). The bases of social power. In D. Cartwright (Ed.) *Studies in social power* (pp. 150–167). Ann Arbor, MI: Institute for Social Research.

Elias, S. (2008). Fifty years of influence in the workplace: The evolution of the French and Raven power taxonomy, *Journal of Management History*, 14(3): 267–283.

## Research objectives

We made the point earlier in this section that the research objectives are developed as a result of careful consideration of the literature. Make sure that they:

- relate to and are developed from your research question(s);
- relate to and are developed from your review of the literature;
- are specific, measurable, achievable, realistic and timely (see Chapter 1 and Table 1.7).

## Method

This will be one of the more detailed sections of your research proposal. It flows directly from your research objectives and shows how you will go about achieving them. In the method section, you have the opportunity to show the assessor the extent to which you really understand the research process through ensuring this close connection between research objectives and method. For example, if one of your objectives is 'to establish the influence of price promotions on supermarket bread sales', you will need to think about ways in which you may quantify the effect price has on sales. This may be done, for example, through the examination of sales records. Whether it is possible to collect the data is an important consideration here: that is a potential assessor concern that you must address in the proposal. This example also raises the issue of validity and reliability (see section 5.6). A key question that will be going through your assessor's mind will be 'are the methods being proposed here likely to deliver credible results that can lead to sound, valid conclusions?' It is vital that you think this through thoroughly when preparing the method section of your proposal. You should justify your choice of methods in the light of the question about credibility. So in defence of any questioning of your research methods, you can answer, 'I chose to collect data this way because I feel this will provide valid and reliable data'.

Your method section can be divided into two parts: research design and data collection. In the research design part of the section, you should explain your overall strategy, for example a case study or a survey strategy, alongside two other aspects of your research design. These are, first, the location of your research and, second, the research population from which you will select your sample (section 6.2). If your research is to be carried out in one organisation, then the location is straightforward and needs no further elaboration. However, if your research topic is not concentrated in one organisation, then you will need to detail the locations. So, for example, a study of the introduction of a new distribution strategy by Internet retailers may mean choosing a sample of retailers among whom you are carrying out a comparative study. In this case, you would need to explain why you chose the participant organisations. Your reasoning here will be judged against the extent to which your choice of organisations is consistent with your research objective and the need to provide credible data. You may be proposing a project which is even more generic, say, a study of the effect of changing consumer preferences for music subscription services on the music industry. Here you would need to explain why you chose this sector.

Secondly, in this part of the section on research method, you will need to describe and justify the population from which you propose to collect data. This may be a small sample of employees that you propose to interview, a large sample that will receive a questionnaire (Chapter 6) or a number of companies about which you can access secondary data (Chapter 4).

The method section should also include an explanation of the way in which you intend to carry out the research. It could involve, say, questionnaires, semi-structured or unstructured interviews, analysis of secondary data or a combination of data collection techniques. Again, it is essential to explain why you have chosen these techniques. This explanation should reflect upon whether this is the most effective way of meeting your research objectives and providing credible data.

The data collection section should be much more detailed about how specifically the data are to be collected (Chapter 6). For example, if you are using questionnaires, you should specify your population and sample size and how your sample will be selected. You should also clarify how the questionnaires will be distributed, the likely response rate, and how the data will be analysed. If you are using interviews, you should explain how many interviews will be conducted, how long they will last, whether they will be audio-recorded and how they will be analysed. You should show your assessor that you have thought carefully about all the issues regarding your method and their relationship to your research objectives and data credibility. Don't worry about the necessity to provide precise detail. It is normally not necessary in the proposal to include precise detail of the method you will employ, for example the content of an observation schedule or questionnaire questions. In this section, you will also need to include a statement about how you are going to adhere to your university's ethical code (see section 3.8).

## Timescale

This is a useful part of your research proposal. Clearly breaking down the research process into a series of steps will show you whether it is reasonable to expect the various tasks to be done within the timescale. For example, it is no good taking three months to do your literature review if your project has to be submitted in two months. More tellingly, it will show clearly how much time is to be available for data collection and analysis. The time required here is often far more than anticipated. This is for a number of reasons, not the least of which is the degree of dependence that you may have upon your respondents from whom you are collecting your data. Analysing the data also often takes far more time that anticipated (Chapter 7). This is particularly so if you have a limited amount of experience with any software that is being used for analysis.

Devising a timescale is also an important part of the research proposal because it enables your assessor to assess the variability of the work you propose. You can follow all the advice in this chapter, and in this text, and produce a beautifully crafted, intellectually coherent research proposal only to be marked down with the damning comment 'an excellent proposal but one which proposes research that could not possibly be done within the timescale'. Discussing your plans with your supervisor should avoid this happening. Experience of reading many proposals usually gives supervisors a good idea of what is practicable in a given timescale.

**Table 8.1** An example timescale for a research project.

| Task | To be completed by: |
| --- | --- |
| Begin research idea formulation and first coverage of literature. | 1/10/2017 |
| Main part of literature research completed, research questions and objectives defined. | 20/11/2017 |
| Research proposal submitted. | 30/11/2017 |
| Make arrangements for data collection. | 31/12/2017 |
| Literature research finished and review written. | 31/12/2017 |
| Secondary data research. | 31/12/2017 |
| Primary research and analysis. | 20/2/2018 |
| Draft written report. | 31/3/2018 |
| Revised draft written report. | 15/05/2018 |
| Final submission of written report. | 30/5/2018 |

### Resources

It may be that you are asked to list the resources required for the completion of the project you propose. This also will assist your assessor in assessing the viability of your proposal. We explained in section 8.2 that you should detail direct costs involved, such as travel and possible accommodation expenses and indirect costs, most particularly your time.

We also mentioned in section 8.2 the importance of data availability. Your assessor will be concerned about approval from any organisations in which you are planning to conduct your research and may well require written evidence of this. You will also need to convince your assessor that the response rate to any questionnaire that you send is likely to be satisfactory.

You should also be able to convince your assessor that you can undertake the analysis of your data satisfactorily. This is often an aspect of the research process that is ignored when the proposal is submitted. It is important that you describe the resources you have available for data analysis purposes. This may include computer software and the appropriate skills to perform the analysis, or help in learning these skills in an appropriate time.

### References

You may be tempted to impress your assessor (and fellow students!) with a long list of references at the end of your proposal. This is not necessary. Do bear in mind the point we made in section 8.2 that simply listing references to those sources which you have consulted is not what is required. You should list only those references that clearly use the literature to inform the choice of topic, the question(s) and objectives and the research approach, strategy and methods. Be careful to ensure that your references are in exactly the format required by your university (section 2.7 and Appendix 1).

## 8.5 The style you should use to write your research proposal

We have included a section a number of dos and don'ts on writing style in this chapter. It will obviously be very relevant to those who are writing the project report. We hope it will also help those of you who are doing the research proposal without progressing to the full project report following the conduct of the research. The points we make in this section are sufficiently generalised to meet all research writing needs.

### Do write clearly and simply

You are unusual if you enjoy the style in which much of the material you have to read for your university work has been written. We hope you find the content interesting (it would be worrying if you didn't!) but the style, well that's a different matter. We agree with the American academic C. Wright Mills (1970: 239–40), who, you can see from the quote that follows, was unimpressed by the writing of many of his academic colleagues.

> The ... lack of ready intelligibility [in scholarly writing], I believe, usually has little or nothing to do with the complexity of the subject matter, and nothing at all to do with profundity of thought. It has to do almost entirely with certain confusions of the academic writer about his own status ... To overcome the academic prose you first of all have to overcome the academic pose ...

This is not to say that you should trivialise what you write in your research proposal or report. Far from it. You will be dealing with a serious subject for a serious purpose so your writing should reflect this. But you can be serious and clear at the same time!

An example will illustrate our point. Consider the following two statements.

1. The research proposed here is seeking to gain an understanding of the ways in which those factors which are closely associated with the relationship between consumer preferences for security and economy are reconciled when the consumer purchasing decision for delivery is made in the Internet seller auction sector.
2. When sellers on Internet auction sites decide which carrier to use, they consider both security and cost. In this research I aim to establish how these two factors influence the purchasing decision.

Both statements say the same thing. But the second uses 34 words rather than 50. This is 32% fewer words! So the 'wordy' research proposal which takes 1,000 words could do the same job for 660. Just consider the benefit to you of asking the assessor to do 32% less work! In addition to this obvious advantage, you will be conveying the same meaning in a much clearer way, so not only will your assessor have to read fewer words but those which are read will be digested much more easily.

## ⬤ Do write simple sentences

Not only does the second statement in the example above use fewer words while conveying the same meaning but it uses two short sentences rather than one long one. Look at your writing and break up those long sentences. Use the simple rule: one idea – one sentence.

Research writing is often difficult because you are writing about ideas and facts and usually working out relationships between the two. Long, complicated sentences usually mean that you aren't sure about what you want to say. This is quite understandable. But shorter sentences are much better for explaining complex information because they break the information up into smaller chunks which are easier to follow.

One more golden rule: avoid the embedded clause! Consider these two sentences.

1. While confidentiality is of the utmost importance, it is necessary to bear in mind the practicalities of organisational life, therefore respondents will be interviewed individually insofar as this is possible, although privacy may not always be possible for the same reasons of practicality.
2. I plan to interview the respondents individually in as setting which will be private and therefore conducive to confidentiality. This depends upon the availability of suitable rooms.

Sentences with lots of clauses and exceptions confuse the audience by losing the main idea in a jungle of words. Don't put all your ideas in one sentence; separate your ideas and make each one the subject of its own sentence, like in sentence 2 above.

## Do be careful with spelling and grammar

Spelling and grammatical errors detract from the quality of your work and make it look less credible and authoritative. It's too easy to say that the word processing software you use will do this job for you. It won't tell you that you have used 'practice' and 'practise' or 'moral' and 'morale' in the wrong context. Try to get a friend who is a good speller to check your work so you don't make these errors.

Common grammatical errors can irritate the assessor. All assessors have their pet hates! So avoid simple mistakes such as referring to one interviewee as 'they'; calling lots of data 'it' rather than 'they' (a single piece is 'datum'); using clichés such as 'the real world' to refer to that which exists outside the university. Again, persuade a critical reader to check your writing for you. You may not avoid all the grammatical pitfalls, but at least you may not fall into the obvious ones.

## Don't use jargon

All disciplines have their jargon, and business is as guilty as most. The meaning of terms like 'buy-in' are clear enough to us, but nonetheless they have the potential to irritate your assessor. There are perfectly good words to use which are correct English and the irritated assessor may ask 'what is wrong with "gain agreement"'?

Jargon should not be confused with technical terms. Some technical terms are perfectly valid. Here it is useful to put a glossary of technical terms in the appendices. However, do not assume that your assessor will have your level of knowledge of the subject and, in particular, the context. Try to put yourself in the position of the assessor. As part of a research writing workshop, we ask students to assess research proposals. Some of these are written by students who use their own organisation as a context for the research. The students assessing these proposals are usually amazed at the assumptions that their fellow students make about the assessor's prior knowledge.

### ● Do beware of using a large number of quotations from the literature

In your research proposal you are unlikely to use many quotations from your literature sources. Yet, one or two may lend authority. However, it is important that you use these to illustrate, or emphasise a point that you are making rather than insert it to make your proposal 'look good'. We should stress here that the point that you are making must be your point. If you are using a quotation that is largely unexplained, it is that author's point alone. In general, it is better to explain other people's ideas in your own words. In that way, you can really gain an understanding of what the author means and convince your assessor of your understanding.

When it comes to the project report we feel that quotations from the literature should be used sparingly. Sometimes we read draft projects that consist of little more than a series of quotations from books and journal articles that a student has linked together with a few sentences of her or his own. This is unacceptable. It tells us very little about the student's understanding of the concepts within the quotations. All it shows is that the student has looked at the book or journal article and (hopefully!) acknowledged sources correctly. Using quotations in this way means that line of argument becomes disjointed and difficult to follow. That doesn't mean that you should never use quotations. But we advise you to use them in moderation to create maximum impact in supporting your storyline.

### ● Do be careful when using personal pronouns

Often project reports are written in a rather dry and unexciting style. This is partly because the convention has been to write impersonally (e.g. 'it was decided to interview a small sample . . .'). Here, the writer is distanced from the text. Some writers anonymise themselves by referring to themselves as 'the author' or 'the researcher'. Our view is that, where appropriate, your writing is much livelier if you use the first person ('I decided to interview a small sample . . .'). We say, 'where appropriate'. This is because your research strategy and methods may dictate your choice of personal pronoun. It may be useful to ask yourself, 'Am I inside or outside the data collection process?' By 'inside' we mean that the researcher is an intrinsic part of the data collection. This may be the case with interviews. However, with questionnaires, the researcher is 'outside' the data collection process. Many academics, but not all, use the broad rule; only if you are inside the data collection process is it appropriate to use the personal pronoun.

Do check this with your supervisor. There may be conventions which you are expected to observe. Some researchers think that excessive use of 'I' and 'we' casts doubt on your ability to stand outside your data and to be objective.

### ● Do be careful when using tense

Rather like the use of person, there are no clear rules about the correct use of tense in academic writing. We usually recommend that you use the present tense when referring to previously published work (e.g. 'Smith notes in his earlier article . . .') and the past tense when referring to your present results (e.g. 'I found that . . .'). Although there are exceptions to this rule, it serves as a useful guide.

## Do be careful when using gender

No doubt you will already have been warned about use of language that assumes the gender of a classification of people. In business and management, the most obvious example is the constant reference to managers as 'he'. This is not only inaccurate in many organisations, it also gives offence to many people of both sexes. It is easy to avoid falling into this trap. Instead of 'I propose to interview each senior manager in his office', it is more appropriate to write, 'I propose that each senior manager's office will be the setting for the interview'. (In an early draft of another book we have written, we referred to a particular writer as a 'master craftsman' before deciding it would be more suitable to change this to 'an expert in the field'!)

In the event of your research having an international dimension, it is a good idea to be aware of any country-specific or national guidelines on the non-discriminatory use of language.

## Do preserve anonymity

It is likely that you have given your participants or respondents (and the organisations) from whom you collected data an undertaking that you would not disclose their identity in your written work. You will need to conceal their identity in your research proposal or report. Normally you can do this by inventing pseudonyms for organisations (as in Research in practice 8.2, where AAA and BBB were used) and not to name individual participants or respondents. It may make your work a little less interesting to read, but in such cases, you have no choice. Anonymising may also allow you do be rather more critically evaluative than you could have been with named participants or respondents.

## Do successive drafts of your work

In section 8.3 we recommended that you continually revise your research proposal, keep each successive draft and treat the report as 'work in progress'. This point applies to all you're writing. Your style and content will be refined, sharpened and clarified with each successive version.

## 8.6    How your research proposal will be judged

Your module guidelines should make clear the assessment criteria against which your research proposal will be judged. In this final section, we offer three guidelines. These may be in your published assessment criteria, and they summarise much of the material already covered in this chapter in particular and this text in general. We offer them here to emphasise their importance.

## ◼ The extent to which the components of the proposal fit together

The main components of your research proposal should fit together in one coherent and seamless whole. These are:

1 The introduction. This should contain an explanation of the reasons for conducting your research and include a summary of the previous published research, covering relevant theories in the topic area.

2 Your research question(s) and objectives, which should be based on the material in the introduction.

3 Your research design, including the proposed method, which should flow directly from these research question(s) and objectives.

4 The time that you have allocated, which should be a direct reflection of the methods you employ and the time available.

5 The resources that you need, which should be a direct reflection of the methods you employ and your own skills.

## ◼ The absence of preconceived ideas

Your research should be a voyage of discovery. As a broad rule, if you know the answer to the research question already – look for another topic! Having preconceived ideas will stunt your creativity and lessen the enjoyment you derive from the research process.

## ◼ The viability of the proposal

This is the answer to the question: 'Can this research be carried out satisfactorily within the timescale and with available resources?'

We end this section on the content of the research proposal with a complete proposal (Research in practice 8.3) for you to consider. This should not be seen as ideal. Indeed, you should review its content in the light of the points made in this chapter to conduct your own assessment.

---

### Research in practice 8.3

**Research proposal**

**Research proposal**
**Mr C.D. Eff, MBA (part-time)**

**Knowledge Management in High-Technology Manufacturing SMEs:**
**Key Strategies to Maintain Competitive Advantage**

**Research Question**

This research is designed to answer the question 'What are the key features of a Knowledge Management Strategy which can contribute to competitive advantage for UK knowledge-based small and medium sized enterprises (SMEs) in the high-technology manufacturing sector, and why are these features evident?'

### Knowledge Management

Growth of the field of knowledge management (KM) was began in the 1990s and has been ongoing (Hislop, 2013). This has been driven by the evolution of a 'knowledge economy' where businesses must continually adapt and use their knowledge effectively to maintain competitive advantage. Teece (2001) attributes superior performance to the ability of firms to be good at innovating, protecting intangible and difficult to imitate knowledge assets and using those assets effectively.

Knowledge management has often been described as comprising three elements: people, processes and technology (Edwards, 2011). (It is important to stress that the term processes refers to the business processes of the organisation concerned, not just to its knowledge management processes.)

These three elements link together, each of them having a reciprocal relationship with each of the other two. For example, people help design and then operate processes, while processes define the roles of, and the knowledge needed by people.

Tidd et al. (2001) state there are five main types of KM strategy. These are ripple (bottom-up continuous improvement), integration (functional knowledge into processes), embedding (coupling systems, products and services), bridge (novel combination of existing competencies) and transfer (existing knowledge in new context). The optimum knowledge strategy is likely to be a mix of these and will depend on the structure and culture of the organisation, the market environment and the availability of resources.

### Knowledge Sharing and Organisational Memory in High-Tech SMEs

For large organisations, organisational design and formal procedures form the basis for knowledge integration. In contrast, for high-technology SMEs, the role of senior management is far more important in the integration of technological knowledge and devising strategies to exploit knowledge competencies. Tidd et al. (2001: 56) state that it is the manager's 'level of technical and organisational skills' which determine whether they 'will be able to develop and commercially exploit a firm-specific technological advantage'. As firms grow, it is clear that organisational design, processes and culture need to be developed to maintain and foster the environment of knowledge sharing which was inherent in the smaller organisation.

The five main learning activities described by Garvin (1993) are 'systematic problem solving, experimentation, learning from experience, learning from others and transfer of knowledge quickly and efficiently throughout the organisation'. For high-technology SMEs practice is often lacking in the application of past experience and the systematic recording and sharing of often tacit knowledge throughout the business. Rather as suggested by Hutchinson and Quintas (2008) these firms manage knowledge in informal ways which are both structured and deliberate.

### Research Objectives

The aim of this research is to understand the characteristics of the firms and their products which determine the success of different types of KM strategy. The research objectives are:

1. To identify KM strategies in operation in SMEs in the high-technology manufacturing sector.
2. To analyse the importance of KM and understand how the strategies and practices in operation contribute positively or negatively to competitive advantage.

→

3. To understand the practices which enable the development of organisational memory and why these are evident.

4. To understand the characteristics, structure and products of a firm which determine the success of different types of KM strategy and why these are significant.

5. To develop a list of key practices and a route for implementation of a successful KM strategy for an SME in the high-technology manufacturing sector.

**Research Methods**

*Research Approach and Design*

The analysis of the research will be largely quantitative, highlighting patterns. The findings will be compared to theory in order to describe the patterns which exist. An inductive approach will be used in order to develop theory as a result of the research findings, although there will be an element of deduction in that the structure of the research will based on the academic literature.

The research will be based on two case study organisations using:

1. structured interviews with a senior manager in both of the case study organisations;

2. questionnaires to all employees in both of the case study organisations.

The cases chosen all have the following characteristics: located in the SME high-technology manufacturing sector, possessing a significant R&D function as a basis for product development and are UK based. The method of selection of case studies was through personal networking and sampling to find a number of organisations with the required characteristics. Effort was also made to select organisations with different characteristics such as markets, sizes and life-spans. Within the case studies the respondent will be senior managers who understood the KM practices and business environment. I intend to interview one management participant from each organisation. The questionnaire respondents will be either all, or at least 10, of the employees working in research or related areas, depending on the size of the company.

A semi-structured interview will be held with a senior manager in each case study organisation to gain company information such as number of employees, number of research staff, annual turnover, market sector and products. The interviews will include open ended questions to discuss the KM practices in order to gain an understanding of the approach taken, the structure and effectiveness of the KM practices and how and why certain strategies work whilst others are less effective. Each respondent will be asked to answer identical opening questions, although follow-up questions are likely to differ.

The questionnaire delivered to employees in each organisation will be used to establish the practices and individual perceptions in the organisation. The aim is to gain an understanding of how the KM strategies work through gaining the opinions and understanding of the employees. The questionnaire will have closed questions with set responses in order to map the KM characteristics of the organisation. There will also be a few open questions for participants to make comments on the various aspects of KM in their organisation.

My approach to the design of the questionnaire is as follows:

- Preliminary framework built on the review of theory from academic literature prior to design of questionnaires and structured interviews
- Pilot interview – restructure the questions as necessary

- Pilot use of questionnaire - restructure the questions as necessary
- Structured interviews – notes taken during interview and audio-recording to produce a full record immediately after interview
- Questionnaire explained and handed out/collected during session

*Data Collection and Analysis*

I intend to perform research in my own organisation, called here AAA, for which I have been granted access to carry out the interviews and questionnaire. In addition, I believe that I require one further organisation to make a comparison of the KM practices and their effectiveness. I have contacted five organisations and have obtained a verbal agreement for access from one of these (called BBB). I am therefore confident that I will be able to gain the required number of participating organisations.

In order to make the process run smoothly and to obtain a speedy and efficient response to the questionnaires I intend to run one or two sessions in both organisations where all of the participants will be present and during which I will hand out and collect the questionnaires. This will both ensure a high response rate and that the correct participants answer the survey. In addition, it will enable me to explain clearly the aims of the research, control how the survey is administered and make clear the type of information required for the open-ended part of the questionnaires.

Analysis of the structured interviews will be mostly qualitative, with the interviews used to understand the business environment, characterise knowledge strategies and canvas individual opinion on their effectiveness. Quantitative analysis of the questionnaires will be used to map the characteristics of both organisations and discover patterns in the responses within organisations. Consideration of the data and patterns found in both organisations will be used in conjunction with academic theory to try to explain the findings and answer the research objectives.

*Validity and Reliability*

I will attempt to achieve internal validity through the use of multiple sources of evidence, structured interviews and questionnaires. The design of questions will be based on understanding of the theory from the literature and pilot testing of the interview and questionnaire will be used to make sure questions are understood as intended.

I have ensured external validity through the use of multiple cases to examine whether findings can be generalised across both organisations. There is no requirement to make a statistical analysis of the results for generalisation here as the approach chosen examines practices and their effectiveness. The aim is to explain the findings and explore generalisability through a comparison of findings with theory.

Reliability is pursued through structured interviews with questions derived from the literature in order to examine cases in same way. In addition, the surveys reinforce the interviews and obtain views from a wider group. The questionnaires will all be administered at the same time and in controlled manner with explanation to ensure participants all understand research in same way.

**Research Ethics**

Respondents will be given a clear written description of the purpose, scope and intended outcomes of the research. The type of information required for the research will be clearly stated as will the policy for anonymity and confidentiality.

→

The research will be carried out in a way that will ensure confidentiality of the participant organisations and the individual participants in the surveys. The organisations which participate in the research will only be referred to by their pseudonyms AAA and BBB and not be named in the project. Interview participants will not be named and the questionnaires will be anonymous.

The interview questions and questionnaire will be designed to examine only the practices of KM, no confidential product or customer information will be required.

**Timescale and Resources**

The plan for the research project timescales is shown below.

- Literature review. I have already performed a background literature search to help formulate research ideas. I plan further extensive period of research before writing the literature review. This will be completed by December 2016.

- Questionnaire/Interview Design. I have a questionnaire which needs adapting for use. I intend to design the structured interview and questionnaire after the majority of the literature review is complete, will both be piloted and their design reviewed. This will be completed by December 2016.

- Interviews and questionnaires. I plan to visit participant organisations to carry out data collection during January and February 2017.

- Data Analysis. This will be completed by the end of March 2017.

- Project draft completed by end of April 2017. Final submission end of May 2017.

The main resource required to carry out the research is my time, I have the support of my employers to carry out this research and I will be able to take days out of work to visit the other participant organisation. I have the means to visit the participants and also to analyse the data and write up the project report.

**References**

Edwards, J. (2011). 'A Process View of Knowledge Management: It ain't what you do, it's the way that you do it'. *The Electronic Journal of Knowledge Management*, 9 (4), pp. 297-306. Available online at www.ejkm.com

Garvin, D. A. (1993) 'Building a Learning Organization', *Harvard Business Review*, 71(4) pp. 78-91.

Hislop, D. (2013). *Knowledge Management in Organisations* 23rd ed. Oxford: Oxford University Press.

Hutchinson, V. and Quintas, P (2008), Do SMEs do knowledge management?: or simply manage what they know? *International Small Business Journal*, Vol. 26, No. 2, pp 131-154.

Teece, D.J. (2001), 'Strategies for Managing Knowledge Assets: The role of the Firm in Structure and Industrial Context' in Nonaka, I. and Teece D.J. (Eds.) *Managing Industrial Knowledge: Creation Transfer and Utilization*, London: Sage.

Tidd, J., Bessant, J. and Pavitt, K. (2001), *Managing Innovation: Integrating Technological, Market and Organizational Change*. Chichester: Wiley.

## Summary

- Writing a research proposal is important because: it clarifies your ideas and helps you organise those ideas; it shows you have a good knowledge of the existing work; it demonstrates to the assessor(s) that the research is viable; it ensures that your research meets the requirements of the university and your programme.

- It may helpful to begin your research proposal at the start of the research process and treat it a 'work in progress' by amending it as you progress through the process of preparing the proposal.

- The content of the research proposal is likely to be: research overview; title; introduction to research; research questions(s); literature review; research objectives; method; timescale; resources required and literature references. The main points to consider when writing the research proposal or report are: to write clearly and simply; to use short, simple sentences; exercise care in spelling and the use of grammar; avoid jargon; beware of using large numbers of quotations from the literature; the use of person, tense and gender and the preservation of confidentiality and anonymity.

- Among the criteria against which your research proposal will be assessed will be the extent to which the various components of the research fit together and the absence of preconceived ideas.

## Thinking about your research proposal

→ Look again at the idea of the six honest serving-men (section 8.2) to generate some initial headings for your research proposal. Your headings may respond to the following 'prompt questions': What are the research questions I am seeking to answer? What are my research objectives? Why is the research I propose significant? When are the key dates in the research process? How will I go about collecting the necessary data to answer the research questions? Who are the key participants in the research process (e.g. gatekeepers, respondents)?

→ Study the brief given to you detailing your university's requirements for the research proposal and note the key sections that you should include in your proposal.

→ Look again at the brief given to you specifying your university's requirements for the research proposal and ensure that you are aware of the assessment criteria that will be used to grade your proposal.

→ Consider the advice given in section 8.5. on the use of person in your writing. In the light of this advice and that from your supervisor, decide which person is appropriate for you to use.

## References

Kipling, R. (1902, reprinted 2007). *A Collection of Rudyard Kipling's Just So Stories*. London: Walker Books.

Mills, C.W. (1970). On intellectual craftsmanship. In *The Sociological Imagination*. London: Pelican.

Saunders M., Lewis, P. and Thornhill, A. (2016). *Research Methods for Business Students*. (7th edn). Harlow: FT Prentice Hall.

Smith, A. (1904). *An Inquiry into the Nature and Causes of the Wealth of Nations* (5th edn.) London: Methuen and Co.

# Appendix 1

# How to reference

Within business and management, two referencing systems predominate, the Harvard style and the American Psychological Association (APA) style. These are both author-date systems where all the sources are listed alphabetically in the 'references' or 'bibliography' section using the authors' family names. If there is more than one work by the same author or originator in this list, they are listed chronologically. If there is more than one publication by the same author from the same year, you need to include a, b, c etc. immediately after the year. Do not forget to ensure that these letters are consistent with the letters used for the references in the main text.

Increasingly we read electronic versions of books and journal articles. For such versions, it is usually acceptable to reference them using exactly the same format as printed books and journal articles, provided the copy you have read is a facsimile copy. Otherwise you need to reference them as explained in Table A1.1. Facsimile copies have precisely the same format as a printed version, including page numbering, tables and diagrams, other than for the copies of journal articles, which are published 'online first'. **Online first** refers to forthcoming articles that have been published online prior to appearing in journals. They therefore do not have a volume or part number, and the page numbering will not be the same as the final copy. When including an 'online first' copy in the list of references, you should always include the DOI (digital object identifier) as part of the reference. The DOI provides a permanent and unique identifier for that document. Where there is no DOI, it is usual to include the document's URL (Uniform resource locator – usually its web address). As the URL is not permanent, the date when it was accessed is also included in the reference.

## The Harvard style

The Harvard style is an author–date system, a variation of which we use in this book. It usually uses the author's or originator's name and year of publication to identify cited documents within the text. All references are listed alphabetically at the end of the text. The style for referencing work in the text and in the references or bibliography is outlined in Table A1.1.

Table A1.1 Using the Harvard style to reference

| To cite | In the text | | In the references/bibliography | |
|---|---|---|---|---|
| | General format | Example | General format | Example |
| **Books and chapters in books** | | | | |
| **(first edition)** | *1 author:*<br>(Family name year) | *1 author:*<br>(Silverman 2007) | Family name, Initials. (year). *Title.* Place of publication: Publisher. | Silverman, D. (2007). *A very short, fairly interesting and reasonably cheap book about qualitative research.* London: Sage. |
| | *2 or 3 authors:*<br>(Family name, Family name and Family name year) | *2 or 3 authors:*<br>(Berman Brown and Saunders 2008) | Family name, Initials. and Family name, Initials. (year). *Title.* Place of publication: Publisher. | Berman Brown, R. and Saunders, M. (2008). *Dealing with statistics: What you need to know.* Maidenhead: Open University Press. |
| | *4+ authors:*<br>(Family name et al. year) | *4+ authors:*<br>(Millmore et al. 2010) | Family name, Initials., Family name, Initials. and Family name, Initials [can be discretionary to include more than first author] (year). *Title.* Place of publication: Publisher. | Millmore, M., Lewis, P., Saunders, M., Thornhill, A. and Morrow, T. (2007). *Strategic human resource management: Contemporary Issues.* Harlow: FT Prentice Hall. |
| **(other than first edition)** | As *for* 'Book (first edition)' | (Anderson et al. 2014) | Family name, Initials. and Family name, Initials. (year). *Title.* (# edn). Place of publication: Publisher. | Anderson, D.L., Sweeney, D.J., Williams, T.A., Freeman, J. and Shoesmith, E. (2014). *Statistics for Business and Economics.* (3rd edn). Andover: Cengage Learning EMA. |
| **(edited)** | As *for* 'Book (first edition)' | (Saunders et al. 2010) | Family name, Initials. and Family name, Initials. (eds.) (year). *Title.* Place of publication: Publisher. | Saunders, M.N.K, Skinner, D., Gillespie, N., Dietz, G. and Lewicki, R.J. (eds). (2010). *Organizational trust: a cultural perspective.* Cambridge: Cambridge University Press. |

| To cite | In the text | | | In the references/bibliography | |
|---|---|---|---|---|---|
| | **General format** | **Example** | | **General format** | **Example** |
| **(e-book)** | *As for 'Book (first edition)'* | (Saunders 2013) | | Family name, Initials. (year). *Title*. [name of e-book reader]. Place of publication: Publisher. | Saunders, J.J. (2013). *The Holocaust: History in an Hour* [Kindle e-book]. London: William Collins. |
| **(chapter in an edited book)** | (Chapter author family name year) | (King 2012) | | Family name, Initials. (year). Chapter title. In Initials. Family name and Initials. Family name (eds) *Title*. Place of publication: Publisher. pp. ###–###. | King, N. (2012). Doing Template Analysis. In G. Symon and C. Cassell (eds) *Qualitative Organizational Research*. London: Sage. pp. 426-50. |
| **Dictionaries and other reference books** | | | | | |
| **(where author known)** | *As for 'Book (first edition)'* | (Vogt and Johnson 2011) | | Family name, Initials. (year). *Title*. (# edn). Place of Publication: Publisher. pp. ###–###. | Vogt, W.P. and Johnson, R.B. (2011). *Dictionary of statistics and methodology: a nontechnical guide for the social sciences*. (4th edn). Thousand Oaks, CA: Sage. pp. 31-2. |
| **(where no author or editor)** | *(Publication title year)* | *(The right word at the right time 1985)* | | *Publication title*. (year). (# edn). Place of Publication: Publisher. pp. ###–###. | *The right word at the right time*. (1985). Pleasantville, NY: Readers Digest Association. pp. 563-4. |
| **Reports** | *As for 'Book (first edition)'* | (Gray *et al.* 2012) | | Family name, Initials. and Family name, Initials. (year). *Title*. Place of publication: Publisher. | Gray, D.E., Saunders M.N.K. and Goregaokar, H. (2012). *Success in challenging times: Key lessons for UK SMEs*. London: Kingston Smith LLP. |
| **(no named author)** | *(Originator name or Publication title year)* | (Mintel Marketing Intelligence 2008) | | Originator name or Publication title. (year). *Title*. Place of publication: Publisher. | Mintel Marketing Intelligence. (2008). *Designerwear: Mintel marketing intelligence report*. London: Mintel International Group Ltd. |

*(continues)*

Table A1.1 Using the Harvard style to reference *(continued)*

| To cite | In the text | | In the references/bibliography | |
|---|---|---|---|---|
| | **General format** | **Example** | **General format** | **Example** |
| *(online)* | *As for* 'Book (first edition)' | (Thorlby *et al.* 2014) | Family name, Initials. and Family name, Initials. (year). *Title of report.* Available at http://www.remainderoffullInternetaddress/ [Accessed day month year]. | Thorlby, R., Smith, J., Williams, S. and Dayan, M. (2014). *The Francis Report: One year on.* Available at: http://www.nuffieldtrust.org.uk/sites/files/nuffield/publication/140206_the_francis_inquiry.pdf [Accessed 20 Mar. 2014]. |
| **Journal articles** | | | | |
| *(print or facsimile)* | *As for* 'Book (first edition)' | (Rojon *et al.* 2011) | Family name, Initials. and Family name, Initials. (year). Title of article. *Journal name.* Vol. ##, No. ##, pp. ###–####. | Rojon, C., McDowall, A. and Saunders, M.N.K. (2011). On the experience of conducting a systematic review in industrial, work and organizational psychology: Yes, it is worthwhile. *Journal of Personnel Psychology.* Vol. 10, No. 3, pp. 133–8. |
| *(forthcoming published online first as facsimile)* | *As for* 'Book (first edition)' | (Saunders and Rojon 2014) | Family name, Initials. and Family name, Initials. (year). Title of article, *Journal name.* Available at full doi or Internet address [Accessed day month year]. | Saunders, M.N.K. and Rojon, C. (2014) There's no madness in my method: explaining how your coaching research findings are built on firm foundations. *Coaching: An International Journal of Theory, Research and Practice.* Available at DOI: 10.1080/17521882.2014.889185 [Accessed 6 March 2014]. |

| To cite | In the text | | In the references/bibliography | |
|---|---|---|---|---|
| | General format | Example | General format | Example |
| **Magazine articles** | *As for 'Book (first edition)'* | (Saunders 2004) | Family name, Initials. and Family name, Initials. (year). Title of article. *Magazine name*. Vol. ##, No. ## (or Issue or day and/or month), pp. ###–###. | Saunders, M. (2004). Land of the long white cloud. *HOG News UK*. Issue 23, Oct. pp. 24–6. |
| ***(no named author)*** | (Originator name or Publication name year) | *(People Management 2014)* | Originator name or Publication name. (year). Title of article. *Magazine name*. Vol. ##, No. ## (or Issue or day and/or month), pp. ###–###. | People Management. (2014). Efficiency rule was misused. *People Management*. Mar. p. 17. |
| **News items including newspapers and online news** | | | | |
| ***(article)*** | *As for 'Book (first edition)'* | (Frean 2014) | Family name, Initials. and Family name, Initials. Title of article. *Newspaper name*, day month year, p. ###. | Frean, A. Credit Suisse bankers 'assisted tax evasion'. *The Times*. 27 Feb. 2014, p. 35. |
| ***(article no named author)*** | *(Newspaper name year)* | *(The Times 2014)* | *Newspaper name*. Title of article, day month year, p. ##. | *The Times*. Budweiser's early win, 27 Feb. 2014, p. 33. |
| ***(article published online)*** | *As for other News articles* | (Rankin 2014) | Family name, Initials. and Family name, Initials. Title of article. *Newspaper name*, day month year. Available at http://www.full-Internetaddress/ [Accessed day month year]. | Rankin J. Record number of women make 28th annual Forbes' billionaires list. *The Guardian*. 4 Mar. 2014. Available at http://www.theguardian.com/business/2014/mar/03/record-number-women-forbes-28th-billionaires-list.html?src=linkedin [Accessed 4 Mar. 2014]. |

*(continues)*

Table A1.1 Using the Harvard style to reference (continued)

| To cite | In the text | | In the references/bibliography | |
|---|---|---|---|---|
| | **General format** | **Example** | **General format** | **Example** |
| **(article from electronic database)** | As for other News articles | (Anderson 2009) | Family name, Initials. and Family name, Initials. Title of article. *Newspaper name*, day month year, p. ### (if known). [Accessed day month year from Database name]. | Anderson, L. How to choose a Business School. *Financial Times*, 23 Jan. 2009. [Accessed 20 Mar. 2010 from ft.com]. |
| **(article from news web site)** | As for other News articles | (Gordon 2014) | Family name, Initials. and Family name, Initials. Title of article. *News web site*, day month year. Available at http://www.full-Internetaddress/ [Accessed day month year]. | Gordon, O. Keeping crowdsourcing honest. Can we trust the reviews? BBC News, 14 Feb. 2014. Available at: http://www.bbc.co.uk/news/technology-26182642 [Accessed 4 Mar. 2014]. |
| **Websites** | (Source organisation year) | (European Commission 2014) | Source organisation. (year). *Title of site or page within site*. Available at http://www.remainderoffullInternetaddress/ [Accessed day month year]. | European Commission. (2014). *Eurostat – structural indicators*. Available at http://epp.eurostat.ec.europa.eu/portal/page/portal/structural_indicators/introduction [Accessed 5 Mar. 2014]. |
| **Conference papers** | | | | |
| **(published as part of proceedings)** | As for 'Book (first edition)' | (Saunders 2009) | Family name, Initials. and Family name, Initials. (year). Title of paper. In Initials. Family name and Initials. Family name (eds) *Title*. Place of publication: Publisher. pp. ###–###. | Saunders, M.N.K. (2009). A real world comparison of responses to distributing questionnaire surveys by mail and web. In J. Azzopardi (Ed.) *Proceedings of the 8th European Conference on Research Methods in Business and Management*. Reading: ACI, pp. 323–30 |

| To cite | In the text | | In the references/bibliography | |
|---|---|---|---|---|
| | General format | Example | General format | Example |
| **(unpublished)** | *As for 'Book (first edition)'* | (Saunders et al. 2010) | Family name, Initials. and Family name, Initials. (year). *Title of paper.* Unpublished paper presented at 'Conference name'. Location of conference, day month year. | Saunders, M.N.K., Slack, R. and Bowen, D. (2010). *Location, the development of swift trust and learning: insights from two doctoral summer schools*. Unpublished paper presented at the 'EIASM 5th Workshop on Trust Within and Between Organizations'. Madrid, 28–29 January 2010. |
| **Film, Video, TV, Radio, Downloads** | | | | |
| **(Television or radio programme)** | *(Television or radio programme title year)* | *(Today Programme* 2014) | *Programme title.* (year of production). Transmitting organisation and nature of transmission, day month year of transmission. | *The Today Programme.* (2014). British Broadcasting Corporation Radio broadcast, 11 Apr. 2014. |
| **(Video download e.g. YouTube)** | *(Company name or Family name year)* | (Miller 2008) | Company name or Family name, Initials. (year). Title of audio download. *YouTube.* Available at http://www. remainderoffullInternetaddress/ [Accessed day month year]. | Miller, L. (2008). Harvard style referencing made easy. *YouTube.* Available at http://www.youtube. com/watch?v=RH1lzyn7Exc [Accessed 5 Mar. 2014]. |

*Notes:* Where date is not known or unclear, follow conventions outlined towards the end of Table A1.2. Be warned, most lecturers consider citing of lectures as 'lazy' scholarship.

## The American Psychological Association (APA) style

The American Psychological Association style *or* APA style is a variation on the author–date system. It is explained in full in the latest edition of the American Psychological Association's (2009) *Concise Rules of the APA Style*, which is likely to be available for reference in your university's library. There are small but significant differences between the Harvard and APA styles, and many authors adopt a combination of the two styles. The key differences are outlined in Table A1.2.

Table A1.2 Key differences between Harvard and APA styles of referencing

| Harvard style | APA style | Comment |
|---|---|---|
| *Referencing in the text* | | |
| (Lewis 2001) | (Lewis, 2001) | Note: punctuation |
| (McDowall and Saunders 2010) | (McDowall & Saunders, 2011) | Note: '&', not 'and' |
| (Altinay *et al.* 2014) | (Altinay, Saunders & Wang, 2014) | For first occurrence if three to five authors |
| (Millmore *et al.* 2007) | (Millmore et al., 2007) | For first occurrence if six or more authors; note punctuation and use of italics |
| (Tosey *et al.* 2012) | (Tosey et al., 2012) | For subsequent occurrences of two or more authors; note punctuation and use of italics |
| *Referencing in the list of references or bibliography* | | |
| Berman Brown, R. and Saunders, M. (2008). *Dealing with statistics: What you need to know.* Maidenhead: Open University Press. | Berman Brown, R. & Saunders, M. (2008). *Dealing with statistics: What you need to know.* Maidenhead: Open University Press. | Note: use of 'and' and '&' |
| Varadarajan, P.R. (2003). Musings on relevance and rigour of scholarly research in marketing. *Journal of the Academy of Marketing Science.* Vol. 31, No. 4, pp. 368–376. [Accessed 6 Apr. 2010 from Business Source Complete]. | Varadarajan, P.R. (2003). Musings on relevance and rigour of scholarly research in marketing. *Journal of the Academy of Marketing Science,* 31(4), 368–376. doi: 10.1177/0092070303258240 | Note: Volume, part number and page numbers; DOI (digital object identifier) number given in APA. Name of database not given in APA if DOI number given; Date accessed site not included in APA. |

# Bibliography

Altinay, L., Saunders, M.N.K. and Wang, C. (2014) The influence of culture on trust judgments in customer relationship development by ethnic minority small businesses. *Journal of Small Business Management*, 52(1), 59–78.

Barclaycard (2016). The emergence of 'serial returners' – online shoppers who habitually over order and take advantage of free returns – hinders growth of UK businesses. Available at: https://www.home.barclaycard/media-centre/press-releases/emergence-of-serial-returners-hinders-growth-of-UK-businesses.html [Accessed 20 October 2016].

Baruch, Y. and Holtom, B.C. (2008). Survey response rate levels and trends in organizational research. *Human Relations*, 61(8), 1139–60.

Becker, H.S. (2007). *Writing for Social Scientists* (2nd ed.). Chicago: University of Chicago.

Beynon, H. (1973). *Working for Ford*. London: Allen Lane.

Brinkmann, S. and Kvale, S. (2014). *InterViews: Learning the Craft of Qualitative Research Interviewing* (3rd ed.). Los Angeles, CA: Sage.

Cassell, C. (2015). *Conducting Research Interviews for Business and Management Students*. London: Sage.

Clough, P. and Nutbrown, C. (2012). *A Student's Guide to Methodology* (3rd ed.). London: Sage.

Corbin, J. and Strauss, A. (2008) *Basics of Qualitative Research: Techniques and Procedures for Developing Grounded Theory* (3rd ed.). London: Sage.

Creswell, J. (2008). *Qualitative, Quantitative, and Mixed Methods Approaches* (3rd ed.). Thousand Oaks, CA: Sage.

Department for Work and Pensions (2014). *Small Employer Recruitment Practices: Qualitative Research into How Small and Medium-Sized Enterprises Select Candidates for Employment*. Report No 855, July 2014.

Dragons' Den (2014). Scott Cupit and Swing Patrol on BBC's *Dragon's Den*. *YouTube*. Available at: https://www.youtube.com/watch?v=lHYnxtR1u0I [Accessed 8 November 2016].

Dunsby, M (2016). *Dragons' Den Success Stories: Swing Patrol*. Available at: http://startups.co.uk/dragons-den-success-stories-swing-patrol/ [Accessed 8 November 2016].

Edelman (2016) *2016 Edelman Trust Barometer Global Report*. Available at: http://www.edelman.com/insights/intellectual-property/2016-edelman-trust-barometer/global-results/ [Accessed 28 October 2016].

Ekinci, Y. (2015). *Designing Research Questionnaires for Business and Management Students*, London: Sage.

Eurostat (2014). *Methodological Manual for Tourism Statistics Version 3.1*. Luxembourg: Publications Office of the European Union.

Eurostat (2016). *Tourism: Main Tables*. Available at: http://ec.europa.eu/eurostat/web/tourism/data/main-tables [Accessed 1 November 2016].

Eurostat (no date). *Europe in Figures*. Available at: http://ec.europa.eu/eurostat/statistics-explained/index.php/Europe_in_figures_-_Eurostat_yearbook [Accessed 1 November 2016].

Eurostat Press Office (2016). Organic crop farming on the rise in the EU. *Eurostat News Release 208/2016*. Available at: http://ec.europa.eu/eurostat/documents/2995521/7709498/5-25102016-BP-EN.pdf/cee89f9e-023b-4470-ba23-61a9893d34c8 [Accessed 21 November 2016].

Fenwick, D. and Denman, J. (1995) The monthly unemployment count: change and consistency, *Labour Market Trends*, November, 397–400.

Ghazali, S. (2011). The influence of socialization agents and demographic profiles on brand consciousness, *International Journal of Management and Marketing Research*, 4(1), 19–29.

Gov.UK (2015). *Data Protection*. Available at: https://www.gov.uk/data-protection/the-data-protection-act [Accessed 15 June 2016].

Hair, J., Black, W., Babin, B. and Anderson, R. (2009). *Multivariate Data Analysis* (7th ed.). London: Pearson.

Harvard College Library (2011). *Interrogating Texts: 6 Reading Habits to Develop in Your First Year at Harvard*. Available at: http://bsc.harvard.edu/files/interrogating_texts_six_reading_habits_to_develop_in_your_first_year_at_harvard.pdf [Accessed 12 October 2016].

Henley, J. (2016). Sweden leads the race to become cashless society *The Guardian*, 4 June 2016.

Hofstede, G., Hofstede, G.J. and Minkov, M. (2010). *Culture and Organizations: Software of the Mind* (3rd ed.). Columbus OH: McGraw-Hill.

House of Commons Environment, Food and Rural Affairs (2015). *Rural Broadband and Digital-Only Services, Seventh Report of Session 2014–15*. London: The Stationery Office Limited.

Hudson, S., Roth, M.S., Madden, J.T. and Hudson, R. (2015). The effect of social media on emotions, brand relationship quality and word of mouth: An empirical study of music festival attendees. *Tourism Management*, 47(1), 68–76.

Kipling, R. (1902, reprinted 2007). *A Collection of Rudyard Kipling's Just So Stories*. London: Walker Books.

Leenders, M.A.A.M. (2010). The relative importance of the brand of music festivals: a customer equity perspective. *Journal of Strategic Marketing*, 18(4), 291–301.

Levitas, R. (1996). *Interpreting Official Statistics*. London: Routledge.

Lewin K. (1945). The Research Centre for Group Dynamics at Massachusetts Institute of Technology. *Sociometry*, 8(2), 126–36.

McSweeny, B. (2002). Hofstede's model of national cultural differences and their consequences: a triumph of faith – a failure of analysis. *Human Relations*, 55(1), 89–118.

Mills, C.W. (1970). On intellectual craftsmanship. In *The Sociological Imagination*. London: Pelican.

Office for National Statistics (2016). *Balance of Payments time series dataset*. Available at: https://www.ons.gov.uk/economy/nationalaccounts/balanceofpayments/datasets/balanceofpayments [Accessed 20 November 2016].

Office for National Statistics (2016). *Labour Force Survey*. Available at: https://www.ons.gov.uk/employmentandlabourmarket/peopleinwork/employmentandemployeetypes/bulletins/uklabourmarket/october2016 [Accessed 20 October 2016].

Office for National Statistics (2016). *Retail Industry*. Available at: http://www.ons.gov.uk/businessindustryandtrade/retailindustry#datasets4 [Accessed 31 October 2016].

Oxford Brookes University (2016). *Ethical Standards for Research Involving Human Participants: Code of Practice*. Available at: https://www.brookes.ac.uk/Documents/Research/Policies-and-codes-of-practice/ethics_codeofpractice/ [Accessed 11 November 2016].

Pricewaterhouse Coopers, University of Southern California and the London Business School (2013). *PwC's NextGen: A Global Generational Study*. Available at: http://www.pwc.com/us/en/people-management/publications/nextgen-global-generational-study.html [Accessed 27 October 2016].

Raimond, P. (1993). *Management Projects*. London: Chapman & Hall.

Saunders, M.N.K. (2011). Choosing research participants. In C. Cassell and G. Symons (eds), *The Practice of Qualitative Organizational Research: Core Methods and Current Challenges*. London: Sage.

Saunders, M.N.K. (2012). Web versus mail: the influence of survey distribution mode on employees' response. *Field Methods*, 24(1) 56–73.

Saunders, M.N.K., Gray, D. and Goregaokor, H. (2014). SME innovation and learning: the role of networks and crisis event' *European Journal of Training and Development* 38(1/2), 136–49.

Saunders M., Lewis, P. and Thornhill, A. (2016). *Research Methods for Business Students*. (7th ed.). Harlow: FT Prentice Hall.

Saunders, M.N.K. and Townsend, K. (2016). Reporting and justifying the number of interviews participants in organisation and workplace research. *British Journal of Management*, 27(4), 836–52.

Smith, A. (1904). *An Inquiry into the Nature and Causes of the Wealth of Nations* (5th ed.). London: Methuen and Co.

Sutton, R. and Staw, B. (1995). What theory is not. *Administrative Science Quarterly*, 40(3), 371–84.

University of Plymouth (2016) School of Marine Science and Engineering, Project Marking Scheme. Available at: http://www.tech.plym.ac.uk/sme/mingproject/MScheme910.pdf [Accessed 12 June 2016].

Van Maanen, J., Sørensen, J.B. and Mitchell, T.R. (2007) 'The interplay between theory and method', *Academy of Management Review*, Vol. 32, No. 4, pp. 1145–54.

Wallace, M. and Wray, A. (2016) *Critical Reading and Writing for Postgraduates* (3rd ed.). London: Sage.

YouGov (2016) *Panel Methodology*. Available at: https://yougov.co.uk/about/panel-methodology/ [Accessed 7 November 2016].

# Index